BEYOND THE INVERTED PYRAMID

Effective Writing for Newspapers, Magazines and Specialized Publications

THE MISSOURI GROUP:

George Kennedy
Daryl R. Moen
Don Ranly

School of Journalism
University of Missouri at Columbia

St. Martin's Press
New York

Editor: Jane Lambert
Manager, publishing services: Emily Berleth
Project management: Omega Publishing Services, Inc.
Cover art: Tom McKeveny

For information, write:
St. Martin's Press, Inc.
175 Fifth Avenue
New York, NY 10010

ISBN: 0-312-04058-X

Acknowledgments

Excerpt from The Union Gospel Mission story, by Diana Dawson.
Reprinted by permission of *The Spokane Spokesman-Review.*

Excerpt from U.S. Navy aircraft carrier America story, by Steve Twormey.
Reprinted by permission of the *Philadelphia Inquirer.*

Excerpt from ASNE's 1991 report, "Keys to Our Survival." Reprinted by
permission of the American Society of Newspaper Editors.

Excerpts from article by Jeff Leen. Reprinted by permission of *The Miami
Herald.*

Excerpt from the medical malpractice series, by Joseph Hallinan and Susan
Headden, June 1990. Reprinted by permission of *The Indianapolis Star.*

Excerpt from story on gunshot victim, by Shari Spires. Reprinted by
permission of *The Palm Beach Post.*

"River Accident." Reprinted by permission of The Associated Press (AP).

Excerpts throughout from "The NRA Fights Back," by Paul Houston,
July 30, 1989 Sunday magazine. Copyright © 1989, *Los Angeles Times.*
Reprinted by permission.

Acknowledgments and copyrights are continued at the back of the book on
page 268, which constitutes an extension of the copyright page.

Preface

☐ WHAT YOU CAN LEARN FROM THIS BOOK

Everyone knew when Frank Barrows of the Charlotte (N.C.) Observer was about to write his column. With a six-pack of Tab tucked under his huge arm, he trudged to his desk, opened a drawer, grabbed a pair of earmuffs and pulled them over his ears to block out the newsroom noise. Next, he tied himself to his chair with his own belt. Only then did he write.

Nobody said writing is easy, but it can be easier. We'll show you how. Among us, we have judged scores of writing contests, led hundreds of professional seminars and edited thousands of stories. From this rich lode, we have mined scores of examples of writing. We use these examples to show you how writers tell stories rather than just recite facts.

We're teachers now, but you won't find any horizontal-communications-interfaced-between-units language in this book. First we were writers, then editors. Then as we learned to be teachers, we discovered—painfully at times—that we had to know *why* something succeeded or failed. We learned to *show* by using examples, analogies, figures of speech and anecdotes, by interspersing the expository lectures with narration.

In this book, we *show* you *how* and tell you *why*.

- We show you the difference between describing a scene and putting readers in the scene.
- We show you how to stop fleeing readers with a single anecdote.
- We show you how to move deftly from one idea to the next without losing or confusing readers.
- We show you how to convert data into usable information that readers can scan quickly.
- We even show you how to conquer your fear of numbers. Well, almost. There's only so much you can do with journalists and numbers.

We do all this and more because writers have to work harder to attract and keep busy readers these days. On the one hand, many readers hunger for more depth, more analysis. On the other hand, many are struggling to keep their heads above the avalanche of information. That's why our journey beyond the inverted pyramid heads in two directions.

One is toward writing that starts the videotape of memories in every reader's mind. If we report with all our senses, we can write to appeal to all our reader's senses. Our goal is to make them forget for a few moments the long commute, the lunches that have to be made, the errands that must be run.

The other direction is to service journalism, the writer's version of microwaved information. Many readers who want useful information don't have time or won't take time to read longer articles, but they will scan short stories, lists, graphics and summaries. The stories may not appeal to the gourmet, but they are useful, quick and easily digested.

Because both genres are built on a common foundation, we start with a discussion of characteristics of writers and audiences, then move to the skills of good reporting before we arrive at the techniques of writing to inform and entertain. Then we apply these skills to special writing challenges: service journalism, organization publications, longer articles, opinion and humor.

The free-lance writers among us will find instructions in Appendix A on how to market stories. And for those among us who have to attend weekly Danglers Anonymous meetings, there's hope—and help—in a summary of grammar and punctuation rules and rationales in Appendix B.

In "Information Anxiety," author Richard Saul Wurman tells the apocryphal story of the professor who, on the first day of class, entered through the window and used the wastebasket for a hat rack. His students learned that words are what we say they mean. You can learn that and also why effective writing works by turning to our discussion of general semantics in Appendix C.

This book is based on the simple premise that good writing is good writing, no matter what the subject or outlet. The traditional distinctions between "newspaper" writing and "magazine" writing, between "news" writing and "feature" writing are eroding under the pressures of competition, the preferences of readers and the advances in technology. Most of those distinctions are artificial and arbitrary. Their disappearance is overdue.

That's why we believe "Beyond the Inverted Pyramid" is ideal for advanced news writing, feature writing and magazine writing classes and for practicing professionals who are not satisfied with just being good reporters and average writers.

Being good isn't enough anymore to keep our readers' attention. Readers are jumpier than frogs. The frog's nervous system is such that a frog sitting in water will boil if you raise the temperature gradually enough. By contrast, most readers will jump to something else as soon as you confuse or bore them. If you want to keep their attention, you must entertain as you inform. We believe that this book will show you how to do it with style.

This book is a team effort. We have benefited from the wisdom and suggestions of hundreds of students in our classrooms and professionals in our workshops. For their extra help, we would especially like to thank Ken Fuson of the Des Moines Register, Jeff Leen of The Miami Herald, Diana Dawson of the Spokane Spokesman-Review and Walt Harrington of The Washington Post.

We are grateful, too, to our colleagues across the country who provided us with helpful comments and suggestions: Jack Nelson, Brigham Young University; Thomas Eveslage, Temple University; Joseph A. Mirando, Southeastern Louisiana University; Michael Buchholz, Indiana State University; Joan Schleuder, University of Texas at Austin; Marion Lewenstein, Stanford University; and Kathryn News, Temple University.

And most of all, we want to thank our wives, Robin, Nancy and Eva Joan, for all their patience and support.

Contents

PART II

The best writers are the best reporters. Observing—
watching and listening—is the basic reporting tool.

A wealth of written information—on paper and in
computer files—can add depth to reporting and
understanding writing. Good reporters extend
their investigation beyond the interview.

The most important part of any journalist's job is
getting the story right, in detail and in context.

PART III

The first goal of nonfiction writers is to be believed.
To be believed, you must first be understood.

8 CREATIVE WRITING TECHNIQUES   84

Readers carry a mental videotape of all their experiences. However, most are soon forgotten. Your creative use of language has the power to help them remember these sights, sounds and smells.

9 STRUCTURING THE STORY   102

In architecture, design and writing, form follows function. Here are ways to weave the narration and exposition of a story that will attract and keep readers.

10 REVISING FOR PUBLICATION   122

By following these examples of drafts being revised, you can learn how to improve your own copy, and perhaps even how to get along better with an editor.

PART IV

11 WRITING SERVICE JOURNALISM 137

Learn how to present readers with useful information in the most usable way. This approach goes beyond the simple how-to-do article.

12 WRITING FOR ORGANIZATIONS 148

You may have an interested audience, but you still have to invite them to read, by writing brighter stories that achieve your organization's objectives.

13 WRITING PROJECT AND INVESTIGATIVE STORIES 163

Clarity and coherence are the fundamental qualities of good writing and the most difficult to maintain in long, complex stories. Discipline and organization are the secrets.

APPENDIX B:
THE JOY OF GRAMMAR   223

Grammar doesn't have to be drudgery if you
know the basic rules.

APPENDIX C:
THE LESSONS OF GENERAL SEMANTICS   251

Korzybski and Hayakawa outlined an introduction
of general semantics; these rules are the linguistic
basis for the principles of good writing.

INDEX   269

PART I

Writers and Their Audiences

1

Qualities
of Good Writers

*A writer is a person for whom writing is more difficult than it is
for other people.*—Thomas Mann

The job of a journalist, says the writer Bil Gilbert, is "telling stories to
strangers."

Writers are as varied as the stories they tell. Their backgrounds,
their training, their assignments differ. They may write for newspapers, for magazines, for corporate publications. They have in common, though, an allegiance to James Jackson Kilpatrick's credo:

> Before anything else, we must be WRITERS. We may be known as
> reporters, or critics, or columnists, or reviewers, or editorialists.
> We may specialize in news of business or labor or politics or sports.
> No matter. First of all, we are WRITERS. This is how we make our
> living: We write. We put words together. In the end, the test of how
> well we do our job is not in how well we cover the news, or review
> the movies, or chide a president, or criticize an actor, but in how well
> we write.

Some writers seem born to the role.

Alex Haley, for instance, delighted in describing how he learned
story telling as a boy of 5, crouched behind his grandmother's rocking chair on the front porch of the family home in Henning, Tenn., as
she and her sisters reminisced about their childhood and retold an
oral history linking five generations to an ancestor known as "the
African."

Haley told his first stories to strangers as a 17-year-old cook in the
U.S. Coast Guard, when he began writing love letters for less-literate
shipmates. At $1 per letter, he became a professional writer.

Nearly 30 years later, after having retired as the Coast Guard's first chief journalist and having established himself with polar-opposite magazines Playboy and Reader's Digest, Haley undertook to tell his family's story. "Roots," of course, became an international bestseller. Haley remained a writer with more stories to tell.

Diana Dawson is a storyteller, too. In her first decade of pursuing Kilpatrick's craft, she has written no books, but she has told the stories of burn victims and their healers, of children and their abusers, of derelicts and their basketball team.

"Whenever I get the chance, I find a lot of satisfaction out of being able to do a story that shatters people's stereotypes and helps them see their world in a slightly different light," she says. The story of the Union Gospel Mission and its championship basketball team gave her such a chance.

She wrote of one player and of the team:

> Rex Brockman, as compact as a caboose, steadily chugs past the defensive man to the basket, missing his layup by a breath. Consistent but reserved, Brockman says only that he came from Montana in search of restaurant work. He no longer grieves over departed teammates. Already this winter they've lost one of six mission players to booze and another to employment.

And, after another victory on the road to a second league title:

> Quiet congratulations all the way around and the men return to a team huddle. Randy Altmeyer begins a closing prayer: "Lord, thank you for this time we had. Thank you for none of us getting injured. Thank you for the sportsmanship."
>
> Amens echo around the circle.
>
> "And thank you, Lord," Deckard adds, "for Beard's free throws."

Like all good writing, Dawson's entertains, though it doesn't always amuse. It is clear, though not always simple. It is detailed, though not always long. It is elegant, though not fancy.

Good writers also have common characteristics. Writers are:

- Curious
- Widely read
- Full of ideas
- Knowledgeable of their audiences

This chapter elaborates on the first two of these characteristics. The next two chapters will help you to know your audience and show you some sources of ideas.

☐ THE CURIOSITY OF A WRITER

For a writer, the classic five W's and one H (Who, What, Where, When, Why and How) are not just elements in an inverted pyramid lead. They are the recurring questions, often subconscious, that guide the working life. A good writer is, first of all, a good reporter. And a good reporter is full of questions.

The questions that led Alex Haley to write "Roots" were fundamental and intensely personal: Who am I? Where did my people come from? Why and how? His search for the answers led him from Henning to Virginia courthouses to the National Archives to West Africa.

Diana Dawson's questions were less personal but still intense. Who were these marked men, these derelicts? What, if anything, lay behind their beards, their scars? How did their reality square with society's stereotypes? Her search led her to mission houses and basketball courts.

The same writer's curiosity prompted Cal Fussman, while a sports reporter for the St. Louis Post-Dispatch, to visit the players of a high school coach who was stricken by cancer. Startled by the reaction of one player, he questioned another. After he had interviewed eight players, he felt justified in quoting one in his story:

"Everyone wanted to get rid of him," the player said. "But we didn't want to get rid of him this way."

The story concluded:

Marler will be rooting for his team in the stands at Kirkwood High Thursday. The Pioneers will try to win one for the coach they don't really want.

An unremarkable story is made remarkable by curiosity at work.

Curiosity led Paul Theroux to a Peace Corps stint in Malawi immediately after college. Twenty-five years and 26 books later, Theroux explained to an interviewer why he had spent an entire year riding trains throughout China: "I wanted to be there long enough to see change, and things did change. I took the Chinese proverb 'We can always fool a foreigner' as a personal challenge." He met the challenge in his book "Riding the Iron Rooster" (the name of one of the trains he found).

Of his curiosity, Theroux explained, "I'm not just curious; I'm nosy."

Few writers match Theroux's wanderlust or productivity, but the good ones invariably are nosy. They may not want to know what's over the next hill, but they do want to know what's behind the next face.

Every writer needs to answer Who and What and Where and When. Good writers hunger to understand Why and How. The best writers follow their curiosity until it leads to the goal articulated by The Washington Post's Bob Woodward: "the best obtainable version of the truth."

☐ READING IN ORDER TO WRITE

Good writers read widely. If you would write well, you must know what good writing is—the look, the sound, the feel of it. Read poetry, read fiction, read journalism.

Poetry is the most overlooked and possibly most valuable source of guidance for writers who would perfect their craft. The best poets are the most efficient users of the language. Making each phrase do the work of a paragraph, creating images with a single line, they use words precisely. Read e e cummings for the discipline of his art, Edna St. Vincent Millay for imagery, and John Neihardt for soaring eloquence. Then emulate those masters.

When the American Society of Newspaper Editors began offering an annual prize for writing, the first winner was Everett S. Allen of the New Bedford (Mass.) Standard-Times. Allen told how, as a young reporter covering a fire, he got the idea of using an iambic line in his story. Most reporters recall iambic verse vaguely, if at all, from some survey course in poetry. Allen put it to work: "Ten pumpers roared throughout the night in Sawyer Street."

Later, after rescuing a sea duck that had been caught in an offshore oil spill, Allen was intrigued with the idea of her struggle for survival. His description is poetic:

> I did not sleep that night. Several times, I went to the bedroom window, squinting futilely into the deep shadows, where Ida waged the battle that each of us must fight essentially alone. There was no sound, no movement, nothing but interminable silence. I thought of her dead,

one big, funny foot outstretched awkwardly and her soft head unmoving on the wooden floor of the house, and I could neither stand the image nor put it out of my head.

At daybreak, I ran out, bracing myself.

Behold, she stood, the wild sea rover. Her eyes were like jewels in the fresh morning. Feet apart, chest out, and bill high, she made one demand of me—and I knew what it was. I shucked and hand-fed her a pint of quahaugs, joyous at the arrogance of her reborn appetite, unmindful of the fact that she nipped me unmercifully and unintentionally.

Take a moment to read that excerpt aloud to yourself. Savor the cadence, the imagery, the precision. Allen has brought the wild sea rover, and our language, alive.

The best novelists have the good reporter's eye for detail and ear for choice quotes. A good reporter who wants to be a good writer should study what those novelists do with their material. Magazine journalism long has borrowed such literary devices as narrative, metaphor, internal dialogue, vignette, first-person observer. Newspaper journalism is now starting to do the same. (A note of caution is in order here. Poets and novelists are free to create their characters, their images, their imagined reality. Journalists are not so free. For a journalist, facts are basic. Accuracy is the first requirement of good journalistic writing. So some devices of the fiction writer are off-limits to the journalist. In journalism, composite characters and invented dialogue are not elements of good writing. They are lies.)

Still, read Hemingway for pacing, for the mastery of the simple sentence, for the expert detail. Read Faulkner for his exploration of character, for the control that saves complexity from confusion. Read John Steinbeck for the use of dialogue, for the drama of everyday events. Read Kurt Vonnegut, Annie Dillard, Tom McGuane, Alice Walker, Eudora Welty.

The best contemporary writing, however, may well be in journalism. The styles and subjects vary widely, but if you look closely, you will find some essential qualities. You also will find that all of it is based solidly on good reporting.

Here, for example, is an excerpt from Steve Twomey's prize-winning report for The Philadelphia Inquirer on the U.S. Navy's aircraft carrier named America:

It is hard not to love the dance of the carrier deck—the skill, beauty, and sheer guts of men launching and landing warplanes on a 1,000-foot slab on the sea.

Seventy-five times on an average day, up to 400 times during crises such as Libya, America's crew members dodge sucking jet intakes and whirring props to hitch aircraft to the catapults and send them flying. That many times, they help them home and snare them and park them. They can launch planes a minute apart. They can launch and land at the same time. They can do it in the dark or in the rain. Their average age is 19½.

Engines whine, then race—and a plane disappears from the deck in 2.5 seconds. Its exhaust heat bathes launch crews. The air reeks of jet fuel. Steam seeps from the catapult track. The next plane is already moving forward to take the "cat stroke," and there's another behind it. Noise overwhelms the deck. All the while, the carrier slices through the blue.

"There's no way to describe it," said an A-7 pilot aboard America. "There's no way to see it in a movie. You've got to come out here and smell it and see it. It's too dynamic. The whole thing's like a ballet."

Twomey comes as close as any novelist could to standing his readers beside the flight deck. He uses the same techniques of description, of metaphor, of pacing. But he doesn't make it up.

Read Tom Wolfe, who more than anyone else created and defines the new journalism that grafts literary techniques onto in-depth reporting. Read Truman Capote, whose "In Cold Blood" was the precursor of a new genre, the nonfiction novel, also exemplified by Norman Mailer's "The Executioner's Song." Read Hunter Thompson, whose bizarre imagination and irreverent viewpoint make his self-indulgent wordiness bearable. Read Ellen Goodman and William Raspberry, two of the most perceptive critics of American society. Read Thomas Boswell, perhaps the finest sportswriter working today. Read Tracy Kidder, who has applied the techniques of literary journalism to subjects as varied as computers, home building and elementary school teaching. Read Elizabeth Drew, Mike Royko, Teresa Carpenter, Bil Gilbert.

Read them both for content and technique. Experiment with the styles of these masters until you settle on a voice of your own.

☐ QUESTIONS AND EXERCISES

1. Think of three good writers you know. How do their characteristics compare with those of the writers described in this chapter? Interview one or two of them. Are they curious? Widely read? Full of ideas?

2. What does the word "WRITER"—in James Jackson Kilpatrick's sense—mean to you? Are you a WRITER?

3. Curiosity test: Without moving from where you are, list five things that you wonder about. How might you turn that wonderment into stories?

4. Read any good books lately? Which ones? What was good about them? How would you describe the writing style of each author? Which is closest to your own style?

5. Stretch yourself. If you usually read fiction for fun, assign yourself a poet to study, or vice versa. If your usual journalistic fare is Spin or Rolling Stone, sample Washington Monthly. If your newspaper of choice is USA Today, try The Wall Street Journal. Ask yourself about the differences in style, in subject matter, in audience.

2

Knowing Your Audience

Writers are people who have readers—Malcolm Cowley

The American newspaper industry, worried that readership is declining, is filling the last decade of the 20th century with an activity that has long been a staple of the magazine industry—audience research. In Boca Raton, Fla. Knight-Ridder Inc. recreated its already-profitable News as part of a research and development effort the company calls the "25/43 Project," after the age group on which it is focused. The Gannett company is involving all its 80-plus newspapers in what it calls "News 2000," an attempt to revitalize papers for the next century. The first step in this project, too, is intensive study of the audience of each paper. And the American Society of Newspaper Editors (ASNE), conducting a series of national studies, titled its 1991 report, "Keys to our Survival."

That title might serve as a description of audience research itself. Understanding your audience is key to the survival of any publication, or of any writer. Let's look at how editors and their bosses study audiences, how they use what they learn and what all that means to you as a writer.

The ASNE study provides a good example of audience research on a grand scale. The organization hired MORI Research, which devised an elaborate questionnaire and administered it, by telephone and mail, to more than 1,000 people selected at random from across the country. Then the researchers analyzed the results by computer. Here are a few of the more significant findings:

- People's attitudes toward newspapers seem to fall into one of four broad types, which the researchers named Loyal Readers,

At-risk Readers, Potential Readers and Poor Prospects. About 55 percent fall into the "loyal" category; 13 percent each into "at-risk" and "potential", and 19 percent "poor prospect".

- Both "at-risk" readers, those who read papers regularly but aren't satisfied with them, and "potential" readers, those who appreciate newspapers but don't read them regularly, tend to be younger, busier, less educated and less attached to their communities than are "loyal" readers.

- Several topics that have broad interest but that many respondents said aren't well-covered now could be "leverage" topics to attract and hold more readers. These include: your own city; your neighborhood; your region; health and health care; news that's helpful with everyday living; schools and education news.

- To complicate matters, "at-risk" and "potential" readers disagree about what they want from newspapers. The "at-risk" readers want papers that are more efficient, easier to use, simple. "Potential" readers want more explanation, more depth, more detail.

- But even "loyal" readers would welcome substantial changes in their newspapers.

Next, using the results of the national study, five newspapers created prototype sections to test with readers some ideas that the study suggested as promising. For example, The Orange County Register in California created a local news section designed to appeal to "at-risk" readers. The experimental section had shorter stories with bigger headlines, no jumps to another page, more attention to school coverage, more follow-ups on earlier stories, lots of brief items and more maps and graphics.

Editor N. Christian Anderson concluded, "Here's the bottom line: They liked it. A lot." In fact, he added, not only did the target group like the new section by a 6–1 margin, but "loyal" and "potential" readers liked it by a 3–1 margin. The Register is incorporating into its existing local section some of the most popular concepts.

By contrast, The Portland Press Herald in Maine tested a general news prototype designed to appeal to "potential" readers but found that the prototype actually was more appealing to "at-risk" readers.

The implications of this kind of audience research for writers should be obvious. The interests of readers (and sought-after readers) point editors toward both topics and types of presentation that, in turn, shape the assignments, opportunities and even the story-telling styles of writers. For example, the reactions of readers to the prototypes in Orange County, Calif., seem likely to mean for writers at the

Register that they will be spending more time looking for stories about education. Those stories probably will be shorter than they used to be, and they will be told more with the aid of maps, charts and lists than with only words arranged in paragraphs.

☐ GOODBYE TO ALL THAT

In learning to follow the findings of audience research, newspaper editors and writers are venturing down a path that has been familiar to magazine journalists for decades. This difference in timing is due mainly to a long-standing difference in the economics of these two branches of the same print medium.

Until recently, newspapers have enjoyed, in most cases, high levels of stability and prosperity (with profit margins frequently exceeding 20 percent per year) based on monopoly or near-monopoly status in relatively small geographic areas. Newspapers in North America are, with few exceptions, local. Nearly every town of any size has a newspaper. Few have more than one. Until recently, readers and advertisers had few choices. So publishers and editors had little need of audience research. The audience, whatever it was, was theirs.

That situation has changed dramatically. Today, audiences and advertisers have an array of sources and outlets ranging from neighborhood newspapers to worldwide cable television networks. Lifestyles have changed just as dramatically. Households are smaller. Single-parent families are common. So are families in which both parents are employed. People are busier, more mobile, less interested in public affairs. Newspaper readership is down. Newspaper advertising is threatened. The industry is in turmoil.

☐ THE MAGAZINE JUNGLE

In other words, newspapers are entering the chaotic world of competition and constant change that has been the working environment for magazines almost since their beginning. With few exceptions, magazines have never enjoyed the geographic isolation and monopolistic stability in which newspapers grew fat and happy. For magazines, it has always been a jungle out there. And, like plants or animals trying to survive in a real jungle, magazines typically live or die on their ability to find a niche in the economic ecosystem. For the publishers, editors and writers of magazines, knowing their audience always has been key to survival. Here's an example of the kind of audience research that is common in the magazine industry.

With about 13,000 consumer magazine titles on sale at any one time, you might consider if any niches remain unfilled. Publishing companies know that some do. What the companies don't know, without research, is whether the niche is big enough to support a profitable publication or exactly what that publication should be. Several years ago, the Meredith company thought it saw a niche for a magazine devoted to woodworking. Some publications already existed, of course. They ranged from the broad-spectrum, such as Popular Mechanics, with some attention devoted to woodworking, to the highly specialized, such as Fine Woodworking. Meredith envisioned a magazine called, simply, Wood. Its intended audience would be hobbyists and professionals with a wide range of skills but a shared interest in making things from wood.

First, Meredith staffers created the general concept. Then they set out to test it with potential readers. Those readers were defined as men between 20 and 59 who claimed high interest in woodworking and who possessed, among them, a wide range of abilities. A research firm gathered 10 such men for a focus group session intended to test reactions to plans for content, appearance, frequency and price of the proposed magazine.

What emerged from the focus group was a set of preferences: for a monthly magazine priced at no more than $2 per copy; against use of slick paper or color illustrations if they increased the price; for heavy emphasis on practical advice and detailed plans; against material that would be esoteric or overly complicated. And what emerged from Meredith's analysis of its audience research was a publication that found its niche. A decade later, Wood is thriving.

For a would-be Wood writer, the message should be equally clear. The topics will be practical, not esoteric, but with some variety in the degree of woodworking expertise required. The writing will have to be simple but detailed, the concepts tested, the directions crystal-clear. And there will be a demand for plans and diagrams instead of beautiful color photography.

Another magazine, Country America, makes its message to writers explicit in a set of guidelines for free-lancers. Here's a sampling from those guidelines of what you'll need to know if you intend to write for Country America's audience:

Editorial Philosophy: Country America celebrates and serves the country way of life including country music.

Country America Readers:	Mainstream America whose values include: freedom, honesty, patriotism, individuality and loyalty. They are people who consider themselves: down-to-earth, straightforward, neighborly, hard-working and honorable.
What Makes A Good Country America Article?	The ideal Country America article will be light on copy with potential for several color photographs. Think visually. The magazine will serve the needs and interests of people who live in the country or identify with traditional country values and lifestyles found throughout the nation. Country America provides feature stories on travel, cooking, recreation, crafts, homes, gardening, traditions and people.

You may write for both Wood and Country America. You may even find yourself read by some of the same people who buy both magazines. But you'll certainly need to bring different tools to the workshop than to the country. That's no news to experienced magazine writers. It is rapidly becoming accepted among newspaper writers, too.

☐ AUDIENCES AND WRITERS

Your work as a writer is shaped from concept to execution by who your audience is and what kind of relationship your publication has or wants to have with that audience. Different publications seek to attract the same audiences in different ways. And different publications deal with the same topics in different styles for their different audiences. Here's an example of the same topic as reported by four publications. As you read, think of the writer-reader relationship.

Many physicians, especially those interested in medical research, are readers of the journal Science, the goal of which is to convey original research results directly from the investigators to their colleagues. Many of those same physicians also read American Medical News, a trade journal published by the American Medical Association. The News focuses not on pure science but on the practicalities and economics of medical practice.

The discovery of ddl, as reported in Science:

> The purine analog 2′,3′-dideoxyinosine (ddl), which has anti-retroviral activity in vitro was administered for up to 42 weeks to 26 patients with acquired immunodeficiency syndrome (AIDS) or severe AIDS-related

complex (ARC). Ten of these individuals were AZT-intolerant. Eight dose regimens were studied. The drug was orally bioavailable and penetrated into the cerebrospinal fluid (CSF). . . . Further controlled studies to define the safety and efficacy of this agent may be worth considering.

The discovery of ddl, as reported in American Medical News:

The federal government is expected to announce that the promising experimental AIDS drug dideoxyinosine—ddl—will become the first compound to be distributed under its recently proposed "parallel track" drug program, which offers HIV-infected people access to medications that are still undergoing clinical trials. . . . The only certainty was that the drug would be distributed free of charge by Bristol-Myers.

The first version, of course, was written by scientists for scientists. The technical language that is impenetrable jargon to most people is the stuff of everyday communication among initiates. Now look at the second version. Same topic, different focus. These physicians are being told about the discovery in fairly simple language, but with the emphasis on the mechanism and economics of the distribution. Two tools required of the second writer, but not of the first, are the ability to translate from "scientist-speak" to standard English and at least some background in medical economics.

A promising discovery in AIDS treatment is news far beyond science and medical circles. Here's how the same story was told, on the same day as the first two articles appeared, in The New York Times and in USA Today.

The discovery of ddl, as reported in the Times:

A promising experimental drug for the treatment of AIDS has produced improvements in patients without causing toxic side effects, a new study has shown.

Preliminary studies of the drug, dideoxyinosine, or DDL, have been so encouraging that researchers are rushing the drug into expanded tests involving nearly 2,000 patients to compare it with AZT, or azidothymidine, the only drug approved for the treatment of AIDS.

And the discovery of ddl, as reported in USA Today:

An AIDS drug that may be less toxic and more effective than AZT shows high promise in early human trials, scientists confirm in a report today.

National Cancer Institute scientists have been optimistic about the drug DDL for several months and already have planned large studies of it.

At least in theory, both these stories are written for the general public. But the differences are obvious. Those differences are traceable directly to the papers' audiences and attitudes toward those audiences. Both distinctions are important to writers, as they are to readers. The Times is America's elite newspaper. For decades it has been accepted as the prime source for the government, business and social leaders of the nation. Its style, verbal and visual, is austere and authoritative. USA Today, self-styled the Nation's Newspaper, was conceived as a second read, a useful and convenient supplement for travellers and others who want a quick fix on the state of the world in a format that lends itself to easy comprehension.

So it shouldn't be surprising that the two paragraphs quoted above from the Times contain 65 words, of which 31 have multiple syllables. The two USA Today paragraphs have just 48 words, 22 of which have more than one syllable. Which has more detail? Which is easier to read?

The moral of this story isn't that any audience or any level of discourse is inherently better than any other. It is that communication has both senders and receivers. Effective communication requires that messages sent—stories told—be about topics that interest the intended audience and be in language that audience understands.

Researchers have devised, and some publications use, formulas for measuring how understandable a story is. These are called readability measures. The two best known are named after their creators—Rudolf Flesch and Robert Gunning. Those and other measures are available in software programs that can be used in any computer system. Readability estimates use mainly word and sentence length. The results usually are stated in terms of the grade level of reading ability required for easy understanding of the copy tested.

One newspaper that relies on readability measures to help its writers communicate with their audience is the Lexington (Ky.) Herald-Leader. Editors there regularly use, and encourage their writers to use, the Flesch formula as one way to make sure they are writing stories readers can easily understand. The importance of such testing is suggested by a study conducted by William C. Porter and Flint Stephens. They compared newspaper editors' estimates of readability to the results of a test using the Flesch formula. Their findings were sobering. The editors consistently estimated stories to be four to six grade levels below the Flesch scores for readability. That is, the editors thought the stories were much easier to read than they actually were.

The study was small, but consider its implications. If editors overestimate the readability of stories, chances seem good that they will publish material their audiences won't understand. If that happens, you're not really communicating. When in doubt, test your work.

☐ LEARNING YOUR AUDIENCE

There are two equally important aspects to this writer-reader relationship. The first is making sure you know as much as you can about who your readers are. The second is making as sure as you can that you're communicating with them.

Start learning your audience by finding out what the publication for which you're writing already knows. Nearly every newspaper and magazine these days does audience research. Not enough of them make sure the results of that research reach the people to whom it matters most—the writers. So ask. Ask who the readers are, what they're interested in, what your publication is trying to tell them. That last point is important because, as we've already seen, editorial goals and approaches may vary widely even when the intended readers are much the same people. If your editor doesn't know the answers to your questions, wander over to the advertising or circulation departments. Somebody there probably does. And that somebody is likely to be both surprised and delighted that a writer really cares. You should care. Your success is at stake.

The final measure of your work is whether it is read and understood. Don't be shy asking about that, either. Some newspapers, and more magazines, do regular samplings of their readers to assess interests and tailor content. Ask what is being learned. If your publication isn't doing that sort of research, do a little yourself. Readability measures can help you assess the likelihood that people can grasp what you write. To find out whether they like it, you may have to ask them. Don't just ask your sources and your family members what they think, though even those assessments are better than none. Sound out acquaintances, eavesdrop at parties, interview total strangers. After all, you do your reporting in large part by asking questions of strangers. Why not ask a few if they're reading what you write?

Remember Ed Koch, the New York mayor who became a national figure for a while? His standard question, asked of constituents, reporters, anybody at all, was "How am I doing?" Maybe writers shouldn't wait for circulation reports or performance evaluations to try to find out the same thing. Just as politicians need followers, writers need readers.

In both cases, it pays to stay in touch.

□ QUESTIONS AND EXERCISES

1. Pick up a copy of Wood or Country America magazine. Using what this chapter tells you about the relationship each of these publications seeks with its audience, analyze the writing. Do the magazines seem to be following through on their promises? What do the differences between the magazines tell you about the differences between the audiences?

2. Read your local newspaper and see what you can tell about who the audience is. Does the audience for Page 1 seem to be the same as the audience for the Sports page? The feature section? The opinion page? The comics? What might the differences mean for writers?

3. Now do a little reporting. Interview an editor and a reporter for the newspaper you have just analyzed. Who do they think their audience is? Do they agree? How are they trying to communicate with their audience? Based on your analysis of the paper, do they seem to be succeeding?

4. Re-read the last piece you wrote. (It makes no difference whether it was journalism, fiction, poetry or a personal essay.) Now think about who its audience is or might be. Who would you like to reach with your writing? What, if any, changes in style or word usage will you have to make in order to increase your chances of effective communication?

5. Rewrite that piece for the audience of your local newspaper. Rewrite it again for Rolling Stone. Examine the differences and think about what they show of the differences in audience. Which style, which audience best suits you as a writer? Why?

3
Finding Ideas

An idea is a feat of association.—Robert Frost

As taxpayers were being asked to spend millions of dollars to build new sports facilities in Buffalo, David Montgomery, a staff writer for the Buffalo News, and his editor frequently talked about the irony that the city's orchestra had to cancel the last two weeks of its season for lack of funds.

The talk moved to more serious thinking. One day the editor put on Montgomery's desk a list of particulars: The city and franchise owners were getting ready to spend $130 million to expand the baseball stadium, $27 million to build facilities for the World University Games and $90 million for a new auditorium so the professional hockey franchise wouldn't leave.

Soon after, a press release announcing the publication of John Naisbitt's "Megatrends 2000" book arrived. The release said that Naisbitt predicted that arts will replace sports as the dominant leisure activity in the 1990s.

Montgomery bought the book, in which he read that one Broadway theater sold more tickets in the late 1980s than the New York Yankees and New York Mets combined.

Additional reporting led him to the National Endowment for the Arts, who told him that spending on arts tickets had surpassed sports tickets ever since 1984. After investigating, he was able to report, "More people attend arts and cultural events in Buffalo than attend professional sports games." He followed that lead by comparing the amount of money citizens were being asked to spend on sports to the amount allocated to support the arts.

The origin of that story is typical. Journalists bounce ideas off each other. A writer reads and wonders: How does that affect my city or my audience?

Even creative people work to find story ideas. Usable story ideas usually aren't found on ceilings, though many a journalist has spent hours studying the ceiling in search of a story. Ideas come to those who read and wonder: How does that affect people who read my newspaper or magazine? Ideas come to those who talk to people and wonder: If these people are curious about that, are others? Ideas come to those who read and talk and wonder: Is there a pattern or relationship?

Occasionally, an idea appears in a flash, an uninvited but welcome guest. More often, ideas lie hidden, like diamonds, waiting to be discovered. You can search randomly and find some of them, but if you search systematically, you are more apt to find more of them and find them more often. In this chapter, you will learn how to use both people and paper as sources of stories. You will also learn the benefits of the creative process involving two or more people.

☐ PEOPLE AS SOURCES OF IDEAS

If you are wondering what would interest people, ask them. Here are six ways.

1. Talk to people. Writers usually talk to dozens of people a day. All of them are sources of information, but they can also be sources of story ideas. Either in the small talk before an interview or after the interview, ask them to suggest stories they would like to see in your newspaper or magazine. Ask them what their colleagues and neighbors are talking about over coffee. A writer who occasionally talked to county extension agents discovered that each spring they answered scores of questions from callers wanting help with their gardening. The newspaper produced a useful story entitled "The 10 most asked questions from gardeners."

2. Set aside 20 minutes a day to call five people, selected at random from the phone book or a subscription list. You would be awash in story ideas.

If you are interested in writing for hunting publications, talk to people in the local gun or archery clubs. Those who are interested in writing for religion publications should talk to clergy and the laity.

3. Ask yourself and others, "How do you spend your time and money?" The answers to that question will clarify what really interests people. For example, people spend a lot of time at work, but newspapers don't cover the workplace systematically. What are workers' con-

cerns: The safety of their pension plans? Job security? How to please the boss? How to get along with co-workers? Day-care for children?

You might also get some less-important but interesting ideas: How to eat lunch on $5 a day. Is the brown bag being replaced by decorated lunch boxes? How electronic mail is being used as an underground communication system. The funniest things people have done for other peoples' birthdays. The best office pranks.

Outside of work, keep following peoples' time and money. Are they rushing from work to pick up children at day-care centers? Do they spend most of their time transporting children to and from school and recreation activities? How many movies do they attend a week? How many movies do they rent? How many times do they eat out? How many tapes and CDs do they own? The answers to each of these will lead you to stories. Some people want to know the new video releases. Some want movie and album reviews. Some want to know how to register their children for soccer or basketball. Some want to know how to find a good piano or dance teacher. Some want to know how to find a safe child-care center. Or they want to be able to compare prices and services.

4. Use polls. Researchers are talking to people about their concerns and interests. Read the results and wonder: If polls show that people are concerned about the availability and cost of medical insurance, what stories does that suggest? What are the people who are telling pollsters that companies and individuals ought to do more to protect the environment doing—or failing to do—in your community? If you are a newspaper journalist, you follow that trail in the area. If you work for a magazine or are a free-lance writer, focus on the publication's audience. An agricultural magazine might be interested in an article exploring whether farmers are environmentalists or polluters. A golf magazine might be interested in whether golf courses enhance the environment as green spaces or whether the fertilizer pollutes area streams.

5. Eavesdrop. Writers should always have their antennas up. When you are in a restaurant, at the mall, on the street or at a sporting event, what are people talking about? Take notes.

6. Talk to yourself. What interests you? What do you do when you are not working? What organizations do you participate in and why? What affects your life and why? How do you deal with your daily problems?

Joe Kennedy of the Roanoke (Va.) Times & World-News turned a near-tragic personal experience into an issue story with a strong human angle. His wife and child were injured in a car accident. The seat belt caused life-threatening injuries to his 6-year-old son. Kennedy wondered how common it was that the belt, meant to protect someone, injured them instead.

The answer: often. His story was one that would attract the attention of any parent of small children.

The story need not be as dramatic. Have you, or someone you know, just bought a car? A writer could use that experience to tell another potential buyer how to save money by talking to experts and reading the right publications. Look around in your home or apartment. What do you need to know to keep it up? Where do you look in your city to find a dependable cabinetmaker? How do you find someone to build an addition or replace the roof? Do you know what to look for when buying new carpeting? What are the trade-offs between price and quality in windows, in washing machines and dishwashers, in microwaves and refrigerators, in televisions and CD players? If you have these questions, so do many of your readers.

☐ PAPER AND ELECTRONIC RESOURCES

You and your readers are awash in information. Your job is to identify the interesting, the useful, the significant. You have more sources than ever. Here are some of them.

1. Electronic data banks. Data banks are merely a systematic way of storing paper files. They save you time because they are organized by many different headings. Instead of rummaging through dozens of envelopes full of clippings, you can now ask the computer to search for key words. If you were Joe Kennedy looking in the traditional filing system, you would probably look under seat belts. You would get dozens of articles you don't want. But in an electronic data base, combine the key words "seat belt" and "safety" and you quickly narrow your search while drawing on a larger body of publications.

If you are a staff writer, you have access to your newspaper or magazine library, now probably on electronic data base. You probably also have access to national data bases, such as Dialog and Dow Jones News Retrieval. Anyone can access some of the same information through libraries, for a fee, or subscribe to them through a modem hooked to a computer.

Data bases that include large numbers of newspapers among their sources are excellent sources of trend stories. Someone examining a data base in the early 1980s might have seen enough stories on smoking restrictions in public places to recognize that what had been an essentially local story was on the verge of becoming a national trend.

Even before electronic data bases became available, futurists such as John Naisbitt spotted trends by analyzing and categorizing clippings from hundreds of newspapers. Data bases have made the task of spotting trends cheaper and faster for Naisbitt, and they have also made the information available to journalists willing to look for patterns.

2. Newspapers, magazines and books. Naisbitt spotted an apparent contradiction between interest and public spending for sports and arts. The Buffalo News made it a local story. Writers must read widely and wonder: What about my readers?

The daily newspaper carries a wealth of story ideas waiting to be found. Read the auction ads and wonder why a family or business is selling. Read the legals and wonder why a home is being repossessed. Read the personals and wonder who places those messages and why. Read the brief about an assault victim and wonder how such victims fare a year later.

Read specialized publications, especially the newsletters, to get a jump on the crowd. Readers of Supermarket News, for instance, would have realized early that microwaves were no longer a luxury item. Supermarket News was telling its grocery managers of the need to devote more shelf space to microwavable products.

That news, in turn, would turn the writer on to many other stories. At first a luxury, microwave ovens became a necessity, in part, because of the rapidly increasing number of households where both spouses

---

EXAMPLES OF SPECIAL-INTEREST
PUBLICATIONS

Trends in Housing
Stores
Trains
Carpenter
Business Insurance
Building Material Retailer
Cereal Foods World
Byte
Dairy Foods
Bookseller
Lodging
Marketing News
Trends in Biochemical Sciences

were working. They were also needed in the increasing number of single-parent households. Those demographic changes signaled revolutionary upheavals in the kind of information newspapers and magazine audiences would need. Instead of time-consuming recipes, the emphasis turned to meals that could be prepared quickly. A writer following the microwave trail would have found a growing need for day-care facilities, would have found the latch-key children syndrome first, would have realized that a growing number of readers needed help raising children without a spouse, would have understood the reason for the rapid increase in fast-food restaurants. The next trend is lurking in several of the specialized publications, in magazines such as American Demographics, or articles and books by futurists such as Naisbitt.

Read the obituaries and wonder about a story of life, rather than death. That's what a reporter for the Columbus (Ind.) Republic did when he noticed that a man who for years had sold brooms on a city street had died. He followed the standard obituary with a story of the man's life. It ended this way:

> Ferrenburg never considered himself handicapped.
> "I can hear birds sing. I can hear little children," Mrs. Michaelis said her father replied when asked whether he would rather see than hear. "I'd rather be blind anytime than deaf."

Read the advertisements in phone books. Compare the phone book from five years ago (libraries often keep old copies) to this year's. Has there been an increase or decrease in the number of doctors? Of specialists? Perhaps that will lead you to a story about changes in health care availability. Are there new categories of businesses? Perhaps you'll discover a trend story.

3. Read statistics. Each set of numbers conceals several interesting stories. Look at the number of phones installed over the last five years in your city and follow your instincts. Business story: How does the number of phones correlate to rising population? To the growing popularity of fax machines? Lifestyle story: How many families now buy their children a separate line?

Your city or local utility has data on the amount of water used. Enterprising reporters have even been able to correlate water usage to television commercials on popular telecasts such as the Super Bowl. Others might be interested in per capita usage, especially in areas of the country where water is in short supply. Correlate electric usage to temperatures or times of the day and do a lifestyle story. Track housing permits by number and amount.

Reporters for the Fresno (Calif.) Bee produced an interesting and important story when they looked at the number of teenage pregnancies in their coverage area. This is how their story started:

> We're No. 1.
> Teen-age girls in the central San Joaquin Valley are more likely to have babies than anywhere else in the state. And, since California tops the country in teen pregnancies, we may very well lead the nation.

Mine the richest of all statistical books, the U.S. Census Bureau reports. You can profile blocks within cities, let alone neighborhoods, by looking at the statistics on income, number of people in each household, education, number of appliances, and yes, even the number of toilets.

4. Anticipate. Editors love to hang a story on a peg. The national park system turns 125 in 1997. Want to do a story on ballooning? The 60th anniversary of the Hindenburg disaster will be in 1997. Earthquakes? An estimated 60,000 people died in an earthquake in Italy in 1693 and 1,100 died in an earthquake in Yugoslavia in 1963. Either would serve as a peg for a story in 1993. Several newspapers and magazines will find an angle for a 10-year anniversary story of the Exxon Valdez oil spill.

Nearly every publication has its annual holiday story timed to coincide with New Year's, Valentine's Day, Hanukkah and Christmas. Those stories are planned weeks, even years, in advance.

☐ THE CREATIVE PROCESS

So far you have been working primarily off your own wits. Get help.

When it comes to creativity, one and one equals three. One person suggests an unformed story idea; another counters. The first responds. The brainstorming continues until a fully formed idea takes shape.

At the Orange County (Calif.) Register, that process led to the establishment of new beats to cover shopping malls and traffic. Those ideas came out of brainstorming discussions about how people were spending their time and money. Journalists realized during the talks that shopping malls had become the new village greens, that malls were more than places to shop; they were also social centers for the young and the old. GO, Girls Only magazine knows this, too. That's why it published an article about a typical afternoon at the mall for three teen-age girls.

The Register also realized that its readers were spending a significant portion of their lives commuting to and from work. That, in turn, leads to stories about road conditions, new roads, road repairs, new routes, car pooling, road safety and others.

The Cincinnati Enquirer staff decided it wanted to create a bond with readers. One response was to start a weekly column in which staff members would write first-person columns on personal experiences. They also are finding stories to help people at work, stories about baby boomers and stories about youth culture, none of which would have come up on traditional beats.

The News of Boca Raton, Fla., used readership surveys and focus groups to help define reader interests, then brainstormed ways to meet the demand. The paper expanded its entertainment coverage, invited readers to contribute front-page opinion pieces and added many "how-to" features.

Not all writers have the luxury of working on a staff, but they can engage friends in the same type of creative session.

☐ FINDING ANGLES

When John Zeaman, art critic at the Hackensack (N.J.) Record, visited an exhibit by artists who had been supported by state funds, he was astonished by the lack of quality. He wrote a review panning the work. After reading the review and questioning him, his editor suggested another angle: Was the state's art council spending its money wisely?

They even had a peg. For several previous months, a national debate raged over National Endowment for the Arts grants that had produced what some considered pornography. Zeaman's new angle is summed up in statement about the exhibit that ". . . its deficiencies are serious enough to raise fundamental questions about New Jersey's program giving fellowships to artists."

No story idea works until you have found the angle appropriate to the audience of your publication. Scores of publications have published stories about the national debate over the quality of education, but each of them looks for its own angle. Here are a few examples:

The New York Times:	A series of schools that are successful despite the odds.
The Colorado Springs Gazette Telegraph:	Problems that teachers encounter, such as children whose families couldn't afford to buy them glasses, children who come without clean clothes, children who come to school hungry and tired and stressed out because of problems at home.

Washington Monthly:	Schools need to teach values, too.
The Economist:	How to encourage deprived kids in the classroom.
USA Today:	Top high-school students criticize the quality of secondary education.
The Los Angeles Times:	Poor schools threaten the standard of living in the United States.
U.S. News & World Report:	The problem of education is not as bad as many think, but there are some steps that need to be taken to improve education.
Newsweek:	How to teach our children.

Those are examples of news publications putting a different spin on the same general subject. SHAPE and HEALTH are examples of two magazines that would appear to have similar content, but they have distinctly different markets. While SHAPE is writing about calcium supplements and devotes a significant amount of space to exercise regimes, HEALTH is examining the claims of manufacturers who market stay-young products and informing readers about a strain of chicken that lays low-cholesterol eggs.

Ask, talk, brainstorm, read. Put yourself in your readers' shoes. Find the angle that will interest readers—and editors—and you won't have to search the ceiling for ideas again. At least, not as often.

☐ QUESTIONS AND EXERCISES

1. Read your local newspaper and list at least five story ideas. Clip the article, listing or advertisement from which your idea originates.

2. In a nationally circulated, general-interest magazine, find three ideas for trend stories that could be localized in your community.

3. In a special-interest publication, find five story ideas that you could localize.

4. List five story ideas that you obtain by talking to other people about what interests them.

5. Using a national data base, find a story that has been done in at least six publications. Analyze the stories and show the differences in the angles each publication pursued.

PART II

Reporting Well
to Write Well

4

Human Sources: Observing and Interviewing

There is only one trait that marks the writer. He is always watching. It's a kind of trick of the mind and he is born with it.—Morley Callaghan

☐ INTRODUCTION

There are two ways to capture the detail that sets the best writing apart from the ordinary. One is recounted by a character in Evelyn Waugh's classic satire on journalism, his novel "Scoop." One reporter is describing to another the exploits of the legendary foreign correspondent Wenlock Jakes:

> Why, once Jakes went out to cover a revolution in one of the Balkan capitals. He overslept in his carriage, woke up at the wrong station, didn't know any different, got out, went straight to a hotel, and cabled off a thousand-word story about barricades in the streets, flaming churches, machine guns answering the rattle of his typewriter as he wrote, a dead child, like a broken doll, spreadeagled in the deserted roadway below his window—you know.
>
> Well, they were pretty surprised at his office, getting a story like that from the wrong country, but they trusted Jakes and splashed it in six national newspapers. That day every special in Europe got orders to rush to the new revolution. They arrived in shoals. Everything seemed quiet enough, but it was as much as their jobs were worth to say so, with Jakes filing a thousand words of blood and thunder a day. So they chimed in too. Government bonds dropped, financial panic, state of emergency declared, army mobilized, famine, mutiny—and in less than a week there was an honest to God revolution under way, just as Jakes had said. There's the power of the press for you.
>
> They gave Jakes the Nobel Peace Prize for his harrowing descriptions of the carnage—but that was colour stuff.

The honest way is more difficult. Writer Bil Gilbert summarizes it: "Observation is the basis of everything." Legend has it that the ancient Druids forced candidates for the priesthood to study an oak tree. A failed candidate would be nailed to the tree whose details he had not captured.

Druidic discipline is not practiced in newsrooms, but the precision of observation it was intended to encourage should be. Not every good reporter is a good writer, but every good writer is, above all, a good reporter. Reporting IS observation.

Of the qualities that distinguish good from bad writing, three depend directly on observation. They are clarity, precision and appeal to the senses. The others—pacing and transition—lend grace and power to the expression of what you have observed.

Observation is an active, not a passive, process. Clarity, precision and appeal to the senses seldom are achieved just by looking or listening. You usually have to seek out information that is not readily apparent. The reporter's main research tool is interviewing. All reporters interview, but few interview as well as they might. Fewer still get beyond the interview to other sources of information and understanding. Documents, the records of business, government and personal life, can be invaluable in answering questions and providing detail. Even the methods of social science offer help for the writer who would be a better observer.

This discussion of reporting is intended to help you become a better observer by showing you how to use the tools of interviewing and research and how to ensure the accuracy of your observation.

The best writers are the best observers.

☐ OBSERVING

Here's a keen eye at work. The eye and the writing belong to Jeff Leen, a reporter for The Miami Herald.

> Johnny Paul Witt, a Tampa sex killer who murdered an 11-year-old boy for the thrill, went to his death in Florida's electric chair Wednesday, nearly devoid of emotion.
>
> Witt, who spent 11 years on Death Row, passed up most of the traditions of the execution ritual. He did not request a minister, refused to order a final meal and made no final statements. Prison officials said that as the end neared, Witt was "uncommunicative."
>
> Witt, 42, the 12th man put to death in Florida since 1979, was the 39th executed since the U.S. Supreme Court lifted its moratorium in 1976.

Witt was condemned for the 1973 murder of Jonathan Kushner, son of a University of South Florida professor. Tuesday night, the U.S. Supreme Court refused his final appeal.

An omelet, rolls and coffee laid out for Witt went untouched Wednesday morning.

Gaunt, pale and wobbly, Witt walked into the Florida State Prison death chamber just before 7 a.m. dressed in a white shirt, blue pants and white socks without shoes. He bit his lip nervously.

When prison Supt. Richard Dugger asked Witt for any final words, he mumbled, "No, I don't have any."

At 7:04 a.m., an executioner paid $150 for the job pulled the switch. Witt was pronounced dead at 7:10.

In a cow pasture across a country road from the prison, seven death penalty protesters and nine supporters gathered for a muted display that lacked the props and skits of past executions.

This is a news story in the hands of a skilled reporter. Notice the detail that helps the reader visualize the event and understand its context. The condemned man wasn't just uncommunicative. He "did not request a minister, refused to order a final meal and made no final statements." We even learn the menu of the breakfast Witt didn't eat. The point: *Specific examples convey reality far more effectively than can any generality.*

Leen doesn't just tell his readers that Witt looked ill. He was "Gaunt, pale and wobbly . . ." We learn the details of his dress, down to his socks. And there weren't just a group of protesters across the road. We get numbers, a brief description of the road and a characterization of the field in which they stood.

Here's Leen's summary of what he was doing with this story:

"Watching the execution was a more powerful and unsettling experience than I anticipated. A somber, subdued tone crept into the hard news story I wrote. In my lede I chose to contrast the sensational nature of Witt's crime—he suffocated a child he planned to rape—with the emotionless way he went to his death.

"The rest of the story is a fairly straightforward rendering of facts with a few personally observed details thrown in for immediacy. . . . The intent of the story is to provide information as quickly and efficiently as possible in a very small space."

The intent of this example is to show you that the precision and detail gained from expert observation play an important role in the seemingly most routine of stories, the coverage of a single event.

However, Jeff Leen had more than the routine in mind on this assignment. He also wrote a personal account of the execution for

The Herald's Tropic magazine. Now he shows us another level of observation. Watch.

> The chair, handmade of oak, sits behind a pane of glass in a chamber not much bigger than a large bathroom. You look at it like no chair you have ever looked at in your life. You look at it as if you expect to see something other than a chair. You look for the death in it.
>
> But all you see is an old-time frame chair that might be one of a crowd around a farmer's dinner table, except that it is made for a giant; the headpiece would tower over the top of your head. It is 61 years old but well-cared for: The dark-stained wood gleams, the grain in the slats and arms stands out like pinstripes.
>
> If you sat in the chair, you would look out on rows of folding metal chairs in a second small room where 40 people are jammed together, trying to erect a proper silence. Sitting in the first two rows are men dressed in suits: judges, prosecutors and detectives. In the second two rows are journalists, more casual in slacks and blazers.
>
> A dozen prison guards stand off to the left. Some are at attention, hands behind their backs. All of them keep their eyes on the empty chair. On the peach-colored wall behind the chair are three beige telephones. On the wall to the left is a clock. It is 6:58 A.M. There are no windows except the one between the two rooms. The lighting is bright and even, eliminating all shadow. Four men in the room are making the final preparations.
>
> There is nothing but the sound of people trying to be quiet.
>
> Before we are ready, a door opens and they bring him in. He is gaunt and pale. The veins stand out against the smooth white skin of his cleanly shaved head. His eyes are set deep in the pale shaved head, already a skull. His eyes are on the floor. He wears a white button-up shirt and dark blue pants that fit badly. He makes his final walk in white socks without shoes. . . .
>
> "Johnny Paul Witt," he is asked. "Do you have any last words?"
>
> "No," he mumbles, looking down. "I don't have any."
>
> A leather strap secures his chin. A leather cap is fastened to the bald head. A heavy cable is screwed into the cap, which contains a mesh of wires and a small sponge soaked in saline solution to keep the flesh from burning.
>
> A dark hood is pulled down, slowly swallowing the face.
>
> There is sound that might be a sigh or a groan or a whimper.
>
> There is a "thunk."
>
> It takes less than two minutes.
>
> Afterwards, the prosecutors, judges and lawyers seem subdued. They had been closest. Some wipe their eyes and sniff. Some of the guards have tears in their eyes. The journalists don't seem to know how to react. There is a discussion about whether the last words were "No, I don't have any" or "No, I don't have." There is odd nervous laughter during the discussion. We are divided about equally on the matter.

About this piece, Leen says modestly, "The story is little more than personal observation." Observe, if you will, this observation. Not only is the observation detailed and exact—"The chair, handmade of oak . . . 61 years old . . . dark-stained wood gleams, the grain in the slats and arms stands out like pinstripes"—but the new is made understandable by comparison with other detail remembered from the familiar. The death chamber is "not much bigger than a large bathroom." This awesome chair is "an old-time frame chair that might be one of a crowd around a farmer's dinner table."

Compare this description of Witt himself to the description that was appropriate to the news story. Compare the news story summary of the execution with this description of preparation for the killing. This detail chills.

Now Leen shifts his focus again to the living. He conveys mood by observation. He even shows something of the human uncertainty of journalism itself in the aftermath of the certainty of death.

The writer says of his work that he has filled it with "closely observed detail designed to paint mental images for the reader." His goal, unlike a news account, "is to make the reader feel along with the writer."

The segments reproduced here don't capture the full force of the narrative, but they are enough to show the power of precise language fueled by detailed observation.

Like Jeff Leen and other fine writers, you too can:

1. **Look for the significant detail.**
2. **Look for the revealing anecdote.**
3. **Look with your mind, as well as your eyes, open.**
4. **Prepare before you start to look.**

No two snowflakes are identical, but their differences are seldom important. No two people, no two situations, no two oak trees are identical, either. Your job is to sort out the important differences.

The first step is to look closely. Suppose you are looking at a successful banker. Look at the clothes. You'd expect them to be tasteful and expensive. Do they look it? Ask where she buys them. (You can find out from the store how much they cost.) Look at the face. You'd expect signs of maturity, of firmness, of good living. Are her eyes bloodshot? That could be a sign of close study of a balance sheet or of a martini glass. Make a note to find out. Is she deeply tanned? The banker could be a golfer, a sailor or a sunlamp addict. Find that out, too. How is her hair cut? Is it trimmed close or styled and full? That may be a clue to her outlook on life. Look at the hands. Are they manicured or nail-bitten? Any sign of callouses? Do you detect a slight tremble? Those are clues, too. Look at the desk, at the wall decorations, at pictures of spouse and children (or note their absence). You may find indications of importance, of ego, of outside interests, of family situations.

The next step is to sort out the significant from the trivial. Those characteristics that might be expected may yield a picture of your subject as a banker like any other. Maybe she is. But the characteristic that doesn't seem to fit, that surprises you, that catches your attention may be the tipoff to what sets this banker apart from the others. Don't jump to conclusions. Fortify your first impressions with all the other evidence you can find—in further observation, in interviews, in assessments from others. Then, taking the sum of what you have learned, piece together the mosaic.

Jim Atwater, in Smithsonian Magazine, told the story of one of the bloodiest battles of World War I. He began with a look at the battlefield.

> On the Newfoundlanders' field of battle the old trenches can still be seen. Smoothed and softened by time, they lie like a gentle range of miniature mountains and valleys. They are grassed over, but narrow; sandy paths wind along the bottoms of the trenches. In the intervening years, enough people have felt compelled to stand where the men had been to wear away the turf. A crag of rocks and bushes rises steeply ahead, topped by a great, dark, metal statue of a caribou, the symbol of the Royal Newfoundland Regiment. His magnificent antlers are lifted high. He is looking out toward the German lines.

Scene-setting is a good way to convey important information and put it in context at the same time. Another way to do the same thing is with the anecdote, or vignette. An anecdote is a sort of story within a story. It may help to set a scene or to reveal the character of a person or a place. It may be used as a lead or in the body of the story. You will be more successful as a writer if you succeed as a reporter in capturing the telling anecdote.

Here's an anecdote that helps Mark Davis of the Tampa Tribune bring life to what could have been a chore for both writer and reader, a description of on-the-job training. Ride along as newly hired Richlene Young learns to drive a road roller.

> They went through the instructions as Barney pointed out the levers that controlled the machine. He also noted that it had a control that shook the 15,000-pound roller. When it vibrated, the roller banged

moisture out of the earth so asphalt would adhere more readily to the road bed. Young was entranced.

They put the roller in gear, and it lurched as it chugged toward the southeast corner where workers dodged cars as they followed a barricade trail. Barney showed her where to use the roller, and she uncertainly aimed the behemoth toward the road-bed and curbing. Sitting eight feet in the air, her hard hat dazzlingly white in the canopy's shadows, she watched the traffic pass by.

She began to feel at home atop the clattering machine as she pushed levers and the machine, miraculously, responded to her directions. It tickled the bottom of her boots, and she enjoyed the sensation. It felt like home.

The best scenes or anecdotes are those that, like these, add something other than entertainment, though that is desirable, too. Look for the anecdote that will tell your readers something about the subject of your story, as Mark Davis told his something of both roadbuilding and of one young roadbuilder.

When you hear a good anecdote or see it unfold before you, try to catch exact quotes and details, jot down the circumstances and names of participants. One way to get good anecdotes is to ask for them. No, you can't expect a perfect response if you say, Please tell me a good anecdote. But you can ask specific questions that may yield the recollection you want. Ask, What's the funniest/saddest/dumbest/ most embarrassing thing that has happened to you since you were elected? People savor such memories. Often they're willing to share. And once you have a good one, share it with your readers. Don't save it for the entertainment of the coffeeroom gang.

It's fair use to boil down the anecdote to its essentials, even if some participants or some quotes must be left out. It is unfair and dishonest to distort the scene or the quotes to make the anecdote funnier or more pertinent. The rules of journalism demand that you shape your writing to your material, not the other way around.

The most serious obstacles to accurate observation and fair use lie in the mental baggage we all carry—the preconception, the stereotype, the prejudice. They distort vision, leading you to see only what you expected to find, instead of what may really be in front of you. No human being can exorcise them, but all writers must learn to identify their mental baggage and to keep it checked.

Though some would deny it, most writers begin reporting most stories with at least some idea of what they will find. There is nothing inherently wrong with that. In scientific research, the same sort of preconception is called the hypothesis. It is accepted as the essential starting point for any research project. The scientific method demands that the scientist, in testing the hypothesis, look for evidence to disprove it. That high standard of detachment is not always met, even in science. But it is the standard that every writer should apply to his or her work.

It's fine to begin with an idea of your likely conclusion, so long as you keep your eyes and your mind open to evidence that may suggest a different conclusion. Careful observation will turn up the evidence; an open mind will accept it.

Scientists have another tool more writers would do well to borrow. In science, it is called reviewing the literature. No reputable researcher launches a study without carefully combing the journals of the discipline to learn everything possible about the research already done, the questions left unanswered, the methods others have found useful.

Too many writers reinvent the wheel with every story. An hour spent with a computer data base, the clippings in your newspaper morgue or down at the public library often can save days of relearning what somebody before you has already reported. In reviewing the literature, writers, like scientists, often can improve their ideas about what questions to ask and where to look for the answers. The section on interviewing will offer more specific suggestions.

If you prepare before you look, look with an open mind and look for the significant detail, you will find, more often than not, the material with which to write compellingly.

☐ INTERVIEWING

When you interview someone and come away with only facts and figures in your notebook, you have done yourself a great disservice as a writer. Why? Because the interview usually offers your best chance of picking up the good quotes, the enlightening anecdotes, the bits of humanity you need to bring life to any story. The facts and figures could be, and often should be, gathered from documents, which are more reliable and less likely to impart misunderstanding than most human sources. Humanity, though, is best transmitted person-to-person.

Here are some tips for getting the most from interviews:

1. **Prepare beforehand**
2. **Put your source at ease**
3. **Listen**
4. **Record what you hear (and see)**
5. **Get it right and get it on the record**

☐ Preparation

A good trial lawyer never asks a witness in the courtroom a question to which the lawyer doesn't already know the answer. The lawyer doesn't want to be surprised, so he or she does extensive research before the trial begins. A writer's life is full of surprises, but homework is no less important. Without it, you may not know what questions to ask. You may not understand the answers you get. You may even be questioning the wrong person.

When the San Jose (Calif.) Mercury News assigned Peter Carey to fly to Guyana to cover the aftermath of the Jonestown massacre, his first stop was not the ticket agency. It was the public library. He found a book on religious cults, read it and called the author. He knew a great deal about the phenomenon he was dealing with before he left home. That's an example worth following.

Of course, librarians and journalists today have access not only to books on the shelves but to information from newspapers and magazines, technical reports, scholarly studies, statistics—all through computer data bases that are available at relatively low cost in newsrooms, libraries and even via modem-equipped home computers. Nexis, Dialog, CompuServe and other databases enable writers today to research stories and background themselves for interviews more quickly and more completely than ever before. The best writers use their computers for more than word processing.

Your goal as an interviewer is to find out all you can about the person you're going to be talking to and the subjects you'll be asking about. Nothing warms a source's heart and loosens a source's tongue like the intelligent questions of a well-prepared reporter. (Of course, as you'll see below, there's more than one way to take advantage of your preparation.)

The conventional wisdom has it that, if you are working on a profile or an investigative piece, you should delay interviewing the central figure until you have done the rest of your reporting. The reasoning behind that advice is that the more material—facts, anecdotes, clues to personality and character—you have gathered, the more likely it is that this key interview will be productive. Often, however, there are even better reasons for talking with the central figure or figures as early in the reporting as possible. Frequently, these key interviews will suggest avenues for exploration that you might not otherwise find until much later, if at all. Sometimes, a key interview can save you from trekking down dead-end paths.

You: "Tell me, Senator, where'd you get the $2 zillion to buy that cable television company?"

The Senator: "I inherited that last year from my Aunt Wilhelmina. Didn't you see her obit in the Times? I have it right here."
You: "Oh."

☐ Establish Rapport

The first few minutes of any interview set the tone and, in most cases, determine the success. Usually, those first minutes are best spent gaining the subject's confidence, demonstrating your knowledge and preparing the way for the more serious questions to come. Award-winning reporter Ken Fuson of the Des Moines Register has a standard response to questioners seeking the secrets of his interviewing success:

"I always tell them not to underestimate the power of stammering. Seriously, I spend so much time hemming and hawing and trying to form a coherent question that the poor souls I'm interviewing feel the least they can do is spill their guts."

Fuson quotes Eugene Roberts' description of the legendary reporter Homer Bigart:

> Bigart seemed capable of everything. He had awesome techniques. He could slam through the wall or pirouette around it. He made instant sources but knew how to work the records. He idolized fact and made friends with nuance. His secret weapon, though, was to bumble.
> Homer Bigart would show up on a story, stuttering the asking, "Wh - wh - what's goin' on?"
> And everyone would be helping poor old Homer.
> They helped him to two Pulitzer Prizes.

Fuson takes from that example an important lesson. Every writer should learn it.

"Don't be afraid to look or sound stupid. One of my strengths as an interviewer is that I don't pretend to know a whole lot—it's not an act—so it forces me to ask simple, elementary questions. And that, in turn, plays off two basic human emotions: (1) the need for people to talk about themselves, and (2) their desire to teach others. If you ask a banker about the Federal Reserve, or a farmer about the set-aside program, or an astronaut about aeronautics, he or she won't laugh in your face if the question is a simple one. Most people love to explain what they do. Let them help you. Only television reporters ask eloquent, three-part questions at the drop of a press conference."

Occasionally, if you know the source to be hostile or if time is short, you will have to dispense with the preliminaries. But otherwise, begin by asking a few questions the source will be glad to answer. The questions themselves will depend on the point of the interview. For a personality profile, good starting points would be family, hobbies or a recitation of the source's rise to prominence. For a harder story, it's often a good idea to start out with a few inquiries about facts you already know. That's a quick test of veracity.

If your research has turned up a flattering anecdote or a bit of esoteric information, work it into the interview early. Most people respect knowledge, and everybody responds to flattery.

❏ Listen

Interviewing is an active, not a passive, process. The best interviews usually are those that most closely resemble conversations. It's a good idea to enter every interview with at least a general understanding of what you want to get out of it. It's a good idea to have a set of questions prepared, at least mentally, beforehand so you can make sure you cover the important ground. But many interviewers make a great mistake by sticking to their predetermined course when the interviewee suggests potentially profitable digressions. Remember that your interviewee knows more about herself and her business than you do. She may have answers for which you don't have prepared questions. Listen.

Practice listening to yourself, too. Ken Fuson: "I would recommend that young reporters use a tape recorder for one reason: to hear themselves conduct an interview. About the fourth time you hear yourself cutting off somebody right when they are saying something interesting, you'll relearn an important lesson—to shut up and listen."

Listen, if your interviewee wants to talk about the impact of her mother's death or about the treachery of a trusted associate when you had in mind a simple success story. Listen and encourage. The best way to solicit more information may be simply to indicate your sympathetic attention. You can do that with nods of agreement, murmurs of sympathy, pauses to encourage elaboration. Lean toward the speaker, watch her. Act interested. That should be easy. You should BE interested.

Listen and ask for more. Even the most helpful interviewee doesn't know what you need for your story. And not everyone wants to be helpful.

Ask for the evidence. "How do you know that?"

Ask for details. "Exactly how much? How many? How big?"

Ask for reactions. "What did you say then? How bad was it?"

Ask for other sources. "Who else knows about that? Who's out to get you? Who are your biggest supporters?"

Ask the hard questions. "Have you ever been arrested? Were you fired? Were you drunk? Have you been unfaithful?"

Pulitzer Prize-winner Eric Nalder of The Seattle Times still reminds himself of the adage: "There are no embarrassing questions. There are only embarrassing answers." The corollary might be that the only embarrassing question is the one you neglect to ask.

While you ask, be prepared to give some answers. The people from whom you want information may well want to know why you want it, who you are and why they should talk with you. Ken Fuson recalls the time he knocked on the door and asked to interview an 85-year-old man who had been charged with robbing a bank. The old man's wife asked, "Why?"

Fuson toyed with a variety of possible answers. "Finally, I just told her the truth, that it's not every day an 85-year-old man is arrested for robbing a bank. We could write a story about her husband from the police reports, but I'd rather find out who he is from the people who know him best.

"From the back of the house came a voice: 'Let him in.'"

To that, Nalder adds a piece of advice. "Don't lie under any circumstances. It will always come back to bite you." You're not under oath; you don't have to tell the whole truth all the time. But don't lie. Experience has taught Nalder that the more you give your interviewee, the more you're likely to get in return.

☐ Record What You Learn

The best interviews are interesting conversations. You're not just out for entertainment, though. Your pursuit of a story dictates that you capture what you hear, see and think during interviews. Experienced writers differ over the best techniques for recording information. There probably is no single best technique for all writers and all situations.

A few writers rely on memorization. The late Truman Capote, author of "In Cold Blood," was the best known. Capote claimed to have trained himself to remember interviews with more than 95 percent accuracy. The benefits of using your memory as your recording device are obvious. Memory is unobtrusive, nondistracting, portable and requires neither ink nor batteries. Its drawbacks are equally obvious. Memory provides no evidence for later referral. It is subject to challenge by other memories. Worst of all, it is notoriously unreliable.

Still, sometimes there is no alternative. You may get caught with no other equipment handy. Or the situation may prevent your pulling out notebook or tape recorder. In such cases, you can improve your results if you:

Concentrate on the key facts and phrases. Try to memorize everything and you're likely to wind up with nothing. So try to pick out the nuggets and grab them. Recite a key phrase to yourself to help remember it word for word.

Seize your first opportunity to write down what you have. Go to the restroom. Step outside for a cigarette or a breath of fresh air. Jot down the most important material. Then, as soon as possible, search your memory banks and write down as much as you can recall of the rest, including context, description, tone.

When you can, tape record. Tape-recording is the only way to be sure of capturing extensive quotes exactly. It also offers some protection against charges of inaccuracy or distortion. And the use of a recorder can free you to watch more carefully, listen more closely, respond more quickly. If you want to tape an interview, be open about it. Explain its value as a protection to the person being interviewed. Set up the machine with a minimum of fuss, then proceed. Usually, your interviewee will get used to the recorder quickly.

Some sources are inhibited or intimidated by tape recorders. Some don't want their words preserved. And recorders do malfunction, especially when mechanically inept writers have forgotten to check the batteries or to make sure there's a blank tape inserted. At best, a tape recorder leaves you with a mass of undigested information, offering the opportunity of delightful hours of relistening and transcribing.

That leaves note-taking. In Great Britain, accurate note-taking has such a high priority that a command of shorthand often is required of aspiring reporters. Few American writers face that requirement, but note-taking is no less important for those who also use tape recorders.

You'll improve your note-taking if you:

- Don't try to write down everything. That's both hopeless and useless.
- Do try to get down exact quotes you think you'll want to use.
- Do write down anecdotes, names, addresses, titles and numbers.
- Do write down descriptions of your source and of the scene.

If you feel yourself falling behind, in danger of losing something you want to preserve, don't hesitate to buy yourself time to catch up. One way to do that is simply to ask the speaker to wait a moment. Most interviewees will be happy to do whatever is necessary to have their words captured fully. If you suspect your source is one of the exceptions to that rule, you can be a little devious. Interrupt to ask for clarification or amplification of some point. It doesn't matter much which point, because while the source is clarifying you're writing down what was said earlier.

No matter what your method of capturing the moment, remember that what appears between quotation marks is supposed to be the exact words of the speaker—no matter what the U.S. Supreme Court may have said on the subject. You'll never be able to render a quote faithfully if you haven't recorded it, on pad or on tape, word for word.

❑ Getting It Right and on the Record

At the end of the interview, take a few minutes to sum up. Go over any tricky spellings. Recheck any mathematics or technical information. Reconfirm—if you're not afraid of alerting the source to some unwitting admission—your understanding of the central points. Get a phone number you can use for any follow-up questions or double-checking.

Then close your notebook, turn off the tape recorder and keep on interviewing. More often than you might think, even sophisticated sources, thinking the formal interview is over, will make revealing comments. Give them that chance. There's nothing unethical about using post-interview material, so long as you have not agreed that it is off the record.

The problem of off-the-record information is more troublesome that it needs to be. Your life will be simpler if you remember:

1. Nothing is off the record unless you agree that it is. No source should be given the right to declare unilaterally, "That's off the record."

2. You're not bound by any "off the record" claim that is made after the fact. Don't allow a source to make a statement and then try to keep you from using it. Any agreement must be made in advance if it is to be binding.

3. "Off the record" usually means "Don't quote me." A complicated system of levels of attribution has grown up in Washington and threatens to spread. Resist it. If the source means that you can't use the information at all, make her say that. Usually, sources want to protect their identity, not their information.

4. Don't spurn off-the-record information. If the source won't give it to you under any other conditions, take it. You may be able to confirm it from sources you can identify. Often, you can come back later and persuade the original source to go on the record. In any case,

it is almost always preferable to know something than not to know it, even if you can't tell the world where you learned it.

5. If you have any doubt, be sure you and your source have the same understanding about the ground rules. Don't seek that understanding by saying, "I shouldn't use that, should I?" Be positive. Say, "I can use that so long as I don't quote you, right?" Better yet, don't bring the subject up unless the source does. If nothing is said to the contrary, everything said to a reporter is on the record.

In the end, you're the maker and the keeper of the record. How complete it is, how accurate and how revealing will depend to a great extent on how well you observe and how well you interview.

☐ QUESTIONS AND EXERCISES

1. Describe. Write a description of yourself. Show it to a friend. Are you recognizable? Now describe the friend. Does she recognize herself? Move on to a street or a building. Now to an event. Compare your description to others. What have you overlooked? Exaggerated? How sharp is your eye?

2. Now, as Jeff Leen did with the execution, put yourself into the scene you describe. Include your reaction, your point of view.

3. Interview. Ask your grandmother or an elderly friend about the elementary school she attended. Write your version of her description. Do your best to describe the child who went there, too. Now check your accuracy by showing your work to your source. Did you get it right? Keep trying until you do.

4. Interview someone in the news. Write the story of the interview. Check it with the source. How accurate is your reporting? (It might be interesting to ask this newsmaker about other interviews and interviewers.)

5. Persuade another reporter to interview you. Feels different on the other side of the notepad, doesn't it? How? Check your friend's story for accuracy. How does the friend's report compare to your own recollection of what you said and did? Any credibility problems here?

6. If you don't regularly use a tape recorder during interviews, use one. Compare the tape recording to your notes.

5

Documentary Sources: Following Paper (and Computer) Trails

Throughout our lives we all generate a cornucopia of information on which the savvy investigator can feast.—from a chapter introduction in "The Reporter's Handbook"

Most writers get most of their information by interviewing. The best writers go beyond the interview to tap the wealth of material that is available for the looking in an astonishing array of public (and, more rarely, private) records. These records kept by governments, businesses and nonprofit organizations can reveal facts your interviewees don't have or won't reveal. Records, unlike human sources:

- usually are organized logically;
- can be copied, analyzed and reviewed at your convenience; and
- typically are detailed and specific.

Records often suggest human sources you wouldn't otherwise think of. Records usually can be examined without the consent or even the knowledge of the people they concern; people who might not give you the information if you asked for it.

Take a look.

Family Circle magazine ran an article on "cluster diseases," health problems that show up in high concentrations in specific locations and that often indicate the presence of toxic substances in the environment. A deadly cluster showed up in Jacksonville, Ark. After the Jacksonville newspaper attacked the Family Circle report, the magazine's editors decided to investigate further. In addition to interviews, writer Stephanie Abarbanel drew on records from the Environmental Protection Agency, the Arkansas Department of Pollution Control and several chemical companies, together with real estate records and documents from lawsuits filed by victims. The result was an 8,000-word article that spurred state and federal health studies and won for the writer an award from Investigative Reporters and Editors (IRE).

The Miami Herald wanted to tell its readers how low-paid public officials supported lavish lifestyles. A team of reporters interviewed the officials, their business associates, former politicians and lawyers. Then the team turned to the records and examined state financial disclosure forms, real estate documents, automobile registrations, estate records, civil court files and even confidential police investigative files obtained from human sources. The results: indictments, resignations and election defeats of officials including a judge, three county commissioners and a mayor. This project also won a national IRE award.

Francis Dealy, outraged by the drug-induced death of basketball star Len Bias, decided to study the failed regulatory system of college sports. He recalled, "I spent a fortune on Nexis, which provided me with a solid base of already published material. . . ." He dug into the files of the grand jury that investigated the Bias death, the report of a state audit of the University of Georgia and another report of an internal investigation performed by the Methodist bishops of Southern Methodist University. He also interviewed more than 200 people. His book, another award-winner, was called "Win at any Cost: The Sell-Out of College Athletics."

All those stories, like most others, could have been told with information gleaned solely from interviews. None would have the depth or the weight the writers were able to bring to their work by using documents as well as people.

☐ PROFILING INDIVIDUALS

Here's the assignment: Profile the new school superintendent. Here's the deadline: Tomorrow. Here's the problem: The new superintendent, first woman to hold the job, has worked her way up through the system determinedly but quietly. Your newspaper library yields little beyond a few routine promotion stories and Record page briefs on her divorce a few years ago and her remarriage a couple of years after that. She is such a private person that such basic details as her age haven't been reported. And she isn't eager to talk about herself.

Don't despair. Check the public record.

Start with the school district office. Typically, public institutions and major corporations will make available at least brief résumés of key officials. Here you'll find such information as education, career highlights, professional honors. You'll also get some clues about possible interview sources—people with whom she has crossed professional paths.

Then back to basics with the phone book and city directory. The phone book has not only numbers but also addresses (and sometimes, in the Yellow Pages, more possible sources). Say you're researching a lawyer, a plumber, a real estate broker. Others in the same line of work, colleagues and competitors, usually are informed and often are talkative. The city directory can be even more useful. Often, you can learn the name of a spouse, whether your subject owns the home she lives in, her profession and, by turning to the street directory section, the names and phone numbers of neighbors. Look back through previous year's directories, usually available in the public library, and you may be able to learn how long she has lived at her present address and who the neighbors were in the past. More clues, more people you can interview.

Now look at the contents of your own wallet. Driver's license, voter identification card, employment i.d., library card, membership cards, credit cards, family photos. Think how much you could tell about somebody just by examining that material. Remember that much of what's in your wallet is also on the public record and therefore available for examination.

Here's a quick review of some of the public records people carry around with them or generate in the course of ordinary activities.

☐ Driving and Vehicle Ownership Records

In most states, you can get the information that appears on a person's driver's license—name, age, address, physical description, driving restrictions. In many states, you can also get the driving record. If you have the license number of the car your subject drives, you can usually learn to whom that vehicle is registered. From your local tax collector, you can find out what motor vehicles anybody is paying personal property taxes on.

☐ Voter Registration Records

These will show full names, current address (and sometimes a different legal address), party affiliation, often a home telephone number, usually a Social Security number and registration date. Usually, you also can find out which elections your subject has voted in, information that can be especially interesting in the cases of politicians.

☐ Employment Records

Public employees, such as our school superintendent, always leave paper trails. Typically, the law requires release of job title, job description, dates of employment and salary. For some public servants, such as those in the military, more detail may be available. You should be able to learn from the Department of Defense, if you have a soldier's or veteran's name and service or Social Security number, such information as date of birth, dates of service, rank, duty stations, awards and decorations, and even names of dependents.

☐ Education Records

Résumés, campaign materials, even bumper stickers often show school ties. Check them. High schools and colleges, especially public schools, usually will tell you if somebody really holds the degrees she claims. Not everybody does, and exaggerations often are accepted as truth because nobody until you has bothered to check. For those who have what they claim, dates of attendance can be useful. In cases of graduate degrees, it may be worth your while to check the library for theses or dissertations. Topics can be interesting. Names of advisers can be useful. So can lists of activities and honors, which the school or its alumni association often will provide. Old yearbooks can provide details and names of dozens of possible interview sources.

☐ Membership Records

Many a public official has been embarrassed, and a few reformed, by revelations of membership in clubs that exclude on the basis of race, religion or gender. Many a good interview source comes from the ranks of colleagues in Phi Beta Kappa or the Teamsters Union. Résumés and interviews often provide the starting points. Most organizations will confirm membership; many will provide membership requirements or even rosters.

☐ Family Records

Births, deaths, marriages, divorces, adoptions, name changes—all are recorded somewhere. State bureaus of vital statistics, county recorders' offices, the clerks of courts maintain the records, which are available for the asking. Those records will suggest other avenues to explore and other people to interview. Marriages, for example, often are marked by newspaper announcements that usually include names of family members, attendants, the minister and others who know your subject. The court files in contested divorces may contain financial information, allegations (and even proof) of character flaws, and still more names.

☐ Property and Financial Records

In the local tax assessor's office, you can find out what real and personal property your subject (or her spouse) pays taxes on. You can learn something of the value of that property, where it is and how it is being used. In the recorder's office, you can find out when and from whom a home or investment property was purchased. In a few states, you may be able to determine the purchase price. You usually can learn how the purchase was financed and who holds the mortgage. By checking the filings under the Uniform Commercial Code (in the secretary of state's office or some county recorders' offices), you may be able to find out if your subject has taken out a commercial loan. If so, you may be able to discover otherwise-hidden assets or interesting obligations. And don't forget to check the Bankruptcy Court, an arm of the federal court system. Any person or business that declares bankruptcy must reveal assets, debts and creditors. The Probate Court, part of the state system, may have interesting information on inheritances from, say, a deceased relative or business partner.

☐ Criminal Records

Information from these files can be hard to get without a friendly source in law enforcement. Bare-bones information about current cases is usually public. Getting beyond the facts and allegations outlined in arrest reports and indictments usually requires human sources. And getting at even the bare facts in past cases can be difficult. Any public files even on convictions are routinely closed after a few years. Such files on acquittals and dismissed charges often are destroyed. Still, you should never fail to check the criminal court clerk's office. A university president convicted of drunken driving is an interesting tidbit people want to know. An affirmative action officer who has been convicted of sex discrimination is an important story people need to know.

Remember the little-known school superintendent? Once you have spent a few hours with the public record, you'll have both the factual skeleton of your profile piece and enough possible interview sources to flesh out the portrait and breathe life into it. Your subject will be amazed, your readers will be enlightened, your boss will be delighted. And you'll be ready for the next challenge.

❏ EXAMINING INSTITUTIONS AND SYSTEMS

Joseph T. Hallinan, a reporter for the Indianapolis Star, was checking on malpractice among doctors in the state prison system when he found an even more important story. He said later, "One of the record-keepers told me some of the doctors with the most malpractice claims were not in the prisons but in private practice. That's what prompted me to take a look from there."

He and colleague Susan M. Headden found that "a handful of doctors in Indiana went virtually undisciplined after maiming and mutilating scores of patients." That summary and Hallinan's recollection both come from the Star's story announcing that the reporters won the Pulitzer Prize for investigative reporting. Their project, published in June 1990, was an examination of an important part of the state's health care system. Not every such examination wins a national prize, of course, but all provide important public service. Increasingly, journalists are returning to the professional roots of investigative reporting by scrutinizing the performance of the social systems and institutions that affect readers' lives.

The best of these examinations are written in simple, human terms. They are invariably based, however, not only on anecdotes but also on detailed analysis of documents. Often the analysis is aided, as was Hallinan's and Headden's, by computers. Here's the opening of the Indiana series:

> Norma Norwood was suffering pain and numbness in her left hand when she sought help from Kokomo orthopedic surgeon Stephen S. Choi.
>
> Choi told the 55-year-old housewife she had carpal tunnel syndrome, a problem common to middle-aged women that is caused by pressure on a nerve in the wrist. On April 1, 1982, he performed a simple operation to relieve the tension.
>
> But after the surgery, things began to go wrong. Norwood's arm swelled. It became so painful she couldn't stand to have it touched.
>
> Choi thought the arm was infected. It was not until his patient had suffered for two more weeks that he finally rushed her by ambulance to an Indianapolis hand surgeon. By then, her massively swollen arm was rock hard, ice cold and without a detectable pulse.

Infection, the hand surgeon said, was not the problem. Norwood had developed a blood clot in her upper arm that was blocking the flow of blood to the rest of her arm.

A team of surgeons performed emergency surgery, but they were too late.

Gangrene had set in. The arm had to be amputated.

Norwood sued Choi for medical malpractice and won. Three other patients also successfully sued Choi for negligence. Yet the doctor has suffered no penalty of any kind.

What happened to Norma Norwood—and what didn't happen to Dr. Choi—is a pattern that has been repeated countless times.

An investigation by The Indianapolis Star has found that a handful of Indiana doctors have maimed and mutilated scores of patients in this state and nothing has been done to stop them.

They have not lost their licenses. They have not lost their hospital privileges. They have not, in many cases, even paid more for malpractice insurance.

Instead of rooting out physicians who repeatedly cause malpractice, the state has created a system that, in effect, protects them. . . .

This writing is clear, compelling and effective. Notice the humanity, notice the detail, notice the simplicity of language and style. Notice too the straightforward, unqualified summary of the investigation. If you are going to write this powerfully about an issue this important, complicated and sensitive, you must know how to find the facts and how to make sense of them. The tips that follow are intended to be suggestive rather than definitive. A thorough introduction to the analysis of institutions and systems would require an entire book.

In fact, such a book exists. If you don't already own it, you should. It is "The Reporter's Handbook: An Investigator's Guide to Documents and Techniques." It was written by experienced journalists, produced under the auspices of Investigative Reporters and Editors, and published by St. Martin's Press. This chapter draws heavily on "The Reporter's Handbook," but there is much more in the book.

Here are some suggested starting points for your examinations of institutions.

❒ Governmental Agencies

The two keys to understanding any arm of government, from the courthouse to the White House, are knowing what it is supposed to do and how it actually works.

Your best primer on what an agency is supposed to do is the organization's own charter. Read the legislation that created it. Read its policy manual, its operating rules, its annual reports. Then find an expert or two to clarify arcane language and interpret legalese. University scholars can be helpful. So can retired officials. Sometimes you can even find the people who wrote the legislation or the implementing rules.

Important stories often lie in the gap between what an agency is supposed to do and what it actually does. Human sources—the aggrieved, the disgruntled, the reform-minded public citizen—are good guides. But you need the documents, too. Among the most valuable:

Budgets. The budget is the blueprint of what an organization does. You may need to find a fiscal architect to help you read it, but look for:

- major changes that can signal changes in priority, the effects of political pressure or the impact of boom or recession;
- the numbers in parentheses that indicate deficits or losses; and
- the detail pages that explain the overall numbers in the summary.

Audits. Nearly every public agency has somebody looking over its shoulder. This may be an internal auditor, whose reports often go unread but whose job it is to make sure the money is being spent for the purposes it was appropriated and in the ways the rules prescribe. There probably are periodic external audits, too. And sometimes watchdog groups produce their own analytical reports. Get them and read them. In formal audits, look especially at the notes and exceptions, those unobtrusive and carefully worded footnotes in which the auditor may note things that just don't look right or can't be verified.

Minutes. Most public bodies are required by law to keep a record, in writing or by recording, of what happens at official meetings. The Congressional Record is the best known and the least useful, mainly because members of Congress can and do "revise and extend" their actual comments, often in ways that leave the written record significantly different from the real proceedings. Your zoning commission or school board probably has a much more accurate record. Few journalists ever take the trouble to check this record. More should. You may find explanations, justifications, conflicts, policies made and changed—all sorts of substance and trivia that will add to your understanding.

☐ Nonprofit Organizations

Look at the nongovernmental organizations that affect the lives of your readers and that often involve the kinds of interesting and important people about whom you want to write. Private schools and colleges; local and national charities such as the United Way and the Red Cross; fraternal groups such as the Shriners; foundations such as Ford and MacArthur. They raise and spend millions of dollars, they provide services communities count on, they influence private lives and public policy. Yet they seldom are subjected to the critical examination journalists routinely give to governmental agencies. They can be.

IRS Form 990. Here's the exception to the rule that the Internal Revenue Service doesn't reveal tax returns. Under the law, not only are the tax returns of most tax-exempt organizations public records, but the organizations themselves are supposed to make them available for inspection. Inspection may yield such interesting stories as the salaries and other perks of professional do-gooders. Or you may find important abuses.

That's what Joan Mazzolini found when she examined the 990 returns of country clubs in Birmingham, Ala. Putting together human sources with this document, she established that the IRS was violating its own rules by continuing to grant tax exemptions to organizations that discriminated against blacks. Her series in the Birmingham Post-Herald attracted national attention.

Gary Marx and John Wark used 990 forms to show in The Orlando Sentinel that the Shriners, who raise millions from the public every year supposedly to help crippled children, spent most of it on themselves, including the operation of members-only clubhouses and bars and low-interest loans to top Shrine officials.

☐ Businesses

Business reporting is one of the fastest-growing fields in journalism. Even the non-specialist can make use of the same basic documents the most sophisticated business writers use. Those documents fall into two broad categories—those produced by the business itself and those produced by some regulatory agency. The first category is most likely to apply to publicly owned corporations. The second category most commonly applies to such service businesses as insurance companies, hospitals, banks and S&L's.

Corporation records. Secretaries of state have records of who formed corporations and who the top officers are. When a company seeks to sell stock to the public, it opens itself to a whole new level of disclosure. The Securities and Exchange Commission requires a wide range of reports, many of them annual, that tell a discerning reader a great deal about the health and direction of a company. Even a stock offering itself generates a publicly available prospectus that can provide more insight. A helpful booklet for the beginner is "How to Read a Financial Report," published by Merrill Lynch.

Regulatory records. From the routine reports of restaurant inspections to the computer tapes that contain the Environmental Protection Agency's annual Toxic Release Inventory, the governmental agencies that regulate businesses keep records of that regulation. Most are available to the public. For those restaurant inspection reports, see your local health department. For updates on the health of financial institutions, get the reports of the Office of Thrift Supervision (S&L's) and the Federal Deposit Insurance Corporation (banks). State insurance commissioners oversee insurance companies. Other state agencies govern nursing homes, hospitals, trucking companies, agricultural pesticide applicators, private schools and on and on and on.

Sometimes, as with the Indianapolis Star investigation, the real story is the lack of effective regulation. All those stories can best be told by writers who have gone beyond the interview to dig through the documents.

☐ USING THE COMPUTER AS A REPORTING TOOL

Most writers, like the authors of this book, use their computers as slightly more sophisticated typewriters. Increasingly, however, serious journalists are tapping the computer's potential as a reporting tool.

The simplest application is the computer's power to connect you to a worldwide network of source material through the dozens of data bases now available. A subscription to Dialog, CompuServe or Lexis puts the world of information literally at your fingertips. Major newspaper libraries now have staff experts in data-base searching. So do university libraries. Ignorance is no longer an excuse.

Perhaps even more significant is the inclination and ability of a growing number of journalists to use the computer for the purpose for which it was created—data analysis. A good example is the medical malpractice investigation by Joseph Hallinan and Susan Headden. A key element of the story was the reporters' discovery that the state regulatory agencies literally did not know who the malpractice-prone doctors were. So the reporters had to create their own data base. They entered the most important facts from every major successful malpractice suit under current Indiana law. Then they created a data base of names of all doctors who had been disciplined. By analyzing—as nobody else had done—these separate but related facts, they were able to show a clear and dangerous pattern of neglect by the regulators themselves.

Other reporters, using commercially available programs, are doing their own public opinion polls, analyzing governmental budgets, making never-before-feasible comparisons, demonstrating previously invisible patterns. The computer is turning out to be the tool that enables reporters to return at the end of the 20th century to the kinds of analysis of social and governmental institutions that the original muckrakers performed with more primitive tools as the century began.

The revolution in electronic generation and storage of information is forcing journalists to use their computer tools for another kind of digging, too. This is the most technologically sophisticated but journalistically most basic work of all. As government and business move from paper to microchip, reporters must follow or be left at the mercy of the information-generators to provide what they will. "Computer-assisted reporting" includes data analysis, but it begins with the location of information—usually in complicated computer programs stored on expensive tapes—and the translation of that information into a form that can be understood and managed by reporters without extensive backgrounds in computer science.

Recently established institutes at the University of Missouri and Indiana University offer instruction and consulting.

In the end, the effectiveness of the computer or any other tool depends on the intelligence and the diligence of its user. The best writers will use all the tools they have to dig into documents for the facts, the figures, the background and the context that are needed for the most effective storytelling.

☐ QUESTIONS AND EXERCISES

1. Investigate yourself. Following the steps outlined in this chapter, find out what the public record shows about you. Any surprises? Any inaccuracies?

2. Pick a public figure and profile her or him from the information available in public documents. What do you learn that you didn't already know? What human sources do the records suggest? What stories do the records suggest?

3. Trace the ownership, history and legal status of the building in which you live.

4. Do the background reporting for a profile of some public person by using one or more computer data bases. Note the questions for interviews, and the potential interviewees, your background check suggests.

5. Get "The Reporter's Handbook." Follow its lead in doing the background reporting on (a) a person and (b) an institution or organization.

6

Ensuring Accuracy

Time equals truth—biographer Robert Caro.

The most important part of any journalist's job is to get the story right. Inaccuracy misleads your readers and erodes your credibility. Getting the story right means more than being sure of the correctness of spellings, of names and numbers, of quotes, although those are essential elements of good journalism. Getting the story right also means getting the context right, being sure of the background, the atmosphere, the tone you are conveying.

Close and careful observation makes possible accuracy both of detail and of context. Clear and careful writing reduces the likelihood of misunderstanding by your readers. There are, however, pitfalls that have tripped even experienced writers. There are also gray areas in which less experienced writers are especially likely to wander astray. And happily, there are guidelines you can follow and techniques you can use to avoid the pitfalls and keep your bearings even in the fog.

☐ PITFALLS AND FOGGY PATCHES

Every journalist knows that you just don't make stuff up. But sometimes the pressures of ambition and expectation lead someone to do it anyway. More than a decade after it unfolded, the case of Janet Cooke still echoes in journalism schools and newsrooms. Cooke, a young reporter with The Washington Post, was assigned to write about the scourge of drugs as it ruined the lives of children. Unable to find an actual victim, she created "Jimmy," whom she described as an 8-year-old heroin addict. Her story was so compelling and so unusual that it won journalism's highest award, a Pulitzer Prize, in 1981. Only after the award was announced did Cooke's editors learn that Jimmy lived only in her imagination. The prize was withdrawn, the writer fired and journalists everywhere were painfully reminded of the permissable limits of imagination.

Imagination, of course, is vital to good writing. Imagination helps you find the outline of a story in a welter of facts. Imagination helps you ask the penetrating question, see the fitting simile. But imagination is no substitute for diligent, detailed reporting. And imagination run wild will lead to lies. Writers are bound by the rules of the genre they choose. Writers of fiction are free to create a reality to conform to their inner vision. Writers of fact, journalists, are less free. Journalists are restricted by the rules of the craft to describing the reality they can observe. The better the writer, the greater the detail and sensitivity of the observation. But distortion of the observation or making up what you haven't observed is a violation of the rules a journalist must live by.

The difficulty of enforcing, or even agreeing on, those rules is demonstrated regularly. In the same year as the Janet Cooke scandal, Michael Daly, a columnist for the New York Daily News, resigned after a British newspaper discovered that characters in a column Daly had written from Northern Ireland were not real. Unlike Cooke, Daly insisted that his characters—whom he named and quoted—were not imaginary but were composites of several people whom he had actually seen and heard. A decade before that, writer Gail Sheehy had published in New York magazine a widely acclaimed story about a prostitute called "Redpants." The central characters in that story, too, turned out to have been composites rather than real, a fact readers were not told.

Both Sheehy and Daly defended their work, but the device they used is indefensible in journalism. The guideline for using any literary device in journalism should be this: A device that adds information is acceptable; one that distorts facts is not. Such techniques as the composite character, compressed time sequences and fabricated scenes or dialogue distort.

Peter Carey, who didn't have to give back the Pulitzer he helped win for the San Jose (Calif.) Mercury News, applies to his own work a rule that all journalists would do well to heed: "I try not to write what I haven't seen and heard."

Even that rule is easier enunciated than enforced. At least two questions arise: How accurately do you record and reproduce what you've seen and, especially, what you've heard? And what's your obligation to readers to reveal the sources and circumstances of what you saw and heard?

The answer to the first question is clear. Not very. Both scholarly studies and journalistic experience show that the ability of even trained reporters to capture quotes with verbatim accuracy is limited. Then writers commonly compound that shortcoming by deliberately altering the quotes they publish. Usually, the alterations are done in the name of clarity, good grammar or the avoidance of embarrassment to sources whose spoken English isn't as graceful as their written language.

The U.S. Supreme Court in 1991 came to consider accuracy in quotes in a lawsuit brought by a psychoanalyst, Jeffrey Masson, against writer Janet Malcolm, whom he accused of libelling him by misquoting him in a New Yorker article. The court concluded that even if Malcolm had confused or deliberately altered some quotes, she had not changed the meaning of what Masson said. Therefore, there was no libel. Most journalists heaved a sigh of relief, although many lamented the court's seeming endorsement of altered—that is, inaccurate—quotes.

The desirability of changing quotes can be disputed, but the reality of the practice cannot. Kevin McManus, writing in the Columbia Journalism Review, interviewed prominent practitioners and came up with four options for handling less-than-perfect quotes.

- Paraphrase, substituting your own words for the speaker's where necessary, without using quotation marks. This, McManus found, is the purist approach.
- "Clean it up." Fix grammatical errors, leave out redundant words and nonverbals such as "uh" and "um," but do that within quotation marks. This is perhaps the most common practice.
- "Make some of it up." That is, fill in partial quotes and make sentences of fragments, again within quotation marks. Those who follow this practice probably wouldn't agree that they are writing a kind of fiction, but they are.
- "Shape quotes for stylistic purposes." Such deliberate alteration is, McManus found, almost universally frowned on by writers and editors. (It does, however, now have the legal imprimatur of the Supreme Court.)

There is another option. That is the option of capturing sources' words accurately by using the techniques outlined in Chapter 5 and then quoting them precisely when their own words are clear and paraphrasing when they are not. This option has several advantages. For one thing, it is honest. For another, your work will be beyond question in the newsroom or the courtroom. And if this were the general practice in journalism, readers would know at all times whether they were getting a source's words or the writer's.

What readers need to know in order to understand and assess a piece of journalism is another question without definitive answers. The question has been posed in critiques of the work of writers as far apart in style and reputation as Kitty Kelley, controversial biographer of Frank Sinatra and Nancy Reagan, and Bob Woodward, award-winning Washington Post reporter and editor whose books explore the inner workings of the White House, Supreme Court and military high command. Both writers rely heavily on unnamed sources. Both freely reconstruct dialogue and scenes they did not witness. Neither provides detailed endnotes or bibliography.

Few journalists take Kelley seriously. Nearly all take Woodward seriously. Stephen Banker's criticism of Woodward, in the Washington Journalism Review, defines the problem with their—and others'—approach. Banker complains that "the building blocks of the narrative rest on air. There are no attributions, no footnotes, no list of sources. The reader is asked to accept what he reads because it comes from Bob Woodward." Is that enough? For Banker and other critics, it isn't. For thousands of readers and for many journalists, it is.

In the cases of both Woodward and Kelley, the writers have track records that provide some basis for trust or distrust. Even from such well-known writers, and certainly from all those with less visibility, readers have a right to expect the greatest possible disclosure of sources and methods. Some sources and some methods are more defensible than others. Here are some guidelines that may save your work from being savaged in a journalism review:

1. Identify your sources. Names are best, but even names may not be adequate. Readers deserve to know a source's reliability and biases. Writers are obliged to provide enough identification to make reasonable judgments possible. Even when, for good reason, you cannot name a source, you should make every effort to let readers know the source's expertise or prejudice. For example, "One experienced military planner observed. . . ." or "A close friend of Mrs. Reagan recalls. . . ."

2. Admit ignorance or uncertainty. Truth is elusive. Claims to omniscience are best left to the pulpit. If you don't know something, be honest with your readers. When causes or connections are unclear, write clearly about the confusion. If you have a scenario but not a certainty, label it for what it is. It's okay to speculate, to suggest, to infer. Just tell your readers what you're doing.

3. Don't quote what you haven't heard. It's hard enough to get a quote right, and in the right context, when you have tape recorded it

yourself. Both literal accuracy and contextual accuracy become next to impossible when you're getting the quote secondhand. That's especially true when, as is usually the case, the person relaying the quote has something at stake in the retelling. What's at stake may be reputation, may be a desire for revenge, may be a hope of reward. What's at risk is your credibility. The only safe way for you as a writer to pass along a quote that was passed along to you is make the distance clear. Don't write, "Reagan said. . . ." if you didn't hear him say it. Write, "Bush recalls that Reagan told him. . . ." Such an attribution is a little longer, but it's a lot safer because it's more accurate.

4. Reconstruct cautiously. One of the most effective narrative techniques is the reconstruction of a scene, a battle, a conversation. It's also one of the most dangerous. The danger is to truth. So be careful. Seek multiple sources. Try to make sure that those sources represent the full range of viewpoints, physical, philosophical or political. Be leery of accepting any single version of events. Be leery of second- or third-hand quotes. And be sure to let your readers in on your methods. Tell them, "All those present agree that the meeting went this way. . . ." or "A friend of the mayor later gave an aide this account. . . ." A small sacrifice of drama yields great gains in accuracy and in reader trust.

◻ TWO APPROACHES TO GREATER ACCURACY

"Time equals truth," says Robert Caro, biographer of Lyndon Johnson. Writer and teacher Steve Weinberg, who quotes Caro, offers that in explanation of Caro's willingness to spend seven years researching a book and his aversion to daily journalism. There's an application, though, to the quest for accuracy that should drive every journalist.

Time equals truth if the time—15 minutes carved from a lunch hour or an extra week wheedled from an editor—is devoted to searching out more sources, seeking expert explanations of complex issues, sitting down for another rewrite. Time equals truth if you use the time to review your notes, reinterview a key source to resolve lingering uncertainties, rework those awkward sentences and confusing paragraphs.

Time and truth have something else in common. Both can be hard to find. As a writer, especially a young writer, you may have to find the time you need for the pursuit of truth by being able to show editors that you'll put the time to good use. You can do that by preparing story proposals, story outlines and first drafts that demonstrate the use you've made of the time you've already invested. You may have to find the time by taking it from your off-duty hours. The best journalism hardly ever fits neatly into 8-hour shifts or 40-hour weeks. The good news about investing your own time is that such investments often pay off in more generous allocations of company time after your investment has yielded good work.

Good work is accurate work. There's one more way, one last step, you can take to ensure the accuracy of your work. You can double-check what you've written with the people who gave you the information.

Accuracy checking, in some variant, has been a staple of magazine journalism for years. The fact-checkers at Time and The National Geographic are legendary in their thoroughness and resourcefulness. Newspapers have not followed their lead. If they did, many of the mistakes of fact and context that plague daily journalism and erode its credibility might be eliminated before publication instead of resulting in post-publication attempts at correction and apology.

The Columbia Missourian, the daily paper published by the University of Missouri School of Journalism, has followed for more than 15 years a policy of accuracy checking that we recommend to every writer. The policy is simple. With rare exceptions, all stories are checked with their sources to make sure they are accurate before they are published. In some cases, sections of the story are read over the telephone to a source. In other cases, especially when the stories are complex or sensitive, sources are invited to read the entire story.

The sources are not invited nor allowed to edit the stories or change their quotes arbitrarily. They are invited and encouraged to correct misspellings, factual errors and mistakes or confusions in context. Any irreconcilable differences over whether somebody actually said what she or he is quoted as saying are referred to the responsible editor. The newspaper always makes the final decision on what to publish.

Sources, many of whom have been misquoted in the past, love the accuracy-check policy. Readers think it makes great sense. Only those journalists who haven't worked with it don't like the idea. Some writers hate the thought of personal conflict or criticism from a source. They know that even people who are misquoted or misrepresented in print seldom take the trouble to complain after the fact. Other writers don't trust their editors to back them up when a key quote or conclusion is challenged. They may need either better notes or better editors. This book should help supply at least the former.

The point to remember, with or without a formal accuracy-check policy, is that the best writers do whatever is required to get their stories right. Before it is anything else, good journalism is accurate.

☐ QUESTIONS AND EXERCISES

1. Both Kitty Kelley and Bob Woodward have been criticized for their reliance on unidentified sources. Get one of their books and read (or re-read) it with an eye on the sources. How many unidentified sources do you find in a chapter? What effect does the use of such sources have on the credibility of the information? How, if at all, would you have handled the source problem differently?

2. Read the front page of the latest edition of The New York Times. How many unidentified sources do you find? How many are unnamed but identified in some other way? Can you suggest to the Times any ways of reducing the number of such shadowy sources?

3. Here's a test of your reporting accuracy: Have a friend write a short statement and then read it to you verbatim. Take the best notes you can. Now compare your version to the original. Sobering, isn't it? How can you improve your accuracy?

4. Take a story from your local newspaper and check it for accuracy. Try to confirm every fact, every spelling, every quote. Is it completely accurate? Almost accurate, with a few small errors? Fundamentally flawed?

5. Now do the same with a piece of your own work. If you relied for background on somebody else's journalism, go back to an original source to double-check that. Contact all your human sources to check both factual accuracy and accuracy of context for each piece of information. How accurate a writer are you?

PART III

How to Write
to Be Read

7

The Essence
of Good Writing

Syntaxation with misrepresentation is tyranny. Those uninterested in the misuse of "disinterested" and those zigging "imply" when they should be zagging "infer," are the fuzzy-uppers of our language, and their laziness should not be accepted as our norm. —William Safire

Robert Gunning, the author of "Clear News Writing" published 40 years ago, was discussing the prose of Ernie Pyle, famed wartime columnist. Like Hemingway, Pyle relied on short sentences marching on the backs of vigorous verbs. Gunning told this story:

> The conclusion of an editorial from an Ohio paper dealing with the writing of Ernie Pyle makes the point. The editorial writer, a former English professor, wrote that Pyle has probably reached more people in his own day with the written word than any other writer that ever lived The reason for this, according to the editorial writer, was Pyle's mastery of the language of the people. 'He writes the language people talk,' the Ohioan said. And from this he drew a lesson with which he closed his piece:
> 'We should all strive to write as we talk—with necessary emendations.'

The editorial writer was honoring Pyle, but he didn't learn much by reading him. "Emendation" is not only a pompous substitute for "editing", but "necessary emendations" is also redundant.

In that one sentence, the editorial writer violated two maxims of good writing: clarity and conciseness. It's easy to do. Still, when you are writing for newspapers, magazines and company publications, you must constantly try to write to be understood by your audience. The author of the following letter was more interested in impressing readers with her vocabulary than with communicating:

> Because of the rapid changes in telecommunications and the growing diversity of related baccalaureate programs, we are attempting to de-

velop a current taxonomy of undergraduate programs upon a theory-to-application paradigm. We are also attempting to see how a program's orientation on this paradigm correlates to student employment after graduation.

That is the opening paragraph of a letter requesting the recipient to complete a questionnaire. If the questions were as abtruse as the cover letter, the response rate must have been low.

The first goal of nonfiction writers is to be believed. To be believed, you must first be understood. To be understood, your writing must be interesting enough to make people read. Here are seven criteria to help you achieve those goals. All good writing is correct, consistent, concise, concrete, clear, coherent and creative. In this chapter we will discuss the first six. Creative writing techniques and their application to nonfiction writing are the subjects of the next chapter.

☐ BE CORRECT

Nonfiction writers must be accurate in fact and context. We must get the numbers, names and sequence of events correct. Misuse of a word destroys your credibility. A scuba diver or firefighter who used an *oxygen* tank rather than an *air* tank wouldn't live long. To ensure accuracy, we must first understand your subject. If you are assigned to a zoning meeting, learn the difference between zoning classifications and then explain them for the reader. One reporter explained it this way:

> "This issue is 31 acres of prairie land, approximately 300 feet south of the south end of Fifth Street.
> On paper, the land is currently zoned 'low-density residential' (LDR)—that is, zoned for single-family homes. In practice, it is zoned 'prairie dog residential.' Thousands of the little critters live there.
> But not for long. The land is owned by Robbins & Stearns Homes, one of the city's largest developers . . ."

When the reporter is comfortable with the content, the story always will be more believable. Often that requires the reporter to work hard, to ask questions and to admit to sources "I don't understand. Can you explain that again?" James Michener, writer of epic books, is unafraid of epic research. When he was gathering information about the Strategic Air Command, Michener decided he needed to fly one of the bombers to write accurately about the planes and the pilots. An Air Force doctor who discovered that Michener had a minor heart ailment refused him permission. Michener went to another doctor, got clearance and was able to fly the bomber.

Once you have the facts right, say it right. Incorrect grammar hinders understanding, embarrasses the writer and frustrates many readers. Like a fog rolling off the river, misplaced modifiers obscure clarity. Sometimes it is incriminating, as a defendant discovered during his trial. Angry at being identified as the person who had committed the crime, the defendant blurted out, "You're a liar. I should have blown your head off . . . if I had been there." Sometimes the result can be both humorous and embarrassing, as in this example from a California newspaper: "The local chapter of Parents Without Partners will sponsor an open toga party on Saturday." If that's true, there may have been fewer parents without partners after the party.

Another way to improve accuracy is to use those literary techniques that are appropriate to nonfiction and to shun those that are not. It is appropriate to use detailed description, recreate scenes, reproduce dialogue, use a narrator to tell a story and tease the reader. It is wrong to create composites because a composite is not real. It is wrong to use mimesis unless the person explicitly tells you what his or her thoughts were. It is wrong to capture the "sense" of what a person said rather than the exact words and put them in quotes. To be believed, you must first be accurate.

☐ BE CONSISTENT

Consistency is a virtue in voice, person, tone and style.

Consistency in voice means that you do not switch from the active to the passive in the same sentence. When you do, it is jerky and confusing.

> "The speakers droned, the senators napped, but finally the bill was passed."

The first two independent clauses are active. The shift to passive in the third not only ruins the parallelism but also will force many people to reread it to make sense of it. It should be:

> While their colleagues napped, the speakers droned, but finally they awoke and passed the bill.

Switching from active to passive in midsentence is like running forward at full speed, then suddenly backing up. (After the painters finished, work was begun by the carpet layers.) It can be done, but not gracefully.

Consistency of person refers to the use of personal pronouns. Most journalistic stories are written in the formal third person: "he said," "she said." A more informal tone is achieved in the second person: "You write best when you write for your readers." The most intimate form is first person: "I am writing this to help you." More than 30 years ago, Rudolf Flesch found that the use of personal words increase interest and understanding. Third person is dispassionate. It establishes a cool relationship between the writer and the reader. Use of the first person establishes a warm relationship. National Geographic and Reader's Digest have an intimate relationship with their readers through their frequent use of stories written in the first person. Intra-company communications are often written in funereal tones when something chattier would be more interesting and easier to understand. Whatever perspective you assume through the personal pronoun, maintain it throughout the article.

Consistency of tone means that once you match your writing to your subject and your audience, you stick with that tone. Most popular magazines are informal; academic journals and some specialized magazines are formal. For better or worse—and it's probably for worse—academic journals are full of ponderous words and comprehension-defying sentences. Newspapers, magazines and newsletters cannot afford to be. This definition of "mood" from The Random House Dictionary is formal and confusing:

> A set of categories for which the verb is inflected in many languages, and which is typically used to indicate the syntactic relation of the clause in which the verb occurs to other clauses in the sentences, or the attitude of the speaker toward what he is saying, as certainty or uncertainty, wish or command, emphasis or hesitancy.

If that were the tone of this book, you would be reading something else. Formality, if not pretentiousness, also produces "aggregate limit" for "total," "commencement" for "start," "terminate" for "end" and "in consideration of" for "because." To paraphrase columnist James K. Kilpatrick, when the temptation arises to use uncommon words, lie down until it goes away.

And last, consistency of style means that you follow your publication's stylebook, a manual containing rules of punctuation, capitalization, abbreviations and numerals. Don't use courtesy titles with some people and last names only with others. Don't abbreviate states in one place and write them out in others. Don't put punctuation inside quotation marks in one place and outside them in others. A mechanic who doesn't know the names of the tools lacks credibility. So does a journalist who doesn't know the publication's style.

☐ BE CONCISE

Concise does not mean short. John McPhee is concise at great length. His novels are welcomed into homes. Newspapers and magazines seek an audience among consumers who are busy with children, work and play. When they pause to read a periodical, readers expect to use their time efficiently. They refuse to meander through thickets of verbiage. Learn from Blaise Pascal, who wrote to a friend: "I have made this letter a little longer than usual, because I lack the time to make it shorter."

Being concise means saying what needs to be said in as few words as possible. Concise writers:

1. Use vigorous verbs. Instead of "His voice went booming through the quiet morning woods," write "His voice boomed . . ." Instead of "The president lowered his head and disappeared into the airplane," write "The president ducked into the airplane." Vigorous verbs are transitive verbs in the active voice. Verbs should do something to someone or something. The passive voice cowers in the intransitive verb "to be." In "Less Than Words Can Say," grammarian Richard Mitchell calls it the "divine passive" because, he says, only God knows who does these things. Consider this: "Accusations have been made that mayoral candidate _____ has not filed a tax return for three years." Who is the accuser? Some reporters retreat into the misty passive to hide their inability to find out the "who." The passive voice allows them to print rumors.

When you don't know who is responsible, use the passive. Instead of "A criminal or criminals burglarized the service station sometime between 1 a.m. and 6 a.m., police said," you would probably write: "The service station was burglarized sometime between 1 a.m. and 6 a.m., police said." You also might use it in the future tense: "At the press conference, the president is expected to be asked whether he will approve the legislation." Still, whenever possible, use the active voice. It is more concise, punchier and assigns responsibility for actions.

2. Eliminate redundancies. Knowing the precise meaning of words is a start. Eliminate the echo, and you'll eliminate unnecessary words. For instance, you don't "remand back" because remand means to send back. In each of these examples, the italicized word says it all:

gathered together, close *proximity, Easter* Sunday, *consensus* of opinion, close *scrutiny,* advance *planning,* absolutely *necessary,* soothing *tranquilizer, compromise* solution, *carbon* copy, totally *destroyed,* broad *daylight* and invited *guest.* For writers the most embarrassing of all is excess *verbiage.*

Then there are the cabooses, words that hitch a ride on another: canceled out, continue on, fall down, open up, rise up, free up and edit down. Unhitch them.

3. Distill your copy. Make every word earn its way. Tighten "over a period of five years" to "for five years." Tighten "registered his objections" to "objected." Tighten "he put the blame squarely on the president's shoulders" to "he blamed the president." When you think you are done, try shortening your copy by one-third. Paraphrase to tighten yawning quotations. Sharpen the focus. For many of us, tightening is a painful process. Told to cut three lines from a 5,000-word piece, Henry James returned the manuscript to his editor with this note: "I have performed the necessary butchery. Here is the bleeding corpse."

4. Delete qualifying and intensive adverbs. One word says more than two. If someone is "really unhappy," perhaps they are "sad." If some is "truly happy," try "ecstatic." Almost, a qualifying adverb, is correctly used in "almost there," but "irritated" is better than "almost angry." "Very" destroys unique. "Truly" casts doubt on honest. "Totally" trivializes devoid.

5. Value brevity. Someone once pointed out that the Lord's Prayer contains 56 words, the Ten Commandments 297, the American Declaration of Independence 300, and the European Common Market directive on the export of duck eggs, 26,911.

☐ BE CONCRETE

Erich Maria Remarque, author of "All Quiet on the Western Front," wrote, "When a man has seen so many dead, he cannot understand any longer why there should be so much anguish over a single individual." Then by concentrating on a few individuals in World War I, Remarque powerfully demonstrated why there is so much anguish. The answer, of course, is that when you know a person, you feel the loss. Remarque did not write about the thousands who died; he wrote about a few. He used concrete examples.

Good writers always do. When Alan Cowell of The New York Times wrote about the ripples that something as simple as an increase of the price of bread had in Egyptian life, he offered concrete examples of the people involved. This is one of them:

> For Hamid, the extra 1.2 cents a loaf had an impact far beyond what one might think. Each family member usually gets one of the flat, dish-like loaves with each meal, so the bread expense for a family of six more than doubled, to the equivalent of $10 a month. This is a quarter of Hamid's income . . .
>
> "If you are earning in a month only the same as an American spends on one meal, then you realize what our problems are and why small amounts matter," said Hamid.

The Egyptian people are anonymous; Hamid is concrete in concept as well as in detail. By being specific, Cowell is able to show you the impact rather than just tell you.

Jean Paul Sartre's advice is as useful for writers as it is for philosophers, "The only sin there is is to make the concrete abstract." When you write in generalities, you are asking readers to fill in the blanks. Look for the specifics in this excerpt:

> No-till corn looked rough early in the growing season. Really rough. So rough that even some veteran no-tillers were wondering if this year's early drought was going to hurt them more than their neighbors who worked the ground. But, just as many no-tillers maintained it would, no-till corn started looking better in mid-July, about the same time corn in tilled ground started looking worse. (Generally, no-till soybeans looked at least as good as tilled beans throughout the season.)
>
> "My no-till fields looked far worse than most tilled fields early," says Cliff Roberts, Kentland, Indiana. "But the worked corn started falling on its face in July, whereas ours held in there."

As Johnny Carson's audience would yell, "HOW ROUGH DOES IT LOOK?" You would do well to adopt Missouri's state motto: Show me.

☐ BE CLEAR

The ability to express oneself clearly is crucial in all fields of work. Of all the futurists in the country, former journalist Alvin Toffler is probably known to more people than any of the others because he can write clearly. His book, "Future Shock" has sold over 4 million copies. The same is true of Carl Sagan in astronomy, John Kenneth Galbraith in economics and Aldo Leopold in ecology.

The admonition to be clear assumes that you want to be understood. That is not true of all writers. Some lawyers, for example, often are obscure for obscurity's sake. To illustrate the lengths to which lawyers will go, someone once translated "Jack and Jill" into legal jargon. It begins: The party of the first part, hereinafter known as Jack, and the party of the second part, hereinafter known as Jill, ascended or caused to be ascended an elevation of undetermined height and degree of slope, hereinafter referred to as hill.

The less people have to say or want known, the more apt they are to camouflage it in obscurity. You cannot conceal duplicity in simple sentences with common words.

Clarity in writing is the result of using words precisely, being grammatically correct and relying on simplified sentences.

❐ Using Words Precisely

Understanding is a prerequisite of using words precisely. Before you describe an oak tree or political convention, you must understand it. Understanding requires close and critical observation. Study the veins on the oak tree's leaf. Feel the texture of the bark. Picture the root system. Find a botanist to tell you how the tree lives and why. Ask yourself the two most important questions: "Do I understand this?" and "Can I explain it to my readers?" Don't be satisfied until the answer to both is yes.

Clarity is impossible without precision. A rose by any other name might smell as sweet, but call it by any other name and you will misinform those who don't know any better while outraging those who do. A pin oak is not the same tree as a bur oak. The people who harvest trees can all be called loggers, but the logger who cuts them down is a faller, and the logger who removes the limbs is a trimmer. A good reporter captures the differences that set one tree, one job, one idea apart from another. The artist Paul Gauguin once explained the key to Camille Pissarro's art: "However far away the haystacks may be on the hilltop, Pissarro will take the trouble to go there, walk around it and examine it." Like Pissarro, good writers convey those precise observations in words that are equally precise.

Precise description appeals to the senses. That oak tree has not just a visual appearance but also texture, aroma, weight, taste and temperature. Its impact on the senses and the emotions will differ if it towers alone on the crest of a hill, stands hidden in the middle of a climax forest or clings, snarled and stubborn, to the crevice of a cliff.

Using precisely the right word means you understand that the thesaurus lists not synonyms but words that are related. Few, if any, words have a synonym. Many have first cousins. Many have a whole family tree of look-alikes, but do not be fooled. Upon closer examination, you will find significant differences. "Claim" means your source lacks proof or there is conflicting evidence; "said" is neutral. "Refute" means your source has proof of error; "rebut" is neutral. Use "allude" when the reference is indirect; use "refer" when it is direct. You infer, but the speaker implies. You repair a damaged building; you rebuild one destroyed. Learn the difference between forego and forgo, loathe and loath, following and after, aggravate and annoy.

In Mark Twain's world, the difference between the right word and almost the right word was the difference between lightning and the lightning bug. These days, the difference often is a lawsuit.

❐ Using Correct Grammar

To be grammatically correct, you must find all your misplaced modifiers, negotiate agreement between your pronouns and antecedents and reel in your dangling participles. Editors' faces turned red when these sentences appeared:

> When Stro-Wold and Dresendofer owned the boar, one could send the other a collection of semen in a thermos and the boar did not have to be transported. Although they no longer share the boar, Marion Strother said they maintain a close relationship and exchange semen.

An indefinite antecedent is a definite embarrassment. Send your sentences into battle in tight formation. Each word, each phrase, each clause should march in lockstep with the word it modifies. When they are out of step, you get this:

> The mayor of a popular resort in the South of France has provoked fury with an edict declaring that bathers will be fined 75 francs if caught undressed by gendarmes.

Those darn gendarmes.

❐ Using Simplified Sentences

And last, to be clear use not just grammatically simple sentences but simplified sentences. Sentences that express a single thought are easiest to understand. So are sentences in which the verb follows the subject, although an occasional sentence inversion attracts attention. Clarity flows from short sentences—"Jesus wept"—and long sentences:

> Oil is the Zen of American enterprise: an exercise in subterranean meditation by a handful of men, baking or freezing in the middle of nowhere, working on a tower of steel that can twist a quarter of a million pounds of pipe down three miles into the earth, through clay and water and poison gas and solid rock, probing for the silent, oozing grease left by countless slug-like creatures that died eons ago in their warm and ancient seas.

That sentence is 80 words and understandable. This one of 46 words is not:

> Nor is sentence combining always an option, even if we assume a plentitude of ideational content in the writer's intention, since semantic constraints governing the grammatically hierarchical arrangement of that content require that much of it occur as subordinate inclusions within the boundaries of orthographic sentences.

Roughly translated, that means (perhaps): Even when the writer has several ideas, combining sentences isn't always an option. Some of the ideas will become subordinate clauses.

People who cannot think clearly cannot write clearly. Words don't fail; writers do.

☐ BE COHERENT

Children are often incoherent when they are learning to communicate. "Where's mommy? I want my toy." The child omits the relationship, if any, between the thoughts. Dad might infer that the child is concerned that mom is missing and wants his toy for security. In fact, there may not be a relationship between the statements at all. Parents put up with incoherence; readers don't. Here are five ways writers can achieve coherence:

1. Avoid non sequiturs
2. Use sentence structures that are appropriate to the content
3. Use conjunctions precisely
4. Use transitions
5. Present the information in logical sequence.

☐ Avoiding Non Sequiturs

As illogical as it sounds, a sentence can be both clear and incoherent. These strange bedfellows are brought together by non sequiturs, two or more ideas that do not appear to be related. This is an example:

> Helen Brady, who is expecting her first child this month, will receive an award at the annual dinner of the Council for the Advancement of Science Writing.

The sentence is clear—Brady will receive an award—but incoherent because the reader does not have enough information to understand the pairing of pregnancy and awards. Let's add the missing link:

> The Council for the Advancement of Science Writing will honor Helen Brady, who is expecting her first child this month, for writing insightfully about her pregnancy.

Now there is connection between the ideas expressed in the sentence. Another example: "Olson, who is 5'2", said the university's financial situation is grave." The meaning of the independent clause is clear, but it makes no sense to include Olson's height there. It is coherent in another context: "Olson, who is 5'2", stood on a chair to unveil the picture."

☐ Using Appropriate Sentence Structures

Even when the ideas appear to be related, you must show the relationship precisely. You do that by choosing the correct conjunctions and sentence structures. A compound sentence carries two or more ideas of equal importance. A compound sentence is inappropriate for showing cause and effect or time sequence. If you write, "The City Council passed the ordinance, and the 250 supporters cheered," your are equating two unequal actions. Readers must infer from that sentence the real meaning. You can clarify it by using a complex sentence to show cause and effect: "Because the City Council passed the ordinance, the 250 supporters cheered." You can also show sequence: "When the City Council passed the ordinance, the 250 supporters cheered." Both communicate explicitly.

☐ Using Conjunctions Precisely

The conjunction also signals the relationship between ideas. The neutral conjunction "and" links ideas but does not comment on them.

Often it is appropriate: "We worship knowledge, and we honor the learned." Sometimes "and" is inappropriate: "We worship knowledge, *but* we respect the uneducated." "But" reports the relationship between the two ideas and relieves the reader from having to infer what is really meant. Your challenge is to communicate explicitly.

☐ Using Transitions

You can meet that challenge by using transitions to tell the reader where you are going. Coherent writing makes sense. By providing continuity and showing relationships, transitions help you make sense. For instance:

> The emergence of the United States as the leading marketer of the world's cheapest fuel was engineered by the federal government.
> Here is how it came about:
> The government imposed price controls . . .

The sentence, "Here is how it came about" moves the reader from effect to cause. That technique of speaking directly to the reader to indicate the next step or direction is one of ten ways to build transitions. The other nine are:

2. Using time sequence
3. Repeating structure
4. Repeating words or phrases
5. Using contrast and comparison
6. Using geographic sequence
7. Using pronouns and demonstrative adjectives
8. Using conjunctive adverbs
9. Using numbers
10. Playing off the last thought expressed in the previous paragraph.

☐ Using Time Sequence

The clock and the calendar provide a logical structure to a story. Writers recreating the final hours before a plane crashes or the last months of a cancer victim's life often use time sequence to organize the story. Within the story, the use of words referring to time such as "then," "since," "next," "before" and "after" all signal time sequence.

Donald L. Barlett and James B. Steele of the Philadelphia Inquirer used time sequence, among other techniques, to steer readers through a seven-part series on why the government lacks an energy policy and what the effects of that are. As an example, let's first look at a Barlett and Steele passage we have edited to remove the transitions:

> The federal government has quietly spent hundreds of millions of taxpayers' dollars building—and abandoning—nearly a dozen pilot plants and experimental facilities to produce synthetic fuels. The plants showed that it was possible to turn coal into synthetic crude oil or natural gas.
>
> The government and its contractors in private industry walked away from the plants, always stopping short of actual commercial production. Under the Energy Security Act that became law in June, the government intends to distribute not just hundreds of millions, but billions of tax dollars to oil companies to construct more pilot synthetic fuel plants and experimental facilities to conduct more tests.

Now let's look at the same passage with the transitions. The transitions are in bold type.

> **Since 1949,** the federal government has quietly spent hundreds of millions of taxpayers' dollars building—and **then** abandoning—nearly a dozen pilot plants and experimental facilities to produce synthetic fuels.
>
> **Time and again,** the plants showed that it was possible to turn coal into synthetic crude oil or natural gas.
>
> **And time and again,** the government and its contractors in private industry walked away from the plants, always stopping short of actual commercial production.
>
> **Now,** under the Energy Security Act that became law in June, the government intends to distribute not just hundreds of millions, but billions of tax dollars to oil companies to construct **yet** more pilot synthetic fuel plants and experimental facilities to conduct **yet** more tests.

The time element moves the passage along logically.

❏ Repeating the Structure

Notice also the repetition in the Barlett and Steele example. Structural repetition is especially effective in speech writing. The ear detects the repetition even better than the eye. Read the Barlett and Steele passage aloud, and you will hear the parallelism. Compare that to the earlier, stripped-down version. Each of the four paragraphs starts with an introductory time reference. As long as the parallelism persists, there is a built-in message telling the reader or listener that the ideas are related.

☐ Repeating Words or Phrases

Sometimes writers repeat words or phrases; sometimes they echo the sentence structure. Both the repetition and the content act as the transition. Writing for The Washington Post, Cal Fussman used the technique when he opened his story about King Jordan. Jordan, who is deaf, had just become the president of Gallaudet University, a school for the deaf.

> A few months ago, King Jordan was a man. He had a wife he liked to sling an arm around and kiss, a teen-age son he'd sweat with on runs around Silver Spring, a teen-age daughter he sang '50s songs with as they washed the pots and pans. His friends weren't acquaintances, they were friends for life.
> And then he became a god.
> It's awkward being a god . . .

☐ Using Contrast and Comparison

Sometimes this technique is as simple as saying "By contrast," or "By comparison." Other times the transition is accomplished when the content is obviously demonstrating the comparison or contrast.

When you use a series of numbers to show comparison, use them in the same order consistently. When you don't, you force the reader to reread them. Compare these two examples:

> Twenty percent of the faculty thinks the quality of the University has declined in the last three years, according to the survey.
> Fifteen percent of the instructors think quality has declined. Twenty-six percent of the professors think it has. Eighteen percent of the associate professors and 17 percent of the assistant professors think it has declined.

Now let's arrange the teaching ranks in ascending order and insert a transitional sentence (in bold type) that explains what is to follow.

> Twenty percent of the faculty thinks the quality of the University has declined in the last three years, according to the survey.

The higher their rank, the more likely faculty members are to think it has declined. Fifteen percent of the instructors, 17 percent of the assistant professors, 18 percent of the associates and 25 percent of the professors think it has declined.

☐ Using Geographic Sequence

Logical progression is evident, too, in Richard Zahler's opening in the re-creation of the eruption of Mount St. Helens for The Seattle Times. In this case, the progression is geographical. Like the sun, it. moves from east to west across Washington.

> In succession, its life-giving light bathed the young wheat stalks of the Palouse and the crops of the broad Columbia Basin. The sun shone on the blossoms and buds of Wenatchee's orchards and hastened the ripening of another bountiful cherry crop in the Yakima Valley.

You can also direct the reader around a place with explicit references to location. Recreating the day of a hotel collapse, David Hacker, then of the Kansas City Times, used geographic references:

> Exactly 44 blocks away . . . at 8021 Pennsylvania, on the Missouri side of the state line, Louis and Mary Katherine Bottenberg were still asleep . . .
> But at 6024 Morningside Drive, in the Brookside section of Kansas City, 27 blocks north of the Bottenbergs . . .
> Next door at 6034 Morningside Drive, where Angela and James Paolozzi lived . . .

Hacker was setting the scene to show how people from all over the city were brought together in the tragedy.

☐ Using Pronouns and Demonstrative Adjectives

"She" or "he," referring to a person just mentioned in the end of the preceding paragraph, provides a transition. Demonstrative adjectives, such as "this," "these," "that" and "those" relate people, places and things to something in the story that preceded them. Although the demonstrative adjective is sometimes sufficient by itself, it is usually more explicit to add the noun after it. Use "That **ideal** fueled the revolution" instead of "That fueled the revolution."

☐ Using Conjunctive Adverbs

Conjunctive adverbs, such as "accordingly," "consequently," "however," "moreover" and "therefore" show the relationship between two sentences. Each of these adverbs, however, has a precise meaning. "Accordingly," and "consequently," for example, show a natural progression from the preceding thought. "However," signals the arrival of contrary information. Therefore, choose carefully.

☐ Using Numbers

Numbers help you map the route whether you are showing how to bake a cake or how to use transitions. When you are presenting steps or ideas, identify the number of them when you introduce them: There are 10 ways to build transitions. They are . . .

After the introduction, treat the ideas in the same order in which you presented them. Words and phrases that show numerical progression include "next," "in addition to," and "last."

The columnist James J. Kilpatrick advocates numbering points as they are introduced. Readers may not understand any better, he suggests, but at least they know when you are finished.

☐ Playing Off the Last Thought

All the of preceding techniques are a way of playing off the last thought, but there is yet another way to move logically from one paragraph to another. That is by playing off the words or idea that ends the preceding paragraph. John Hurst did it in The Los Angeles Times Magazine:

> "Probably some time around 10 years ago," he recalls, "I began to notice the kind of activity that we never saw before. When I was an investigator, we would assure witnesses that they could come forward and testify and nothing would happen because those kinds of things you saw in the movies didn't really happen."
>
> Not so any more. Alston tells of one case . . .

Hurst spins off the last statement in the preceding paragraph with the line "Not so any more."

When you move expertly from one paragraph to the next, as Hurst does, your paragraphs cling to each other like Velcro. When that happens, your readers will stick with you.

When you have mastered all these techniques, you are ready to add your fingerprints to the story. You can learn how in the next chapter.

☐ QUESTIONS AND EXERCISES

1. Compare and contrast the tone among articles from The New York Times, People magazine and your local newspaper.

2. Choose any two pages from this chapter and tighten the copy.

3. Put the following information into a simple sentence or sentences, a compound sentence, a complex sentence and a compound-complex sentence. Tell how the meaning changes. Which sentence structure or structures is the most appropriate?
   a. Congress passed the budget.
   b. The president vetoed it.
   c. The president said there wasn't enough money for defense.

4. Choose any two pages from this chapter and identify the transitions by the categories listed in this chapter. Critique the transitions and identify places where transitions are missing.

5. Select a story at least 15 inches long from a newspaper or magazine and identify the transitions by the categories listed in this chapter. Critique the transitions and identify places where transitions are missing.

8
Creative Writing Techniques

The difference between journalism and literature is that journalism is unreadable and literature is not read. —Oscar Wilde

Gene Roberts, former editor of The Philadelphia Inquirer, tells the story of his first job at a small paper in North Carolina. His publisher was blind, so each morning he would have his secretary read him the newspaper. Once, the publisher called Roberts into his office and said, "Roberts, I can't see your story. Make me see."

That's a reasonable goal for all writers. Readers carry a mental videotape of all their experiences, all the sights, sounds and smells. It's up to the writer to start that videotape rolling, to help them recall sights and smells they have forgotten. Telling doesn't start the videotape; showing does. Reporting with all your senses gives you the means to show. Here writer Walt Harrington shows his readers a relative through marriage:

> While Alex works, Reid leads me toward the house, walking deliberately with his hands stuffed into the pockets of his old green coat. He's a tall man, only slightly stooped with the years. He has been lean all his life, and only recently has he put on a little weight around the middle. He wears jeans, leather boots and a tan work shirt. On his head rests an orange hunting cap: "Burkesville Fertilizer." The hat sits back, angled to the right atop a full shock of chalk-white hair. "Let me put on a dry stick in the stove," Reid says, heading back out the front door for five huge pieces of split cedar. I sit in a creaking chair, one of only three, and survey the single room in which Reid lives. It's as if I'm inside an old, sepia-toned photograph: the "Warm Morning" wood stove in the center of the room, the bare light bulb hanging overhead, the long on-off string running from the light and tied to the bedpost, the dog-eared Bible, the brown cross painted on the unpainted drywall, the strong—and to my

own weak, city-dweller nostrils—nauseating smell of dead mice in the walls, a cold-weather condition that can't be avoided on the farm. Reid is like a movie frame halted in time, the living embodiment of where Alex's family began a century ago.

Using rich detail, full of color and fabric, the writer paints pictures.

Winston Churchill savored good writing. Of him, President Kennedy once commented, "He mobilized the English language and sent it into battle." Churchill used rhetoric to rally a nation; journalists use it to inform, inspire, instruct, interpret and entertain. You may be writing about war; more often, you are writing about common people doing uncommon things. By using pertinent description, analogies, personification, allusions and quotations, you, like Churchill, can win readers in war and peace.

After learning how to apply these literary techniques, you will turn to two devices that give writing individuality: pacing and emphasis. You will conclude with a discussion of how to handle quotations and attribution.

◻ USE SENSORY APPEAL

Journalists, especially newspaper journalists, often get so immersed in ordinances, burglaries, politics and environmental impact statements that they neglect to use their senses. Their idea of the facts often fails to extend to the ambience of the event. Their medium may be black on white, but the world they are reporting is a prism of colors. Listen to speech patterns on the streets, smell victory and defeat in the state-house, touch the hands that build and taste the food the poor eat.

That kind of reporting and writing has only recently been welcomed back to newspapers, where dispassionate reporting became confused with colorless reporting. The muckraker Lincoln Steffens told why he left newspapers for magazines in 1901:

> Reporters were to report the news as it happened, like machines, without prejudice, color, and without style; all alike. Humor or any sign of personality in our reports was caught, rebuked, and, in time, suppressed.

Magazines benefited from that period in journalism, which lasted nearly 80 years. Now the line between newspaper and magazine writing is blurred. Good writers, working for all media, report with their senses. Their work has texture, smell and color.

Once awakened to the richness of the detail available, many writers find ourselves overwhelmed by it. Of the thousands of details you choose from, select only those that are pertinent. Like the crow, the amateur writer clutters the nest with things that glitter. That there was a mild breeze from the south adds nothing to a report of a city council meeting, but both what the public says and how it says it does. An AP reporter picked appropriate detail in describing a fire that kept fire-fighters busy at the Denver airport for days:

> By then, the tank farm was a surrealistic heap of twisted metal. Metal stairs that once wrapped around the tanks clung to the wreckage like a twisted web. On the ground, a thin layer of mist hovered above the foam-topped water that inundated the fuel pumps and storage sheds.
>
> A ghostly set of utility transformers dangled from wires. Radiant heat from the blaze had incinerated the pole.
>
> Hartung's face glistened wet as the wind blew back a fine spray. Depending on which way the breeze blew, he was alternately soaked by the water or baked by the heat.
>
> "You come out of there feeling like you've been through a car wash," he said.

The writer provided the detail; the firefighter added the simile.

Good writing includes reporting on one or more of the five senses: hearing, sight, smell, taste and touch. To convey that ambience, every writer needs to know how to use figures of speech.

☐ HOW TO DESCRIBE

Figures of speech allow writers to compare, to contrast, to breathe life into inanimate objects and to summon an entire culture or a forgotten line in a sentence or two. The four common figures of speech are similes, metaphors, personification and allusion.

Similes compare the unfamiliar with the familiar: Electrons revolve around a nucleus of an atom like planets revolving around the sun. To most readers, the solar system is known; to many, the atom is not. The comparison is not literal. In fact, its value derives from the mental images that writers invoke with comparison. Similes are used to say two things are like each other. They begin with "like" or "as." Author Hunter Thompson uses two similes in the same sentence: "The terrible flashing of the lights made us all seem like ghosts, and the music was like the amplified sound of a Studebaker throwing a rod."

Another writer uses similes to describe the ritualistic gathering of teenagers in a shopping mall: "One group of five girls huddle like football players to discuss plans. Each has spent an hour trying to get her bangs to defy gravity and the rest of her permed, shoulder-length hair to cascade away from her face like a waterfall."

A writing student once was asked to describe her dog without naming the breed. She replied: "He has four legs, short tan hair, pointed ears, a white patch on his chest and stands about a foot high."

"Do it again," the teacher urged, "but this time, tell us what he looks like."

The student thought awhile. "He looks as if he ran into a closed door," she finally answered.

"Ah," another student said. "You must have a bulldog."

For that listener, the simile explained what the facts couldn't.

Metaphors are used to say two things are the same. Describing author and radio personality Garrison Keillor, James Lileks of the St. Paul Pioneer Press wrote, "And there he is. A sequoia in a room full of saplings." Lileks used a metaphor to give you a sense of Keillor's size, both literally and figuratively. The metaphor is a splash of cold water on a hot day; it jerks the reader to attention. Of Ed Koch, former mayor of New York, Saul Pett, Associated Press special correspondent, once wrote: "He is seltzer with a lifetime fizz." Writing about college, a student used a sports metaphor: "College is not real life. It's the on-deck circle."

Like Dr. Jekyll and Mr. Hyde, metaphors have split personalities. A mixed metaphor—one that combines two or more metaphors illogically—is a monster. This letter from an applicant to a journalism graduate school is a model of inconsistent metaphors:

> I launch this missile to probe for information about your graduate program. I enclose my resume, which should indicate what caliber I carry in my holster.
>
> I have toiled in the trenches for a time, and I have reached a point at which the practice of traditional journalism no longer fulfills me. I want to teach our craft, brick by brick . . . With my desire to teach humming in my gut, I have learned from some early research that a master's is required to get a foot in the classroom door.

That career fizzled on the launch pad.

When properly used, similes and metaphors invite us to see, hear, smell or feel familiar things in unfamiliar ways and unfamiliar things in familiar ways. They do not just decorate the story; they help the reader understand the message.

Another way to compare is to contrast. Similes and metaphors establish similarities. Contrast compares to establish the differences. Pett uses parallel structure to contrast the two sides of Uncle Sam:

> The federal government is ridiculed easily for its bureaucratic excesses, its stifling regulations, its intrusive Big Brotherism. But against that, one needs to recall it was the federal government, not the states or private industry or private charity or the free marketplace that sustained the country in the Great Depression and saved it from revolution. It was the federal government that ended slavery in the South and had to come back 100 years later with "swarms of officers" to make that liberation real.

Contrast is also inherent in the word "than" (bigger than, faster than, more than), which ought to be used often by every writer. Pett used it to put the amount of gold at Fort Knox in context:

> To tell it straight out, there are 147,342,320.272 ounces of gold at Fort Knox, more than was ever viewed by all the pharaohs of Egypt or the conquistadors of Spain, or the Hunts of Texas.

☐ Numbers by Comparison

Where two or more writers gather, you can almost smell the fear of numbers. Analogies are not only an antidote to the writer's phobia but also a placebo for the readers.

Some writers fear numbers because they don't understand them. Others fear them because they know they tranquilize readers. The cure is to make the numbers understandable. Start by realizing that one number is complex: The federal government's budget now exceeds $1 trillion. The oil slick covered 500 square miles. The planets Venus, Jupiter and Mars will line up within three degrees of each other. In each of these cases, the writer can make the numbers understandable by using more numbers to contrast and compare.

To explain the federal budget, a Washington Post reporter offered this analogy:

> Suppose somebody paid you $1 for reading each word of news and features in a typical edition of the Washington Post. Since one day's Post is officially estimated to contain 80,000 non-advertising words, you'd have $80,000 after reading one day's paper. In the unlikely event that you read every word of every paper for a year, you'd have a cool $29.2 million. But to read a trillion words and earn $1 trillion, you'd have to read the Post every day for 34,247 years.

Another writer explained that it would take 31,688 years to make a trillion dollars at $1 a second. The same technique can be used to explain city and school district budgets. How much does the city spend annually per resident? How much does the district spend annually per student? Get the average income figures for residents of your city from the census reports. Get the average tax bill from the city. Figure out how long it takes the average citizen to earn the average city tax. Or the school tax. Regardless of the approach, you are translating an incomprehensible number to something understandable to the average reader.

We read of oil spills with frightening regularity, but how many readers can envision a 500-square mile oil slick? Translate it. Readers in California could understand easier if they knew that's nearly four times the size of San Francisco. It's eight times the size of St. Louis and 15 times the size of Springfield, Mass.

By using an analogy, an Associated Press writer helped readers to understand—and find—Mars, Venus and Jupiter on the rare occasion when they were almost aligned:

> Anyone on Earth who looks to the west during the few hours after sunset June 21 will see the planets within 3 degrees of each other— roughly one-third the width of a fist held at arm's length against the sky.

How rare is this alignment? "The last time they were so close, American colonists were arguing with King George about taxes."

You think you understand people's ages because you already know so much about the measurement. But at 15, you thought someone is ancient at 50. Ronald Reagan was a month short of his 50th birthday when John F. Kennedy was inaugurated as the nation's 35th president. Twenty years later, Reagan became the nation's 40th president. At 43, Kennedy was the nation's youngest president; at 69, Reagan was the oldest.

When the age extends beyond the human life cycle, it is even more important for writers to translate. Describing the Christmas tree selected for the White House lawn one year, a writer told readers, "Through 28 presidents and half the country's history, it survived." The pertinent analogy helps us understand how long it took for that tree to grow.

Size and distance are more meaningful when they are expressed in relative terms. If you write, "The speaker was huge," the reader has to fill in what you have left out. Huge in one reader's eye may be 5-feet, 6-inches tall; to someone 6-feet tall, huge might be 6-feet, 6-inches. Readers will grope for a comparison. Distances should be compared to the known, such as a football field or a city block. John Glenn, the first man in space for the United States, ascended 163 miles. The concept of leaving the Earth's atmosphere is difficult to comprehend, but it is more meaningful if you translate: 163 miles is less than the distance from New York to Washington, D.C. And if you really want to put it in perspective, consider this: If all the blood vessels in a normal-sized human body were laid end to end, they would extend 100,000 miles. Nothing is big or small, dark or light, colorful or bland until it is compared to something known. For writers who paint pictures, analogy and contrast are the primary colors.

☐ Personification

Personification is often the application of an extended metaphor. Animals, inanimate objects and abstractions are given human characteristics. The technique is used daily in weather reports (Mother Nature) and often in describing natural disasters. Throughout his award-winning story, David Von Drehle of the Miami Herald wrote of Hurricane Hugo as a person: "First the air yanks, then slips its fingers into the tiny gap between door and door frame, then strains at the heavy steel structure until the door actually *bends.*" Referring to the sale of the Delta Democrat Times, newspaper essayist Paul Greenberg wrote that "for four decades and more it was a voice of reason, character, and Southern courage." Abstractions are personified in uses such as "Time marches on" and "Truth does not blush." Reporters write about the "political arm" of institutions and refer to campaigns as "horse races." Those terms are now cliches. A Newsday writer describing a neighborhood coined a new metaphor:

> The houses have eyes. It is hard to walk down a street in Maspeth without someone coming out to ask you what your business is.

Personification is one way to breathe life into your writing.

☐ Allusion

Allusion is a literary shortcut. It permits you to compare two things, people, places or events in few words. The success of the allusion depends on whether the reader knows or can determine from the context what the meaning is. The AP's Pett writes:

> It is one of the ironies of history that a nation born of a deep revulsion for large, overbearing government is itself complaining, from sea to shining sea, about large, overbearing government.

He is using an allusion, "from sea to shining sea," that is well-known to Americans. When Paul Greenberg wrote of 70-year-old Orval Faubus, the man who, as governor of Arkansas, forced the federal government to use troops to enforce equal rights for blacks, he used an allusion to a legal standard: "he was scarcely a clear and present danger now." Many of his readers probably did not recognize the line as a famous legal test, but it works even for those who didn't.

Allusions often are to classic literature or geography, but they can also be topical. Writers allude to song, book and movie titles, to advertising slogans, to historic events—anything that their audience can be expected to know. Describing a pick-up basketball game among four youths who had dreams of becoming professionals, Harrington of The Washington Post wrote:

> The alley court is the fadeaway hook, the look-away pass, the fantasy of the perfect game, the perfect life, Magic and Isaiah and Michael, played against a squat cityscape of boarded windows and rusted bedsprings, of mediocre grades and bounded experience, of race.

Harrington used only the first names, but even casual basketball fans know he is referring to NBA stars Magic Johnson, Isaiah Thomas and Michael Jordan.

Some readers are challenged by such allusions and even look them up; others are irritated by them. As always, writers must know their audience.

☐ PACING AND EMPHASIS

How writers use pacing and emphasis determines the personality of their writing. The two devices are evident in the fingerprints of each successful writer.

☐ Pacing

In writing, as in art, architecture and music, form follows content. That means that the pacing of the sentences should be consistent with the subject matter. Generally, longer sentences are appropriate for more leisurely and serious topics. They slow down the reader. Short sentences convey action or tenseness.

Pacing serves the same purpose as the musical score of a movie. When the scene is romantic, the music flows quietly like a small stream. When the killer stalks his prey, the music pulses. When the killer strikes, the cymbals crash.

The story began slowly when a reporter for the Nashville Tennessean recounted how a maid had murdered a woman she had worked with for more than 50 years. Nine of the first 10 sentences are between 15 and 37 words. One is five. In that sentence the writer reports, "The mistress slapped the maid." The average sentence length in the story is 29 words. But when the writer is describing the fight and murder, the sentences range between five and 15 words:

> Suddenly, consumed in anger, Alberta pushed the older woman to the floor.
> Realizing she may have hurt Miss Sadi, Alberta tried to step back. The old woman reached up and backhanded the maid across the face.
> Dazed, the maid lunged for the pistol beneath the pillow on the bed. "I'll end it all," she thought, as she pointed the weapon and pulled the trigger.
> The bullet struck the old woman in the head. She made a grunting sound, and the maid realized she needed to shoot again.
> She fired a second shot.

Stories on subjects ranging from murders to emotional debates to athletic competition are served by short sentences at key moments.

Manipulating sentence and even paragraph length, then, helps you to establish the appropriate pace for your story. By coupling changing sentence lengths with a variety of sentence openings, you can avoid boring the reader. Consider the openings in the following excerpt:

> Head Start is housed in a ramshackle quarters on Fourth Street. The local center delivers a variety of services to its 20 preschoolers. The three teachers give them speech therapy, pre-reading instructions and two balanced meals. The most important thing they give the students is love.

If you read the paragraph aloud, your ear will detect the monotonous evenness of the cadence. By varying the openings and the sentence length, this writer has added pacing and changed the emphasis:

> Housed in a ramshackle quarters on Fourth Street, Head Start delivers a variety of services to its 20 preschoolers. The three teachers dish out speech therapy, pre-reading instruction and two balanced meals. And love.

And love. Short sentences—or fragments—jab you. Instead of four sentences with 46 words, there are now three with 34; instead of sentences ranging from 10 to 13 words, they now range from two to 19; instead of having three sentences open with an article, the sentences begin with a past participle, an article and a conjunction. Writers sometimes read their stories aloud to hear the pacing. You may want to count the number of words in each sentence.

☐ Emphasis

Other ways to achieve emphasis, the technique of drawing attention to a word, phrase, idea or group of ideas, include story organization, story proportion, sentence ordering, punctuation and repetition.

Traditionally, news stories have been written in the form of the inverted pyramid. That organization emphasizes the lead, the opening paragraph or two. The essence of the message appears at the beginning of the story. In the narrative form, the essence of the message usually appears near the end. The narrative form is common to the news magazines and other publications less concerned with the timeliness of the information. Compare the way two publications reported the beginning of the Gulf War. First, The Wall Street Journal:

WASHINGTON—The U.S. went to war in the Persian Gulf last night.

Next, Newsweek, which appeared more than a week later:

It seemed almost too easy. With eerie precision, "smart" bombs dropped down air shafts and burst through bunker doors. Cruise missiles, lethal robots launched from warships in the Persian Gulf and the Red Sea, slammed into the Defense Ministry and the presidential palace in Baghdad. Hot streams of antiaircraft fire lit up the night, while bomb explosions bloomed above the skyline. Out in the desert, the Iraqi Air Force hid in its hardened shelters; the few pilots who came up to challenge the intruders were quickly shot down or turned tail and fled to the north . . .

The Journal emphasized what happened; Newsweek emphasized how it happened. The Journal used the inverted pyramid; Newsweek used narration. The Journal revealed; Newsweek recreated.

Within the story, there are four other devices to achieve emphasis: sentence length, which we've already discussed, the order of the sentence, punctuation and repetition.

Normal sentence order is subject-verb-object. (Or, subject-verb-object is normal sentence order.) That sequence sometimes results in "loose" sentences, those which, like this one, ramble on long after the main thought has been completed. That's like telling who dunnit and then expecting the audience to stay around to the end anyway. Periodic sentences, by contrast, do not complete the main thought until the end. This ensures that the reader will see it through. Still, to emphasize you can invert sentences:

> The largest beneficiary of this booming business is none other than the American oil industry.
> The American oil industry is the largest beneficiary of this booming business.
> None other than the American oil industry is the largest beneficiary of this booming business.

The first sentence is periodic: "Who gets it" isn't known until the end. The second sentence is loose. It could end after beneficiary. Inverted, the third sentence emphasizes "who gets it" by abnormal placement. Ideas at the beginning and end of sentences are emphasized naturally. Often, the end provides more punch than the beginning.

A third way to provide emphasis is to set off an idea—dashes are one way (and parentheses are another)—so that it attracts your reader's attention. Both of these devices should be used sparingly. Most of the time when you see parentheses, you see a writer who has failed to write concisely. Use parentheses and dashes about as often as the buzzards return to Hinckley, Ohio.

Repetition, however, ought to be seen and heard more often. Repetition provides both pacing and emphasis.

You can repeat both words and forms. Repeating words is one way to provide transitions. It is also a way of emphasizing the word. The Washington Post's Jean White used the technique while reporting on an auction at the fabled J.P. Morgan estate:

> It was a time when the very rich were rich together, as F. Scott Fitzgerald has described it; a time of private mansions, private polo fields, private railroad cars, private art collections, private yachts. . . .

By repeating "private," White drives home the idea of wealth.

More often, repetition of form is used. Parallel construction is used both to equate and to contrast. In "Changing of the Guard," David Broder quotes from a memo by pollster Patrick Caddell:

> Americans always believed that their country fought only just wars, and that we did not lose wars like other nations. Then came Vietnam.

Americans always believed that every President would at least try to provide moral leadership—that whatever was wrong with the man, the office itself would right . . . Then came Nixon and Watergate.

American always believed that this country was ruled by the ballot, not the bullet. . . . Then came Dallas and all the horror which has followed. . . .

The repetition of "Americans always believed" followed by the contrast in the shorter sentences is parallel throughout. That parallelism establishes a cadence that is often present when writing is meant to be read aloud.

Parallelism, which is repetition of form, depends on strict adherence to the pattern. Whether you use parallel nouns or verbs, phrases or clauses, you need to maintain a consistent form. For instance, instead of this:

The tornado dropped onto the city Wednesday, killing four persons, injuring seven, and caused $2 million in damage.

Write it this way:

The tornado dropped onto the city Wednesday, killed four persons, injured seven and caused $2 million in damage.

In the first example, the writer switched from verb to participles and then back to a verb. The rewritten version presents a series of verbs in parallel form.

Parallelism works on a larger scale, too. Writing about a man whose infant son was kidnapped from a hospital, the Post's Harrington captures the father's agony in a parallel series of "what ifs."

If Rob hadn't overslept that Thursday, if he hadn't stayed home from work, if his old Plymouth hadn't been on the fritz, Rob would never have gone to the hospital earlier than usual to see Jeremiah. He wouldn't have gotten to the sixth floor about 4 that afternoon and found his son sleeping on his stomach, head turned to the left. He wouldn't have held the duffel bag filled with incidentals in his right hand, reached out with his left and softly touched his son's back. He wouldn't have suggested to his wife, Terry, who had slept in Jeremiah's room for the several days he was hospitalized with pneumonia, that they leave Jeremiah and go down to the canteen for dinner. If Rob hadn't overslept, Jeremiah, three weeks old and without sin, wouldn't have been alone for the 20 minutes it took for someone to strike at the righteous.

The writer pounds home the agony of the "ifs" with the parallelism.

☐ HANDLING QUOTES AND ATTRIBUTION

Nothing is more deadly to the rhythm of a story than a quote that doesn't carry its own weight or an attribution that isn't necessary. When wisely selected, quotations help tell and personalize a story. Dull quotes, like leaches, drain stories of their vitality. And for every quotation, there is the question of attribution, a burden that nonfiction writers must learn to bear more graciously.

Direct quotes enhance journalistic credibility and add the human element in the story. But pick up any newspaper or magazine, and you will see them overused. Like candy kisses, too many quotes are sickening. Don't use quotes; use good quotes.

If selected carefully, direct quotes are invaluable. As a general rule, look for the unexpected, both in form and content.

There is nothing unexpected in this quote from a telecommunications engineer: "Revocation of a franchise usually isn't to the benefit of anybody." A paraphrase would have served as well. When an attorney says, "They didn't hire me because I'm good, even though I am. They hired me because they thought I had an in," that's unexpected content. Unexpected form comes from another attorney: "It's the second coming. Cable is hot, it's an item, it's in."

You can capture emotion in direct quotes—"Lord have mercy on me! I've killed my best friend"—and pathos—"But you know what? I had that gun right up to my head. . . . I couldn't do it. I wanted to, but I didn't have the nerve." Quotes can sum up frustration: "This government is driving me nuts. The forms are so complicated, I have to call my accountant at $35 an hour or my lawyer at $125 just to get a translation." They can sum up vision: "I have no apologies for the federal government being interested in people, in nutrition, education, health and transportation. Who's going to take care of the environment and establish standards: You? Me? Who's going to work out our transportation problems: the B&O Railroad?"

Good quotes sing in harmony; dull quotes sing off-key. Compare the preceding to these disharmonious examples:

From a story about unsafe conditions at a plutonium factory: "The problem of occasional undocumented transfer has been addressed by a management review team."

From a story about farmers struggling to meet their mortgage payments: "I owned 180 acres and rented 230 acres," he said. "Sixty-six percent of my land had no interest, so even at 13 percent interest on my FLB loan, true interest was 3 percent. Then the drought hit and the profit potential turned."

As a general rule:

1. Avoid direct quotes with factual, verifiable information. ("I think we held him to 10 points," the coach said.)
2. Avoid formula writing that calls for direct quote, paraphrase, direct quote, paraphrase. . . .
3. Avoid reporting that consists of getting a couple of quotes.

You don't apply the same criteria to each quote when you are using dialogue. You should choose to reproduce a conversation with a person—or run it as a monologue—only when that person is famous, an interesting conversationalist, colorful, has a compelling story to tell or all four. When the subject does not meet at least one of those criteria, your story will be dull at great length.

Cal Fussman recreated the dialogue to illustrate Mike Criner's encounters with racism. The sum of the quotes is stronger than any single one:

> "Where I come from, they don't allow niggers to eat in white restaurants," one of the diners had said at that place in Ogden, Utah, after he'd returned from Iwo Jima and the war in the Pacific.
>
> "Hold on," the owner said. "Mike's a regular customer, a good man."
>
> Criner tensed, not certain whether to get up.
>
> The diner snarled. Criner stood. Should he stay, feel good about himself and make problems for the owner?
>
> "Nigger in a white restaurant," the diner grumbled. Or walk away, feel himself shrivel up inside and spare everyone trouble?
>
> "Mike," the owner said. "It isn't me, but . . . I, uh . . . I have to . . ."
>
> "So you'd prefer I leave?" Criner said.
>
> "At this time," the owner said. "Not all the time . . . Just now . . ."
>
> He headed for the door.

To paraphrase a significant portion of that account would be an act of literary insensitivity. Still, even Fussman compressed some of it to maintain the story line. Compression is the process of editing, not of changing what was said or taking the conversation out of context.

A larger problem with dialogue is how to handle dialect. Even to consider it, you need both a good ear and a working tape recorder. The dialect can be regional, as it was when John McPhee wrote about the New Jersey Pineys, or it can be a combination of regionalism and ethnicity, as it was when Bil Gilbert wrote about Nick Haywood, a black man who was a one-man juvenile delinquency prevention program in Kansas City, Mo. McPhee choose not to reproduce the dialect, though he explained several words that are unique to the Piney's common vocabulary:

> Bill is building a small cranberry bog of his own, "turfing it out" by hand. When he is not working in the bogs, he goes roaming, as he puts it, setting out cross-country on long, looping journeys, hiking about thirty miles in a typical day, in search of what he calls "events"— surprising a buck, or a gray fox, or perhaps a poacher or a man with a still.

Gilbert, on the other hand, used dialect. To reassure readers he wasn't just reinforcing stereotypes, he explained the how and why of what he was doing and concluded, "To render his accent precisely in print is possible, but it may leave the impression that the writer is patronizing Haywood, which is not possible." By explaining his rationale, Gilbert met the problem head-on.

☐ Using Attribution Gracefully

The special burden the journalist bears is the necessity of attribution. Constant repetition of attribution jars the ear. Some journalists' solution is to eliminate too much of the attribution in the interest of smoother sentences.

Journalists walk a delicate tightrope between the need to establish the source of information and the effort to make the story readable. At stake is our credibility.

There are, however, at least five ways to deal with the problem:

1. You do not need attribution more than once in a paragraph for the same speaker if no other name appears in that paragraph or if it is clear who is speaking. Too many writers use attribution in the first sentence of the paragraph and repeat it at the end.

2. You do not need attribution with every direct quote when you have only one speaker. The context will show whether the attribution is needed. If it is clear who the speaker is in the paragraph preceding the direct quote, you do not have to hook another attribution to the quote.

3. You do not have to attribute factual, verifiable material. Information such as "The building was seven stories high," should not be in quotes and does not have to be attributed unless the reporter is unsure of its veracity.

4. You do not have to write, "He says he did . . ." when there is no reason to believe it's not true. Simply write, "He did . . ."

5. You can use a comprehensive attribution when you are introducing a version of events from a single source. For instance: "According to police reports, this was the sequence of events leading up to the fight." What follows may be a paragraph or several paragraphs. The attribution does not have to be repeated throughout them.

Most of these guidelines are put into practice in the following excerpt. The italicized words represent excess attribution. Read it once with the attribution and once without.

> Clement Carls, 40, is from Chicago. He used to be a worker in a steel cable factory there. At 17, he started to drink.
>
> "At the beginning, I just felt good, I got high," Carl says. "But later, I was addicted and drank all day until I blacked out." When he was drunk, *he says* he felt lost. He missed work. Then, *he says*, he lost his job, his car, and finally, his wife.
>
> *He says* he quit drinking in 1970 and stayed away from alcohol for six years. "I started drinking again last year because I had too much time on my hands," Carls says.
>
> He drank at home, in the bar and on the street. Sometimes he started fights. He quit a second time.
>
> "I have caused my mother too much worry," Carls says. "I feel guilty." This time I'm quitting for good," *he says*.

Attribution should bear the burden of proving its necessity. Ask "why" when you use it. If there is a chance the reader will be confused, use it. If not, don't.

❑ Apt Quotations

Writers who read are better writers. And writers who jot down lines that make a point concisely, that carry a phrase well turned, are the writers who turn up with apt quotations. Bartlett's Familiar Quotations and The Oxford Dictionary of Quotations don't have compelling story lines, but they are mandatory reading. The influence of Bartlett is evident in Churchill's rhetoric. Almost 30 years before Churchill told the House of Commons, "I have nothing to offer but blood, toil, tears, and sweat," the Italian general Giuseppe Garibaldi wrote, "I offer neither pay, not quarter, nor provisions; I offer hunger, thirst, forced marches, battles and death." By his own testimony, Churchill read Bartlett's. He borrowed and improved the thoughts he found in it. Churchill loved and used the language as he did his troops.

Quotations are used to support arguments because of their dazzling syntax or for their historical context. Pett used a quote from James Madison, the fourth U.S. president, to set the theme of his article on the federal bureaucracy:

> In designing a government, James Madison said, "the great difficulty is this: you must first enable the government to control the governed and, in the next place, oblige it to govern itself." Has it?

Like Grantland Rice and Red Smith before him, sports essayist Thomas Boswell of The Washington Post shows evidence of culture and education in his writing, not to look down on his readers but to enrich them. In a prize-winning essay about athletes at the end of their careers, Boswell quotes Emily Dickinson ("I like the look of Agony because I know it's true") and John Keats ("vale of soul-making"). As he concludes, he alludes to both Dickinson and Keats:

> Look below the Yankee dollar signs and New York headlines. This is a team familiar with the look of Agony. Its players have been forced to look in the mirror. For most, their baseball world long ago became a vale of soul-making.

As with any literary device, you should not use quotations as a crutch. Don't use them to say the ordinary in the ordinary way. Use them too often and your readers will react as Emerson did, when he said, "I hate quotations. Tell me what you know."

All of these creative writing techniques, from the inventive use of imagery to the unobtrusive use of attribution, are but tools. Perhaps someday you will dare to commit literature with them.

☐ QUESTIONS AND EXERCISES

1. Find examples of description that show the writer reported with each of the five senses. Critique the quality of the description. Does the detail clutter the story or add to your understanding?

2. Find examples of similes, metaphors, personification and allusions. Do the figures of speech help you understand or see better? Can you improve the figures of speech?

3. Write a paragraph personifying a specific building in your community.

4. Find some numbers in a story in your local newspaper and rewrite the paragraph(s) to make the figures more understandable.

5. Rewrite this sentence twice to change the order of the words:

   Cruise missiles, lethal robots launched from warships in the Persian Gulf and the Red Sea, slammed into the Defense Ministry and the presidential palace in Baghdad.

   How do your rewrites change the meaning? The emphasis? Which is the best version?

6. Clip a story from a newspaper or magazine and underline each transition. Evaluate them. Should there be more? Add them.

7. Examine the direct quotations in a feature story from your local newspaper. Which are the best? Which would you leave out or paraphrase?

8. Now take the same story and determine whether all the attribution is necessary. Can some of them be eliminated by using a comprehensive attribution?

9

Structuring
the Story

---

*In conversation, you can use timing, a look, inflection, pauses.
But on the page, all you have are commas, dashes, the amount of
syllables in a word. When I write I read everything out loud to get
the right rhythm.*—Fran Lebowitz

When Shari Spires, a staff writer for the Palm Beach Post, wrote a
follow-up story about a woman whose life had been shattered by a
gunman a year earlier, she chose to start by re-creating the dramatic
moment:

> The first bullet shattered the bones of her forearm and tore through
> the muscles. Its force spun her around like a music-box ballerina.
> The second one hit her in the back like a sledgehammer, knocking her
> to the ground. More bullets hit her, so many and so quickly she couldn't
> count them. The doctors found five.
> As she lay writhing on the sidewalk, she could see people running for
> their lives, and she called out to them, "Help me. Help me."
> Her voice sounded so small and so far away, like that awful dream she
> had as a child in which she would scream as loud as she could, but no
> sound came out.
> Then she heard her assailant's footsteps striding purposely toward
> her. In eerie calmness she looked up as he placed the .38-caliber re-
> volver against her chest and fired.
> The last shot blew out both lungs and sent bullet and bone fragments
> into her spinal column, paralyzing her from the waist down.
> Still Victoria Sando remained conscious, her long blond hair fanned
> out on the sidewalk, her clear blue eyes opened wide in shock.
> The last thing she remembered in the emergency room was the snip-
> snip of the scissors and feeling her new red silk dress slip and fall away
> from her body. The white light overhead was blinding, yet reassuring.
> "I was so afraid of closing my eyes," she recalled recently. "And it was
> so odd. There was no pain. No pain at all."

*Months later she was sitting at home idly rubbing her neck when she dis-
covered a lump that turned out to be a sixth bullet.*

For Spires, purpose determined structure. "That was the most dramatic moment," she says. "I wanted to put the reader right there."
Spires took readers to the scene by re-creating it rather than just telling
them about it.

All nonfiction writers must choose an appropriate structure to tell
their stories. In architecture, in design and in writing, form follows
function. As Spires demonstrates, re-creation can be a way to invite
readers into the story. She intentionally backs into the theme, which
is how the victim's rehabilitation is progressing. She used the focus
structure, and you will examine it along with the inverted pyramid
and chronology. You will also examine how writers can weave narration and exposition to tell stories regardless of the structure.

☐ INVERTED PYRAMID

Despite the efforts of many writers and editors who would like to bury
the inverted pyramid, it remains the basic story structure of newspaper and electronic journalists. It survives because it is the most efficient structure yet devised for communicating news quickly and
clearly. In simplest terms, the information is broken into five categories: who, what, where, when and how. Often, these days, journalists
are adding "why." The writer ranks each of the categories in descending order of importance and then begins with the most important:

> CHICAGO (AP)—A taxi spun out of control on a busy downtown
> street today, struck four pedestrians on a bridge and tossed one of them
> into the Chicago River, officials said.
> Letrice Morano, 15, was pulled from the water and was reported in
> fair condition at Northwestern Memorial Hospital, spokeswoman Mary
> Ascher said. Morano injured her hip, knee and thigh, Ascher said.
> Police Sgt. Richard Hansen said the cab driver lost control of the
> vehicle, which then jumped a small median strip and struck the
> pedestrians.
> "The cab came from my left, spun around a couple of times and hit
> four people," said 24-year-old Cidi Zalik, who was walking behind the
> four women who were struck. "One lady flew into the river."
> The other injured women also were taken to the hospital. Ascher said
> a 31-year-old woman was in good condition with a knee injury, a
> 40-year-old woman was in fair condition with a rib injury, and a 24-
> year-old woman was in fair condition with head and arm injuries.

In the first paragraph, the writer answers who (taxi), what (hit four pedestrians), where (downtown) and when (today). The how appears in the second paragraph (lost control . . .). The rest of the information also is arranged from most important to least important. Although the story lacks important detail (exact location, names of the injured, name of the driver), those are omitted because the Associated Press is writing this for a national audience for whom the names are unimportant. Besides, at the time the story was distributed, the names may not have been available.

Depending on their space and time, a newspaper or broadcast station could give you two paragraphs or all five. Like most inverted pyramid stories, this one doesn't have an ending. It simply stops.

To newspaper and broadcast journalists, this form is so common that few give it a second thought. The inverted pyramid conveys information quickly and efficiently, and because it can be trimmed quickly from the bottom, it increases the speed of production. Its use, in modified form, could even be extended into corporations where managers who get lengthy reports often have to search for the recommendation or conclusion. The same report written with the most important information first—the recommendations—would save that manager time. Its principles are also applicable to newsletters and memos. The ability to recognize the most important elements of a story and rank them is essential to all writers.

Saving the reader time is what the inverted pyramid does best, but in the hands of the creative, it can also be entertaining. Stan Benjamin wrote this lead for Newhouse News Service on a story about how Saudi Arabia dominates OPEC:

> It is written in the desert sands: Twelve horses harnessed with an elephant will go where the elephant wants to go.
> So may it be with the 13 tribes of OPEC.

Benjamin hinted but did not tell the news in the first two paragraphs. It is a space-efficient way to hook readers. The tease leads to the news:

> Sheik Almed Zaki Yamani, petroleum minister of Saudi Arabia, is counting on it, and so are the world's oil consumers as they watch Yamani try to reduce and unify the divergent voices of the organization of Petroleum Exporting Countries.

Another journalist was writing a story about a doctor who lost his job at a Catholic teaching hospital when it was disclosed he had attempted to inseminate a lesbian artificially. The story began this way:

" 'All we wanted was a baby,' the lesbian said." The hook is set firmly. The news—that the lesbian cost the doctor a job—followed immediately.

The opening paragraph, or lead, in any story structure is important, but writers of the inverted pyramid must learn to be especially brief and interesting. Writers using other story forms usually have more time, even if only a few more paragraphs, in which to set the hook. One of those forms is the focus structure.

☐ FOCUS STRUCTURE

This is the news:

> People returning to the state accounted for one out of three people age 65 and older who moved to Minnesota between 1975 and 1980.

This is how the Star Tribune of Minneapolis started the story:

> Like thousands of other Minnesotans, Hazel Holzman retired to a life of leisure in the Sunbelt. Now she's back in Minneapolis for the third time, after outliving two husbands in California and "baking my brains out" in North Carolina.
>
> "The second time I came back, I joked to my daughter that I wanted to live closer to the cemetery," said Holzman, 90, who retired 25 years ago as child welfare director for Minneapolis public schools.
>
> The flow of retirees to the South has obscured the fact that hundreds of widows, frail people and others have begun moving back to Minnesota each year. While the return of retirees is more a trickle than a tide, demographic experts say it could swell as the number of Sunbelt retirees grows and the population age 75 and older increases.
>
> So-called "return migrants" accounted for one out of three people . . .

☐ Personalize the Story

"Don't write about Man," E.B. White advised. "Write about a man." He could as well have said, "Don't write about 3,800 people who moved back to Minnesota; write about one of them." The structure permits the writer to focus on an interesting story, using one or more people as examples, before turning to the universal theme. The structure permits journalists to perform two important functions: making the story interesting and putting it in context. Writers who ignore the power of people to attract readers are failing to take advantage of literary techniques. And no writer is achieving the potential of the story if he or she tells stories about the Hazel Holzmans of the world without relating them to others affected the same way. Rudolf Flesch, whose readability formula is still being used today, was already saying this in 1949 in "The Art of Readable Writing." He wrote then that "Only stories are really readable," and later added, "There's nothing on earth that cannot be told through a hero—or heroine— who's trying to solve a problem in spite of a series of obstacles. It's the classic formula; and it's the only one you can rely on to interest the average reader."

☐ How the Focus Structure Works

The structure that permits writers both to add humanity to a story and process information works like this:

1. Open with a person, anecdote or situation that illustrates the theme of the story.
2. Provide a transition to the theme paragraph.
3. Explain the story line in the theme paragraph.
4. Tease the reader.
5. Provide details to support the theme in the body, preferably by using the person introduced in the lead as the narrative thread.
6. Close, preferably by referring to someone or something introduced in the opening.

Let's look at each of these parts of the focus structure.

Opening with a person—a Hazel Holzman—to illustrate the theme of the story is the most common opening in the focus structure, but writers can also open either with anecdotal or situation leads. For all of them, the two keys are whether they are pertinent to the story and whether they are interesting.

Let's look at examples of anecdotal and situation leads. A reporter for The Miami Herald reported testimony verbatim to build an anecdotal lead:

> LAKE BUENA VISTA, Fla.—It happened in broad daylight on Main Street U.S.A.
> "I was watching the parade, and this Disney character came towards me," Pennsylvania housewife Patricia Reinsel recalled under oath. "He walked right toward me . . . he was just kind of dancing around . . and I was kicked."
> Attorney: "Describe the character as best you can."
> Reinsel: "It was a big brown dog with long whiskers and long ears."

Attorney: "Do you think it was Pluto?"

Reinsel: "Yes . . . yes!!

Hi ho, hi ho, it's off to court we go.

Welcome to Walt Disney World, home of Tomorrowland, Frontier-land—and sometimes Litigationland, where tourists of all shapes and sizes sue the ears off Mickey Mouse.

"We're a target defendant," acknowledges lawyer John H. Ward, who defends many of Disney's negligence cases . . .

The lead is a story within a story. It gives way to the theme para-graph, which informs us that Disney World is sued often.

Re-creating a situation that illustrates the theme of the story is another effective way to weave an interesting opening. It requires re-porting in detail. When done well, the opening sounds like a scene from a novel. This one, however, is from a newspaper's Sunday magazine:

In blood-red letters, the sign on the front window of the Dealers Outlet gun store in suburban Phoenix declared: "Urgent! Act Now! Stop the Gun Ban!" Inside, customers took time out from browsing through AK-47 assault rifles and a flock of other firearms to sign a petition—and to vent their wrath at a local "turncoat," U.S. Sen. Dennis DeConcini (D-Ariz.).

"We are petitioning to protest the semiautomatic gun-control bills before Congress," read the text above a fast-growing list of names. "If we allow the government to become involved in any type of gun con-trol, we are violating a basic constitutional right, the right to keep and bear arms."

The petitioners' target that sunny day last spring was DeConcini, a longtime opponent of gun-control measures who had suddenly switched sides, sponsoring one of the nine bills currently in Congress to ban the sale of assault weapons. "I'm a one-issue voter, and I'm going to do everything in my power to take DeConcini out," George Hiers, a burly man on crutches, vowed as he bought a semiautomatic shotgun for his wife to defend herself with while he's away on hunting trips.

That opening sets up the transition to the theme paragraph:

The attack on DeConcini was stirred up by the National Rifle Assn. in a display of fury that represented far more than retaliation against a former supporter. Long described as "the powerful gun lobby," the NRA is now scrambling to recover from stunning setbacks in the past three years. Over the NRA's opposition, Congress and state legislatures have enacted legislation banning "cop-killer bullets" that penetrate protective vests, plastic guns that can be slipped past metal detectors and "Sat-urday night specials" that are used in many crimes. And most recently, the group found itself caught in the furor over assault weapons that was ignited by the massacre of five children in a Stockton schoolyard last January. Those killings, combined with the increasing use of the weapons by drug dealers and youth gangs, have exacerbated the contentious relations between the NRA and its former allies.

Fiction writers create situations; nonfiction writers re-create them. Done well, these vignettes invite readers to participate in a real-life experience. Readers also remember these kinds of stories better than straight factual accounts. The writer's goal is not just to attract attention but also to help the reader retain the information.

Situational leads often take more space to set up than most newspaper reporters can afford, although even in newspapers, this structure is found with increasing frequency. Some publications allow you more freedom and space to craft an introduction. When Ron Rosenbaum wrote about the lure of questionable cancer cures, he used the basic focus structure but set up the opening slowly. His prize-winning story in New West magazine began this way:

> The captain rapped on the door of my hotel room promptly at 6 a.m. He was eager to get this expedition under way. He had a decision to make, and his time was running out.
>
> First of all, just 30 hours remained on his VA hospital pass. If he didn't make it back in time, they might find out about his peculiar below-the-border mission. Worse, they might search his room and confiscate whatever magic potion he managed to bring back.
>
> And the time was fast approaching when they were scheduled to do that CAT-scan on the Captain's liver, get a picture, give a local habitation and a name to that vexing shadow on his last X-ray. They had already cut a malignancy out of his intestines—this shadow could be the dread metastasis.
>
> "No use pretending you're brave or whistling past the graveyard," the Captain told me as we headed south on 405. "I know I've got it again."
>
> But this time the Captain was going to be ready with a plan of his own. That's why he'd asked to hitch a ride with me on my exploratory trip to the cancer clinics of Tijuana. There were at least a half dozen establishments down there offering every kind of exotic therapy and esoteric substance driven below the border by U.S. authorities— everything from the mysterious decades—old Hoxsey elixir to coffee enema cures, fetal sheep cell injections and three varieties of metabolic enzyme treatments. The Captain wanted to scout them all so he'd have his escape route ready when the CAT-scan delivered its diagnosis.
>
> "I know surgery is not the answer," the Captain declared. "I can say that from experience. I took chemotherapy and it was rough. I couldn't take it anymore, and from experience, from the statistics, I know it doesn't work. So they told me, 'Why don't you try immunotherapy?'

That was equally rough. They inject dead cells in an alcohol base into your back. I still have the scars. Devilish rough. You can see it in the doctor's eyes—they know they're up against something they can't beat."

The Captain does not say the word "rough" from the perspective of a man who's lived a life of ease. Not counting his wartime Marine Corps service, he's spent most of his 60 years working as a mining geologist in one rough place or another, prospecting for platinum in the Bering Strait, seeking rare earths and precious metals in the feverish interiors of Central America. The Captain never minded the physical privations of the prospector's life, he told me—it was malignant fate that had treated him roughly.

"Had a reef of platinum off the Aleutians," he sighed. "Would have made my fortune. I was back in the States getting ready to sell shares of it when a goddamn earthquake wiped it out."

The same thing happened down in Yucatan, the Captain said. Titanium this time, a sizzling vein of it. Another earthquake and it was gone.

These reverses left the Captain—who has no fortune or family to fall back on—at the mercy of the VA when the malignancy first showed up. He complains bitterly of the degrading, no privacy, prisonlike confinement at the hospital, but he has nowhere else to go.

Still, circumstances have not deprived the Captain of his drive, his prospector's instinct, and this time he is on the trail of something more valuable than any of the precious metals he sought in the past. This time the Captain is prospecting for a cancer cure.

The presence of the Captain immediately signals that this is not a technical piece on underground cancer cures but a story about why people who would otherwise know better succumb to their lure. The ten thousand people a year who travel to Tijuana's cancer clinics are merely a statistic; Captain is Rosenbaum's Ahab, a nonfiction protagonist.

☐ The Transition

The transition between the opening example and the theme paragraph is essential to the success of the structure. Without it, many readers will fail to make the connection between the example and the story theme. At its simplest, the transition says, "This person (or anecdote or situation) is representative of many." In Rosenbaum's story about the Captain, we learn about the scope of the clinics in the fifth paragraph. In the eleventh, we find the story line: "This time the Captain is prospecting for a cancer cure." The line is followed quickly by the transition into the body of the story: "So are we all, of course." In the NRA account, the story opens with the petitions against De-

Concini. The transition to the theme paragraph makes the connection explicit: "The attack on DeConcini . . ."

Leslie Phillips shows how it is done in a piece for USA Today (emphasis added).

> NEWTON, N.C.—Cynthia Harton, like any mother, wants her 9-year-old son to know the thrill of scattering a set of 10 pins.
>
> What's stopping her is a 5-inch curb at the local bowling alley.
>
> Harton has been in a wheelchair for 23 years so that 5-inch curb might as well be Mount Everest: She can't scale it to take her son inside.
>
> "I'm segregated because that's the way things are," Harton says. "You don't have to take my word for it. Just pick a community and ask a handicapped person if there's a place they want to go without a ramp.
>
> *Harton and 43 million other disabled people in the USA always have depended on a patchwork of laws and the goodwill of others to incorporate them into the mainstream culture . . .*

If Cynthia Harton isn't typical of the 43 million, then she should not be used as the focus. Pertinence is the test of whether the lead is appropriate. When the focus structure was being developed by magazine writers in the 1920s, leads often had so little relationship to the story theme that it took either great tolerance or no critical faculties to continue reading the stories. The genre has been refined throughout the years, however, so that today writers for both newspapers and magazines use it to perform its dual functions—informing and entertaining—successfully.

☐ Theme Paragraph

In the inverted pyramid, the most important information is presented in the first paragraph. In the focus structure, it is presented in the theme paragraph or paragraphs, which appear near, but not at the top. Notice that in the story that starts with Harton, the theme appears in the fifth paragraph. The theme in Rosenbaum's story about underground cancer cures maintains his informal, first-person tone:

> But this time the Captain was going to be ready with a plan of his own. That's why he'd asked to hitch a ride with me on my exploratory trip to the cancer clinics in Tijuana . . .

That theme paragraph gives way to the narrative. Rosenbaum develops the story chronologically. By contrast, Phillips presents the evidence to support the story line about access for the handicapped in descending order of importance.

As you may have noticed by now, this chapter is written using the focus structure. We opened with an example of a writer—Sheri Spires—who had to select a structure appropriate to her content. That done, we moved to the chapter's theme statement:

> All nonfiction writers must choose an appropriate structure to tell their stories. In architecture, in design and in writing, form follows function. As Spires demonstrates, re-creation can be a way to invite readers into the story. She intentionally backs into the theme, which is how the victim's rehabilitation is progressing. We call that the focus structure, and we will examine it along with the inverted pyramid, chronology and the suspended-interest structures.

You'll hear more of Spires later.

☐ Foreshadowing

At the carnival sideshows, you may see the fat man or the dancing girls for free. That's the tease. The promise is that there is more inside.

When writers tease, it's called foreshadowing. Accomplished writers are like the carnival barkers: They can whip the tent flap open just far enough and long enough to whet your appetite.

Rosenbaum teased: "This time the Captain is prospecting for a cancer cure." Will he find it? Rosenbaum placed this tease at the end of his introduction.

In newspapers and some magazines, where leads to stories written in structures other than the inverted pyramid may consist of several paragraphs, the tease can appear anywhere near the top of the story. Usually, though, it is either in the theme paragraph or soon after it. In many magazines, where introductions replace leads, the tease usually comes before the body or narrative of the story. This opening uses foreshadowing to hook the reader:

> Deana Borman's relationship with her roommate Tricia during her freshman year in college had shattered long before the wine bottle.
>
> Weeks had gone by with Tricia drawing further and further away from Deana. Finally, after repeatedly hearing Trica talk about suicide, Deana says, "I kept telling her how silly she was to want to die."
>
> That made Tricia angry. So she threw a full wine bottle at Deana. It shattered against the wall and broke open the simmering conflict between them. That was when Deana tried to find out what had gone

wrong with Tricia's life, and that was when Tricia told Deana that she wanted to do something to her to get rid of her.

And that was when Deana began to be scared of her own roommate.

For only a second, the tent flap is swished open. We are promised a look at the conflict. We wonder if Deana escapes unharmed. Whether Tricia commits suicide. The lead is full of promise of a good story.

Nonfiction writers often neglect to foreshadow the story; good fiction writers lead readers on as if they were dropping chocolates down a trail. The taste is irresistible.

The good writing in Noriko Sawada's memoir in Ms. Magazine of her life as a youngster is also irresistible:

> Had I been able to forgive my mother during her lifetime and tell her so, I might have spared myself years of feeling hagaii ("itchy teeth," Japanese for helpless anguish tinged with frustration). I had long buried the events that shaped me into a mother-hating adult until they surfaced one evening during a sex seminar when I was well into middle age. Its leaders, in order to purge me of the naughtiness I attribute to sex and the guilt I assume for participating in it, exposed—no, overexposed—me via film to nudity. I had already watched male and female frontal nudes superimposed one upon the other, dissolve and coalesce into unisexual blobs, until I felt no shock, no shame, only boredom at the sight of another naked body.
>
> Then, . . . my mind raced back to my adolescence and an altercation with my mother when she had so enraged me with her deceit that I vowed never to trust her again. For my story to make sense, however, I first must tell about my mother's early life that had the impact of a fist upon mine.

Sawada brings us to the climax—to an altercation she had as an adolescent with her mother—then unexpectedly backs off, closes the tent. First, she says, I must tell you about my mother's early life. The hook is firmly set.

The technique of foreshadowing is not confined to introductions; you can use it as often as it occurs naturally in the narrative. For instance, longer stories that have natural breaks often benefit from teases at the end of each section. Foreshadowing permits you to move into the body of the story with a promise that something interesting will unfold. If it doesn't, the writer is no better than the illusionist. Writing can't be done with mirrors. Techniques such as foreshadowing help bait the reader, but good writers don't promise more than they can deliver. Unlike the carny, who sometimes has disappeared by the time the show lets out, the writer must stick around for the conclusion.

☐ The Body

Perhaps it seems as if it took a long time to get to the body of the story, the primary reason we are reporting and writing. We've introduced our protagonist; we've crafted the transition and stated the theme. We've even been a bit of a tease. Now, at last, we are here. But it really hasn't been all that long: usually as few as three and as many as eight or ten paragraphs.

How the body of the story unfolds depends on the purpose of the story. Is the story revealing the results of an investigation? The information usually will be presented in descending order of importance. Is the story a recreation of an event? It usually will be told in chronological order. Is the story primarily nonfiction entertainment? The writer may collapse time, change sequence or use chronology. Whatever the form, the writer often finds it necessary to take a sideroad occasionally. Flashbacks are one way. Sawada used the technique to move the reader back to her mother's childhood. The challenge is to craft an effective transition. Signal your turns for your readers.

Entertain them too. Anecdotes are oases in the body of any story. Even when you are enjoying a long trip, you need a rest. An anecdote provides a smile, or at least diversion. In Saul Pett's magnificent retrospective about Franklin Roosevelt for the Associated Press, he built this oasis into the middle of his text:

> Through a thousand competing pressures and details, he appeared imperturbably on top of life. With equal aplomb, he took epic calls from Winston Churchill and one from a son asking if the President knew of a diaper service in Washington.

Another president, another anecdote. George Bush recalled for writer Walt Harrington a telling experience from his childhood:

> At 8 years old he came home from tennis and told his mom he'd been "off his game." With uncharacteristic anger, she snapped, "You don't have a game! Get out and work harder and maybe someday you will."

If anecdotes aren't worth their weight in gold, they are at least worth something, as one enterprising American found out. He wrote Kipling, "I understand you are selling literature for $1 a word. I enclose $1. Please send me a sample."

Kipling kept the dollar and replied, "Thanks."

The American wrote back that he had sold the anecdote for $2. He enclosed 45 cents worth of stamps—half the profits minus postage.

☐ The Close

The inverted pyramid is like most lizards: cutting off their tails doesn't affect them. Often the victim of too little space, the inverted pyramid is designed to be cut from the bottom. Little premium is placed on the ending. But writers can't be so blasé about the ending of other story structures. The close, the denouement for fiction writers, gives the writer an opportunity to come full circle. When you have opened with a person who illustrates the theme of the story, the close gives you an opportunity to turn your attention to that person again. The ending should be as strong as the opening. In some cases, they may even be interchangeable. In other carefully crafted closings the writer ties up loose ends. As Pett did, when he wrote about Franklin Roosevelt. His story began with two people:

> It hit people in different ways, all of them bad.
> The first thing that happened in Paul Bethke's house, near Loveland, Colo., was that a dream began to die. He had yearned to be a school teacher but now, at 20, he had to drop out of Colorado State Teacher's College.
> His parents, who ran a small farm, were stone broke. He had one pair of pants, corduroys, and he washed them every week. He drifted, desperate for a job. He would ride boxcars, a hobo, just one step ahead of the railroad cops, this man who wanted to be a teacher.
> The first thing that happened in Harold Ions' house, on a day in 1932 in Ferndale, Mich., was that his father was laid off after nearly 30 years at Ford.
> Then, when they couldn't pay the bills, they lost their electricity. Then, when they couldn't meet the monthly mortgage payment of $35, the bank foreclosed and they lost their home.

Pett then tells how FDR pulled America out of the Depression. Along the way, we are offered glimpses of how Bethke and Ions started rebuilding their lives as beneficiaries of New Deal programs. Pett closed with them, too:

> There is still no official monument to Franklin Roosevelt in Washington, D.C., but out in Colorado and Michigan and across the land, monuments exist in the lives of ordinary people.
> Paul Bethke fulfilled his dream of being a teacher. He taught government and political science for 22 years, doubled as football coach, and ended up as superintendent of schools. He has voted mostly Democratic through the years.

Harold Ions, the auto worker, has voted only Democratic for 48 years. He now has three children, 11 grandchildren and three great-grandchildren.

In the family as a whole, there are eight homes, 15 cars and 16 television sets. . . .

And in the twist of circumstances, when one generation takes for granted what another didn't have, when one man's progress becomes another man's concern over high taxes and the excesses of the welfare state, Harold Ions' son, Mickey, also an auto worker, voted for Ronald Reagan.

The denouement. We have a few loose ends of our own to wrap up. First, let's look in on the migrants who are returning to Minnesota. By now, the writers have introduced other migrants, and they end with one of them:

But the prospect of spending retirement away from ice and snow will continue to draw many to the South. It's the warm winters that Boyden will miss most when she leaves Florida on Tuesday.

"I'm glad I'm coming up in the spring. Right now my blood is strictly Floridian, and it's going to take a while for me to get my body ready for a Minnesota winter."

Now back to Noriko Sawada:

After her funeral, after all the company had gone, my father handed me the missing pieces of the puzzle. He told me about my mother's early life and the baby that she had borne, and about the pact of silence she had sworn him to. I protested that he should have told me sooner; after all I was no longer a child. But of course he couldn't. Only my mother's death released him from his promise. . . .

I wept for a woman who gamely wore her hair shirt of guilt and who was so perverted by the experience that she could not alter the fatal course of her relationship with her own daughter. I wept for a mother who became grotesque in her daughter's eyes, an object for pity.

I wept for myself.

And finally, let's return to Rosenbaum:

I don't know what's in that Hoxsey tonic, don't want to know, in fact, but having immersed myself in the mystique and made a pilgrimage to the shrine I have a strange feeling—yes, a false hope, the American Cancer Society would call it—that the old-fashioned elixir might do me some good someday. I hope it helped the Captain.

☐ CHRONOLOGY

The most radical departure from the story structures we have discussed is also the simplest. You can heed the king's advice in "Alice in Wonderland." Asked where to start, he replied, "Begin at the beginning and go on till you come to the end; then stop." Few nonfiction chronological accounts start at the beginning and run until the end. Most start with an exciting moment as a tease, return to the beginning and then run until the end. That's what Spires did in her story about the shooting victim. Rehabilitation progress is measured in inches, not the stuff of which drama is made. After re-creating the shooting scene, Spires offered a chronological account of the rehabilitation.

A suspended-interest structure is the counterpoint to the inverted pyramid. The outcome is at the end, not the beginning. That is pure chronology, and it works when the story is compelling enough to hook the reader from the beginning. It worked for Time magazine in a story called "A Case of Mommie Dearest?"

On a sunny afternoon last May, just two days before Mother's Day, a parcel arrived at the two-story brick home of Howard and Joan Kipp, in the Bay Ridge section of Brooklyn. The package was addressed to Joan, 54, a supervisor of guidance counselors in New York City's public schools. Standing in her kitchen, Mrs. Kipp tore off the brown wrapping paper and found the Quick and Delicious Gourmet Cookbook. She opened the cover. Suddenly there was a flash, and two .22-cal. bullets tore into her chest. Kipp came running into the room and discovered his bleeding wife on the floor, gasping, "A bomb! A bomb!" Three hours later, she was dead.

The bomb had been rigged up ingeniously. The cookbook was only 1½ in. thick, but someone had hollowed it out and placed inside a six-volt battery wired to gunpowder and three bullets. The police were mystified, as were neighbors and co-workers. Who would want to do Mrs. Kipp any harm? Affable and popular, mother of two grown children, Joan Kipp was treasurer of the Bay Ridge Community Council and was expected to be named vice president the following month. Said her grieving son Craig, 27, to a group of reporters: "It was an irresponsible, violent act that doesn't make any sense at all."

Worse to come? Inside the boobytrapped book was scrawled an ominous note: DEAR HOWARD, YOUR DEAD/ BUT FIRST JOAN/ CRAIG NEXT/ DOREEN TOO/ NO MORE GAMES. The police immediately began guarding the entire family. Since the bomb went through the mail, a federal crime, an investigation was mounted by agents of the U.S. Postal Inspection Service. Said one inspector: "It took a lot of thinking to make that bomb."

By early summer they had quizzed some 200 people. Then, finally, a break: a handwriting expert matched the printing in the book's message to that of one of the suspects. The police subpoenaed a sock belong to the suspect and let a trained German shepherd sniff it; the dog was then set loose in a room containing the remains of the real bomb and four replicas. The animal headed straight for the genuine one, and the sock owner's scent. Last week, 91 days after Mother's Day, police arrested their suspect outside his Brooklyn apartment and charged him with mailing the deadly package—to his mom. The accused: Craig Kipp. The motive of Kipp, an unemployed marine engineer, was not known. Craig's father, for one, stoutly proclaimed his son's innocence, and raised the money to pay the $300,000 bail.

This story was not widely known before Time reported it. If the reporting is thorough, chronology also works for well-known events. Saul Pett recapped the fall of Richard Nixon. Others have recreated the moments leading up to airplane crashes. You can do it with less dramatic events: a fire, a crime, a story of success against odds. A writer who had access to the victims, the cab driver and witnesses could re-create the accident that we reported earlier in this chapter and continue through the convalescence. What each of these efforts have in common is hindsight and a fresh look from the inside.

□ NARRATION AND EXPOSITION

Even if you can't define narration and exposition, you know it when you read it. Narration is Mark Twain telling stories. Exposition is Sgt. Joe Friday asking for "Just the facts, ma'am. Just the facts." Narration arouses emotion, makes you laugh, makes you sad. Narration is more easily recalled; expository writing is more easily forgotten. Exposition is only as interesting as the facts. The story about the cab driver hitting the pedestrians is exposition. Exposition works best when the information has immediacy, relevancy and is unknown to the reader. You use exposition to inform; you use narration to inform and entertain. Exposition states; narration illustrates.

Sheri Spires used narration in her attention-getting lead that opens this chapter. When the event first occurred, hemmed in by deadlines and lack of information, the reporters used exposition to write this lead:

DEERFIELD BEACH—A businessman facing thousands of dollars in payroll taxes stemming from an unemployment claim shot his former receptionist outside an unemployment office, then killed himself at his home after fleeing.

A year later, Spires was able to add telling detail and re-create the scene that readers had never really known. As we have already seen, Paul Huston of The Los Angeles Times used narration to open his NRA story. He moved smoothly to exposition to state his theme, but he used narration often to keep the readers' interest. For instance, at one point, to illustrate NRA lobbying efforts, he took the reader to the Florida legislature. This is narration:

> As the NRA waged its war in the West, Marion P. Hammer, a 50-year-old grandmother with brown bangs, strode to the front of another heated battleground in Tallahassee, Fla., a packed meeting room in the state's House of Representatives.
>
> A subcommittee was getting ready to vote on a bill that would ban a list of semiautomatic assault weapons, and Hammer had asked to speak against it. Only 4 feet, 11 inches tall, she could barely be seen as she took the podium. Her gray slacks, blue ruffled blouse and blue suede jacket complemented her steel-blue eyes but belied her credentials: prize-winning marksman and hardball lobbyist for the Florida NRA . . .
>
> Attacking the crux of the bill, Hammer told the subcommmittee: "You cannot differentiate between semiautomatic firearms that look menacing and your routine sporting firearms because, functionally, they are the same."
>
> Next, she dealt acidly . . .

Narration relies on dialogue, anecdotes and scene re-creation. The difference is small; the impact is large. If Houston had used exposition to report on Hammer's testimony, he might have approached it this way:

> NRA lobbyist Marion Hammer told Florida legislators they should not ban semiautomatic assault weapons.
>
> "You cannot differentiate between semiautomatic firearms that look menacing and your routine sporting firearms because, functionally, they are the same," she told a House of Representatives subcommittee . . .

Instead of re-creating the scene at the Phoenix gun store and using dialogue, Houston could have used exposition. The result would have been a drier, less interesting account:

> Members of the NRA in Arizona are gathering signatures on petitions protesting the proposed ban on semiautomatic weapons.
>
> They are also angry at U.S. Sen Dennis DeConcini (D.-Ariz.) for co-sponsoring the bill.
>
> "I'm a one-issue voter," said George Hiers, a customer in a Phoenix gun shop, "and I'm going to do everything in my power to take DeConcini out."

The expository versions shown here are less interesting than the narrative versions, in part, because the story lacks immediacy. Reading narration is like watching a movie; instead of listening to someone tell you what happened, you listen directly to the speakers. You see and hear and smell and feel the environment. Writers remove themselves as intermediaries. In exposition, the writers observe and listen and then tell you what they saw and heard.

◻ FLASHBACKS

Story tellers use a narrative thread to weave stories. Often the thread is woven around time sequence. Writers need to depart occasionally, to flash back to earlier times, but the chronology remains the main road. Time isn't the only narrative thread. The point of departure could be the clock or the calendar, but it also could be a place, such as a courtroom, or even a bathtub.

That's what Cal Fussman used in The Washington Post Magazine in his story about Mike Criner, a black man who had lost his job, and subsequently, almost everything else, because of bias in his workplace. Under intense pressure trying to hold his family and his life together, Criner often retreated to the bathtub where he tried to wash away his troubles. Fussman used the tub as his narrative thread. From there, he would flash back to tell the story of how Criner fell, and eventually, recovered. In the course of seven magazine pages, Fussman opens with the bathtub scene, flashes back to earlier events and returns four times. Here are a few examples, starting with the lead:

> The bathtub, thank God for the bathtub, Mike Criner was thinking. At least they hadn't taken that away, too. He turned the left faucet, and the steam from the hot water rose over his misery. Here, in the warmth of the tub, was the one place, the only place, he couldn't be touched.
> Why him, Lord, why him? His job, his savings, his car, his motorcycle, his travel trailer, his kids' college tuition, even the food in his refrigerator . . .
> "Mike, c'mon, you've been in there for an hour now."
> "I'll be out in a little bit, Tina. Just let me be a little while longer."
> He grabbed the washcloth, soaped it up and began to run it relentlessly across his arms . . .

Here, Fussman recaps how Criner had been so successful in his job that he was offered a job as a foreman in another printing plant. That was the beginning of his troubles.

> Six years later, Criner would spend entire mornings or afternoons in a bathtub wondering what he'd done to deserve his firing and the subsequent chain of events that left his family without a home or an income. To those who've dealt with racism all their lives, his troubles may seem depressingly unsurprising. To those who've been sheltered from bias, however, or who've preferred to ignore it when they could, Mike Criner has an eye-opening story to tell . . .

This leads Fussman to Criner's new job, and the troubles that immediately followed. Then he returns to the tub.

> "Mike, you've been in that tub for two hours. Are you trying to beat yesterday's record?"
> He felt the water going cold on him again. Maybe Daddy had been right after all. He could remember back in Texarkana, Tex., standing in the grocery store waiting and waiting while all the white people got served first. "Daddy, why don't the man take care of us?" he asked . . .

The tub, Criner's oasis, is Fussman's narrative thread. Once the scene had been established, Fussman is able to move easily back in time and return. The thread permits writers to use flashbacks and return without confusing readers. Fussman had time and space. Associated Press writer Jim Litke didn't when he wrote a story after the second round at the Master's golf tournament. But he was able to use a flashback to contrast the present competition between Jack Nicklaus and Tom Watson with the past (emphasis added):

> After lurching through the front in an even-par 36, Watson dropped the gauntlet with a birdie at No. 10, and Nicklaus almost dropped from sight when he dumped two balls into Rae's Creek fronting the par-3, 12th green and stalked off after a quadruple bogey . . .
> Asked what he thought watching the debacle, Watson grinned slyly. "I said to myself, I've hit the ball six feet from the hole and I hope I make birdie."
> He didn't. But after the bath, Nicklaus started a run of four straight birdies. Watson caught the train at the par-5, 15th with an eagle and matched Jack at No. 16, where both drained sidewinding 30-footers that traveled nearly 50 feet to reach home. *Suddenly, it could have been the 1977 British Open at Turnberry all over again.*
> Playing head-to-head over Scotland's parched links that year, they staged perhaps the greatest final round in the game's storied history. After both carded 66 in the third round, Watson squeezed out a 65 Sunday to Nicklaus' carefully crafted 66. An Associated Press story that day concluded that "the best there is" had simply outlasted "the best there ever was."

But the truth of it was, when they set out Friday, neither man was what he once was . . .

The italics highlight the transitions into and out of the flashback. Brief and effective.

From structure to writing techniques, what we have presented here are guideposts, not straitjackets. Accomplished writers chart their own course, find new routes. The rest of us are thankful for a map. You have to travel the route a few times before you start noticing the sideroads.

☐ QUESTIONS AND EXERCISES

1. Using a short inverted pyramid story about an event, such as an accident, rewrite it in chronological order. (You may have to add some detail that is not available in the original.) Which is more interesting? Why? Which is longer?

2. Find a story written using the focus structure. How many paragraphs are there before the theme statement or nut paragraph? Evaluate the clarity of the theme statement and the transitions into and out of the paragraph(s). Is the opening pertinent to the theme?

3. Find two examples of foreshadowing and evaluate them. Do they entice you to read on? If so, why? If not, why not?

4. Find two examples of anecdotes and evaluate them. Are they interesting? Are they pertinent to the story? Did the writer move into and out of them gracefully? What questions do you think the reporter asked to get them?

5. Using a newspaper or magazine story, find examples of narration. What techniques did the writer use to create narration? Examine the detail, the verb tense, the scene. Is it longer than if the writer had used exposition? If so, is the extra length worth the reader's time?

6. Find two examples of a flashback. How did the writer signal the change in time or location? Is it clear or confusing?

10
Revising
for Publication

Just get it down on paper, and then we'll see what to do with it. —Maxwell Perkins, editor

Having discussed scene setting and description, having compared the strengths and weaknesses of narration and exposition and of similes and metaphors, this writer was eager to try to use the techniques. This is the opening of his first draft:

> The smell is antiseptic, radiating upward from the gleaming plastic tiles that adorn the rooms of her house. Flooding into the eyes from every bend and curve and niche and nook, the color white is everywhere. The walls, counter tops and windows all smile with a cleanliness that envelopes a newcomer; no matter how clean you are, you feel slightly soiled walking by. The inhabitants of the house, although their tasks are august, often perform more simple, banal duties, like nodding reassuringly, that warmly comfort the visitors to her house. But most visitors here are oblivious to the sensations of sight, sound and smell, which pass through them like an X-ray. The visitors here desire only information. They prepare for the worst, hope for the best and accept whichever they receive. For it is the activities that take place in her house that bring the visitors to her doorstep. It is here, in her large house, during every minute of every day, that she hears the twin cries of unrestrained joy and quiet sorrow. In Toni Sullivan's house, visitors come to witness birth and death.
>
> When they arrive, the visitors usually know the outcome of the people they came here to see, but she treats them as she would the patients, with deft skill and placid compassion. A whirlwind of activity when the fingers of death try to reach out and take what is not theirs, she can be serene, quiet and charitable to those visitors whose family members could not escape its clutches. Here, the Carriage pulls in often, kindly stopping for those who could not stop for death.

"It's something that we live with each day. Death, we do our best, of course, to try to stop, but sometimes we can't," said Sullivan, dean of M.U.'s School of Nursing. I don't think we should ever be hardened or blasé about death, but death is inevitable; it will happen at some point to all of us. We try to do our best to delay it for as long as we can, but sometimes we can't. Those of us who have been practicing long enough can tell when it's coming. Sometimes there's just a smell of death."

After her first year on the job, the deliberate and determined 53-year-old is not one to be enveloped by the administrative tasks of her job. So she walks the hallways with the nursing administrator of the University Hospital and Clinics to look in on patients who hear the approaching hooves that draw the Carriage ever near.

The millions of people who are treated each year in hospitals across America, and the many more visitors who have anxiously paced in hospital waiting rooms, would take comfort knowing that the men and women dedicated to saving lives—expert in the passionless logic of medicine—often pray when logic is not enough to save a life.

Comment: *The opening is overwritten (". . . The inhabitants of the house, although their tasks are august . . ."; "It is here, in her large house, during every minute of every day, that she hears the twin cries of unrestrained joy and quiet sorrow.") It is also not pertinent to the theme of the story, which is to be a profile of Sullivan. Many readers might think it was about how the hospital treats its dying patients. Others might think we have a story about Mother Theresa, not a nursing dean. You have many good lines and insightful observations in this opening, but you need to start the story with a scene or anecdote that is pertinent to the theme, and then you need to emerge from it—as quickly as possible—to the theme paragraph. After the hook, tell the readers clearly what the story is about.*

This is the writer's second effort:

The quiet, tree-lined road that leads to Toni Sullivan's home is sprinkled with fallen leaves, each brightly colored and adding to the existing grandeur of suburban Elizabeth, N.J. A fresh breath of fall comes again, and the leaves move from one yard to the next. Nash Ramblers rest in the neighborhood driveways. In front of one house, a man dressed all in white carries bottles of fresh milk to the doorstep. He nods hello to a girl who drops her bike in the driveway and skips past him to the front door.

Inside Toni finds her parents watching the news on television, a new black-and-white set the family recently purchased. Adlai Stevenson is talking about what he wants to do for America. She sees her parents lean forward on the couch. "Democracy cannot be saved by supermen, but only by the unswerving devotion and goodness of millions of little men." Her father, lips pursed, leans back and nods. Later, at the dinner table, her father talks about it again—Toni has heard the refrain a million times—and with the conviction of someone saying it for the first time.

"We have a duty to help those who haven't made it yet." Toni really has heard it all before, but now, at 14, she senses for the first time the passion with which her father speaks and lives the words duty, service and responsibility. Before falling to sleep that night, she tosses in bed, looks up at the ceiling in her room and thinks again about her father's words, and she wonders what service she will perform to help those who haven't made it yet.

Now, nearly 40 years later, Toni Sullivan is dean of M.U.'s School of Nursing, and although she has reached among the highest levels of her profession, she still lives the life of a sonar operator, quietly searching for those who need help.

Comment: *This is a great leap forward. You are using narration to tell the story of an event that had a great impact on Sullivan's career choice. That is pertinent to the theme, which you state clearly in the theme paragraph. The theme paragraph also sets you up with a transition into the body of the story. The last line of the theme paragraph, particularly, uses an appropriate figure of speech. You also have subtly worked in details that set the anecdote in time. Now work on tightening; the opening is still unnecessarily long. The handoff from the milkman to the girl is confusing because it is not clear immediately that the girl is young Toni.*

So goes the process of revision. All writers, beginners and experts alike, benefit from another perspective. Hitler was no exception. His first title for "Mein Kampf" was "Four-and-a-Half Years of Struggle against Lies, Stupidity, and Cowardice."

The relationship between an editor and you needs to be built on mutual respect. Editors need to withstand the temptation to rewrite, at least in the early drafts. Celebrated author H.G. Wells, no fan of editors, once said "No passion in the world is equal to the passion to alter someone else's draft." On the other hand, many editors tell stories of writers who defend their writing as passionately as a mother lion protects her cub.

If you are a free-lance writer, the story is often edited or rewritten in your absence, and more than one editor may edit the story. Sometimes several editors, following the admonition of Maxwell Perkins, will rewrite it. If you are on staff for a magazine or newspaper, you will have the opportunity to work with an editor. You can benefit from the comments, or you can fight it. The best writers assume the editor's good intent, and listen closely. Others fight it because they see it as an assault on their abilities. Everyone benefits from a critique. None of us is capable of looking at our own copy dispassionately, but we can look at someone else's story without a sense of ownership. In the following examples, you can follow that process as a disinterested observer. Then try to apply the comments to your own writing.

◻ FINDING THE FOCUS

Here is the opening to the first draft of a story intended to help readers, particularly those just getting interested in bicycling, to select the proper bicycle (editor's comments are in italics):

All of us remember the day our training wheels were stripped from our bike. The first successful ride was filled with tingling fear and wobbly triumph. Once we got the hang of it, we were sailing down the block at breakneck speed. *All of us? Most of us? Some of us? You are assuming that your memories are the same as your readers. This approach may work in a first-person story; it won't work when you are attributing your feelings to your readers.*

What a feeling of power, control and freedom.

These emotions are returning to 45 million adults nationwide who are hopping on bikes to take part in the latest leisure activity craze.

Have you been considering joining the peddling *Check spelling* masses lately? Do you need an alternative to parking meters and traffic jams? Or maybe that baby fat isn't so cute anymore and you don't want to hassle with a fitness club? Or maybe you feel like gliding through picturesque trails and your car just wouldn't be the same? No matter what your desire, there is a bicycle for you. *Speculation is no substitution for reporting. Find someone who has these questions or had these questions rather than making them up.*

There has hardly been a better time to buy a bike. The bicycling industry is pumping out high quality bikes at enormous rates. The Bicycle Manufacturers Association of America estimates 10 million bikes will be sold this year alone . . .

Comment: *To tell a story, you need to find a person who has recently bought a bicycle. Tell the story through that person. That will help you move from speculation to reporting, from exposition to narration. You still need a theme paragraph; this one acts as a transition to the theme you proposed—to help people make a decision about the bewildering array of bicycles from which to choose.*

Taking the cue, the writer found someone around whom she could weave the narrative thread. But as you will see, she still has more work to do:

Four years ago Brian Bradley entered a triathlon as part of a three-man team. Although he was the swimmer of the bunch, something clicked when he saw all the different kinds of bikes. Four years ago Bradley caught the bug. *Avoid the cliche.*

Now in season, you can rarely find Bradley without his bike. Bradley is not alone. Forty-five million adults nationwide are hopping on bikes to take part in the latest leisure activity craze. *Good first attempt at tying Bradley to the theme. Now try to make the connection more explicit to your theme, which is not just that a lot of people are buying bikes but which ones to buy.*

If you have been thinking about joining the pedaling masses lately, you have picked a good time. There are bikes built for every desire and lifestyle. The bicycling industry is pumping out high-quality, reasonably priced bikes at enormous rates. The Bicycle Manufacturers Association of America estimates 10 million bikes will be sold this year alone . . . *This paragraph still fails to clearly state what the story is about. Tell readers that this story will help them make decisions about bikes.*

Here is the third attempt at a theme paragraph:

If you haven't been in a bike shop since you were a child, you will be confronted with an astonishing array of choices. There are bikes for road riding, for racing, for off-road riding. There are bikes for beginners, and there are bikes for professionals. Which is the right one for you? Experts can save you money and increase your enjoyment of the sport by matching the right bicycle to your needs.

Comment: *Much better. Now you have a structure and a theme paragraph that permits you to focus on the information you have. And readers know what rewards await them if they keep reading. Now think about the best way to help them through the choices. Should it be in the typical story, a mix of exposition and narration? Could a table listing the kinds of bikes, uses and costs be a good way to tell part of this story?*

◻ POLISHING THE DRAFT

Some stories need polish more than revision. The story that follows is one such example. It is a profile of a woman who has had an unconventional life. The names and locations have been changed for use in this exercise.

Lana Preston slouched in her chair in a back room of the Unity Center, fingering through the Nature Company Catalog. *Name of catalog pertinent; nice detail.* Every few minutes, she would pause in her reading to make eye contact with the woman across the table, who spoke of chemotherapy, surgery, massage therapy and the death of her father.

As the woman began relating memories of her father, Preston gently placed the catalog in the middle of the table. She sat upright, tugged on her sky-blue skirt so that it hung lightly over her legs, fluffed her loose white blouse, and pulled at the gold wire barrette that clasped her straight, shoulder-length brown hair. Reaching up to her *Right? Left?* ear lobe, Preston unclipped an earring.

The gaze of Preston's aquamarine eyes did not break from the woman as she *Ambiguous. To whom does "she" refer?* ran her fingers over the soft curves of her lightning bolt *Hyphenate compound modifier* earring. When the woman finished speaking, the room was silent for a moment. In a soft, soothing voice, Preston broke the silence. "Have you grieved for him?"

The woman understood the importance of Preston's question. About one year after the death of her father, she fell ill with lung cancer. *Ambiguous. Who got cancer, Preston or the woman?* Both Preston and many members of the Healing Circle, a support group for people recovering from cancer, believe that emotional and spiritual healing, as well as medical treatment, is an integral part of recovery from cancer. As part of her recovery from lung cancer, the woman has made a concerted effort to grieve for her father.

As moderator of the Healing Circle, Preston works as a specialist in emotional and spiritual healing. She does not have cancer. *She doesn't have a lot of other illnesses either. Not needed, especially if you clear up the first reference.* But she has devoted much of her life to seeking emotional health, both for herself and others.

In 10 years as a professional counselor, Preston has taken a progressive approach to therapy. She did not discover her techniques and theories in psychology textbooks or college classrooms. She learned her techniques while dealing with the painful experiences of her own life.

"I was looking for answers for myself, and I didn't find them in psychology," she says. "I use tools that worked for me."

Preston has spent more than 20 years of her life coping with emotional pain and searching for solutions to problems that began in her childhood.

Preston was playing in a neighbor's yard one summer day when a white truck pulled up beside her house. Two men dressed in white stepped out of the truck and walked into her home. They emerged a few moments later, dragging her mother through the yard. Her mother, dressed only in a bathing suit, was kicking and screaming with all her might as the men placed her in the truck and drove her to Fulton State Hospital.

The girl did not cry or scream. "I just survived by being numb," Preston says. "At the time, I didn't think anything of it. It was normal." *Powerful anecdote. Try composing a better introduction to it so the reader will be teased about what is coming and thus understand it better. You have a flashback here. The transition into it should clearly signal change of time and place.*

Preston's mother was schizophrenic. On several occasions, her father had her mother committed to hospitals. Her father told her that when he married her mother, she had scars on her wrists from restraining manacles. During Preston's childhood, she watched her mother receive electric shock treatments and mood-elevating drugs. Nothing worked. When Preston was 20, her mother committed suicide.

"To me, it seemed like a really horrible, miserable experience. I was really afraid of it happening to me," she says. "My unconscious message was 'Whatever you do, don't let that happen to you.'"

When Preston was 18, she moved to Champaign to attend the University of Illinois. *Abrupt change. Work on a transition to this paragraph.* It was 1968, and the tenets of the counter-culture *Check dictionary.* provided a means for Preston to avoid her mother's fate. While Preston rejected materialism, marriage and traditional female roles as reflections of her mother, the counter-cultural movement emphasized self-fulfillment, even it that meant breaking roles and norms.

"It was very permission-giving to do whatever you wanted to. You didn't have to get married and wear pearls and be a housewife after college," she says. "Being a hippie was safe; it was a way of coping."

In her senior year, Preston met John Dolph. She would not earn her degree for another eight years.

"It was very sheik to drop out of school at that time, and I convinced her to drop out," Dolph says. *Good reporting to track down Dolph. You need to introduce him as the speaker before the quote. Otherwise, it appears as though Preston is speaking until we get to the attribution. Also tell us where he is and what he is doing now. And check the spelling of "sheik."* The couple never married, but a few months after they became involved with each other, Preston was pregnant.

The couple lived in a vegetarian commune and helped open Champaign's first vegetarian restaurant. After a year and a half, the commune sold the restaurant. Some of the members, including Preston and Dolph, decided to live their fantasy of building a homestead. They moved to a Costa Rican farm. *You are about to change speakers; introduce the speaker at the beginning.*

"I thought, 'Wouldn't that be great: to live by the ocean, in the tropics,'" she says. "Of course, instead we had hip waders and machetes."

Life in the country was rough. There was no running water or electricity, and the land was surrounded by a tropical rainforest. *Check the dictionary.* After three months, Dolph left Preston and their son, Bill, to return to the United States.

"That was when Lana began her woman-in-the-wilderness saga," Dolph says. Preston decided to remain in the country, raising her son alone, for another six months. *Did she decide to stay for six months, or did she decide to stay and it turned out to be six months?*

"It was a proving of myself, that I was strong and tough, that I could make it in the jungles of Costa Rica with a baby alone," she says. "I just made myself strong, like a wounded bird." *Wow. Nice quote.*

In 1978, Preston began to do "volunteer spiritual growth work" *Why in quotes?* at the School of Metaphysics. *Where? Is she back in the U.S.?* The volunteer work fulfilled Preston's inner desire *As opposed to outer desire?* to help people with spiritual and emotional growth, but it wasn't enough. While volunteering, she returned to college with a specific goal: to be a professional counselor. *Wordy.*

"I wanted to be credentialed, because I wanted to get paid for the work I was doing for free," she says. Preston earned a master's degree in counseling and personnel services. She now has a private counseling practice and works part-time as a counselor at Columbia College.

As a counselor, *Jarring repetition* she has never stopped seeking her own solutions. She continues to seek what she had been searching for as a young woman: self-acceptance. *Try tightening and smooth the syntax.*

"From my parents, I never received any sense of value. I never felt any affirmation or approval," she says. Her path to finding self-acceptance is paved with "reprogramming" inaccurate beliefs *Can a path be paved with reprogramming?* about herself with such techniques as affirmations, journal writing, anger therapy and massage. She describes these techniques and her own spirituality as a process of "re-parenting."

Preston uses many of these techniques in her counseling, including rebirthing and anger therapy. Her present focus in working with clients is "experiential." If clients are discussing disturbing events, Preston will have them pause to experience their emotions, rather than urging them to continue to talk. *If what follows "experiential" is a definition of the term, make it more explicit. Some readers will have to back up and reread it to understand.*

Preston disagrees with some schools of counseling that believe the counselor should manipulate the client without the client's knowledge. To begin her sessions, Preston asks her clients what they want to accomplish that day. "They know what's best for themselves, better than anyone else," she says.

Preston has not always felt completely comfortable about being a progressive therapist. *Progressive is a mushy word. What does it mean?* "I used to feel weird about my focus and my techniques because I was loyal to the things that worked for me in my own growth," she says. "At times, I've gotten weird reactions about that."

Preston says that counseling techniques in the Midwest are lagging five to ten *Style error* years behind those used on the East and West coasts. Although her techniques are considered progressive in Illinois, they were considered the norm at a class on anger, depression and guilt at the University of Arizona-Tucson last year. "All the people I met out there were into the exact same stuff I was into."

For Ellen Hagan, a member of the Healing Circle, Preston's techniques have paid off. *It's been quite a while since you mentioned Healing Circle. Can you quickly re-identify it? The same would be true of someone you introduce and then leave for a while.* "I don't know if her way is best, because you do have people that come to the group that are more mainstream and some of these ideas are real new," she says. *Fix punctuation.* "But in that sense, the group meets a need for people, for me a different kind of group available from other places." *Quote is not memorable or said well. Should you paraphrase?*

"She helped me get a handle on it. I think I've made a lot of progress in a lot of areas, physically and mentally," Hagan says.

Although Preston has been practicing her own techniques for years, she still works to heal the emotional wounds of the past. *Wordy and ambiguous.* Like the woman in the Healing Circle who faces the pain of her father's death, Preston struggles with her own grief.

"I have a lot of grieving to do about not having a mother I could bond to," she says, "I never let my mother love me. She did love me, but in a needy way, like a leech."

A ginger-colored teddy bear with turquoise earrings on its ears sits upright on the couch in Preston's home. Beside the bear, Preston sits with her legs folded beneath her. She reaches across the couch, picks the bear up, and whispers its name, Edwina. Holding Edwina gently in her arms as if she were rocking a baby, she looks up with wide eyes.

"She's good for healing the child within."

Nice anecdote for an ending. It would be even better with an introduction to it that signals a change of time and location and helps us understand what we are about to read.

Comment: *This woman's story is interesting, even compelling in parts. It is clear that you have spent a good deal of time getting to know her, and she apparently feels comfortable with you. You have a nice mix of exposition and narration, although if your notes and additional reporting permits, the story would be strengthened by additional narration. Challenge each direct quotation to see if it should be paraphrased so that the good quotes stand out. Tighten ruthlessly, especially the opening. Some readers are going to drop out before they get to the theme. Also consider putting the opening scene in present tense to give the reader a better sense of being in the room rather than being told about it by the reporter. Polish the transitions. Try to compose a better theme that not only sums up the story but also foreshadows the rest of the story. Make sure the reader knows there is good stuff to come. You have done a good job. Finish it in style.*

☐ The Next Draft

The writer didn't agree with all the suggestions. She argued that the story couldn't be shorter; in fact, there was much more she would like to include. She liked the scene in the opening and didn't want to shorten it. She questioned the need to provide an introduction to the anecdotes, especially the flashback to Preston's childhood. But in the end, she worked hard to make some changes. Here is the rewritten and edited result:

Lana Preston sits in a back room of the Unity Center and absent-mindedly fingers through the Nature Company Catalog while a member of the Healing Circle talked about chemotherapy, surgery, massage therapy and the death of her father.

Preston puts down the catalog, props her elbows on the round table, rests her chin on her hands, turns her eyes up to the woman, and asks softly "Have you grieved for him?"

About one year after the death of her father, the speaker had fallen ill with lung cancer. Both Preston and the members of the Healing Circle, a support group for people recovering from cancer, believe there is a connection between the health of the mind and body. In order for the woman to recover from her disease, she must sort through the emotions surrounding her father's death.

Preston, the group moderator, knows emotional pain firsthand. She carries scars from her childhood and from the journey fleeing from that childhood. She found her way back to emotional stability, slowly and sometimes, painfully.

Now she uses those experiences to help others travel the same route. Her techniques and theories will not be found in a psychology textbook. But then, her life wasn't mainstream, either.

"I was looking for answers for myself, and I didn't find them in psychology," she says. "I use tools that worked for me."

Those tools are different from those used in the mental health profession when she was a child. She recalls one scarring experience with such clarity that it could have happened yesterday instead of more than 30 years ago.

Then 10, she was playing in a neighbor's yard one summer day when a white truck pulled up beside the house. Lana quickly stepped behind a Chinese elm to avoid being seen. From the safe shadow of the tree, she watched two men dressed in white climb down from the truck and walk into her home. A few moments later, they emerged dragging her mother through the yard. Dressed only in a bathing suit, her mother kicked and screamed uncontrollably as the men placed her in the truck and drove her to Fulton State Hospital.

Lana neither cried nor screamed. "I just survived by being numb," she says now.

Her father later told her that when they married, her mother had scars on her wrists from restraining manacles. Doctors diagnosed Preston's mother as a schizophrenic. She was chained to a bed and given electric shock treatments and mood-elevating drugs. Nothing worked. When Lana was 20, her mother committed suicide.

"I was really afraid of it happening to me," she says. "My unconscious message was 'Whatever you do, don't let that happen to you.'"

She has spent the rest of her life making sure that it wouldn't happen to her. Her first response was to flee.

When Preston was 18, she moved to Champaign to attend the University of Illinois. It was 1968, and the Vietnam-era counterculture provided a means for her to find her own way. While she rejected materialism, marriage and traditional female roles as reflections of her mother, the countercultural movement emphasized self-fulfillment, even if that meant breaking roles and norms.

"You didn't have to get married and wear pearls and be a housewife after college," she says. "Being a hippie was safe; it was a way of coping."

In her senior year, Preston met John Dolph. She would not earn her degree for another eight years. Dolph, now a businessman in another state, takes responsibility for the delay in Preston's education.

"It was very chic to drop out of school at that time, and I convinced her to drop out," Dolph says. The couple never married, but after a few months, Preston was pregnant.

The couple lived in a vegetarian commune and helped open Champaign's first vegetarian restaurant. After a year and a half, the commune sold the restaurant. Some of the members, including Preston and Dolph, decided to live their fantasy of building a homestead. They moved to a Costa Rican farm. That's when fantasy met reality.

"I thought, 'Wouldn't that be great to live by the ocean, in the tropics,'" she says. "Of course, instead we had hip waders and machetes."

Reality was no running water or electricity and being surrounded by a tropical rain forest. After three months, Dolph left Preston and their son, Bill, to return to the United States.

Dolph says that was when Preston began her "woman-in-the-wilderness saga." Preston decided to remain in the country and raise her son alone. She lasted six months.

"It was a proving of myself, that I was strong and tough, that I could make it in the jungles of Costa Rica with a baby alone," she says. "I just made myself strong, like a wounded bird."

Back in Illinois, Preston volunteered to work at the School of Metaphysics. The work fulfilled Preston's inner desire to help people with spiritual and emotional growth, but it wasn't enough. While volunteering, she returned to college to be a professional counselor.

"I wanted to be credentialed, because I wanted to get paid for the work I was doing for free," she says. Preston earned a master's degree in counseling and personnel services. She now has a private counseling practice and works part-time as a counselor at Columbia College.

She is still her own best patient. She has never stopped seeking self-acceptance. "From my parents, I never received any sense of value," she says. "I never felt any affirmation or approval."

She paves her path to self-acceptance by replacing inaccurate beliefs about herself with such techniques as affirmation, journal writing, anger therapy and massage. She describes these techniques and her own spirituality as a process of "re-parenting."

Preston uses many of these techniques, including rebirthing and anger therapy, in her practice. Her present focus in working with clients is "experiential." That is, if clients are discussing disturbing events, Preston will have them pause to experience their emotions, rather than urging them to continue to talk.

Preston doesn't believe in manipulating the client without the client's knowledge. To begin her sessions, she asks her clients what they want to accomplish that day. "They know what's best for themselves, better than anyone else," she says.

Preston has not always felt comfortable with her approach. "I used to feel weird about my focus and my techniques because I was loyal to the things that worked for me in my own growth," she says. "At times, I've gotten weird reactions about that."

Preston says that counseling techniques in the Midwest are lagging five to 10 years behind those on the coasts. Although her techniques are considered avant garde in Illinois, she says they were considered the norm at a class on anger, depression and guilt at the University of Arizona-Tucson last year. "All the people I met out there were into the exact same stuff I was into."

For Ellen Hagan, a member of Preston's Healing Circle, the techniques have paid off. "I don't know if her way is best because you do have people that come to the group that are more mainstream," she says, "and some of these ideas are real new." Hagan says Preston's approach has helped her. "I think I've made a lot of progress in a lot of areas, physically and mentally."

Although Preston has been practicing her own techniques for years, she is still healing her own wounds. Like the woman in the Healing Circle who faces the pain of her father's death, Preston struggles with her own grief.

"I have a lot of grieving to do about not having a mother I could bond to," she says, "I never let my mother love me. She did love me, but in a needy way, like a leech."

Here in her home, she looks secure. A ginger-colored teddy bear with turquoise earrings sits upright on the couch. Preston sits with her legs folded beneath her. She reaches across the couch, picks up the bear and whispers its name, Edwina. Holding Edwina gently in her arms as if she were rocking a baby, she looks up with wide eyes.

"She's good for healing the child within."

To paraphrase Somerset Maugham, there are three rules for writing. Unfortunately, no one knows what they are. That's why this story would be different with another writer and another editor. What is certain, however, is the value of having someone else's perspective. You should seek—and listen to—as many perspectives as you can get. It can be humbling. Sometimes, it can even boost your ego. Whatever the response, learn something from each critique.

☐ QUESTIONS AND EXERCISES

1. Exchange stories with another writer and critique each other's work. Phrase your comments as you would like to see them if they were made about your story. After the critique, talk frankly about

the process. What hurt? What helped? Tell each other what insights you gained. Tell each other what didn't help. Do the same with a second draft.

2. Find a published story that you think can be improved. Ask a group of writers to meet and critique it. Compare the suggestions that come from the different perspectives in the group.

3. Compare your experiences with other writers who have gone through the editing and revision process. What have you and others found most valuable? Least valuable? If you are on a publication staff, involve editors in the discussion.

PART IV

How to Reach Specialized Audiences

11
Writing Service Journalism

Good journalism is service to the community. Successful service journalism is service to the individual.—John Mack Carter, editor-in-chief of Good Housekeeping

In California, the Office of Traffic Safety has watched drivers floss and brush their teeth, cut their child's hair, groom their pets, read, shave and nurse the baby. All this while in a moving vehicle.

You can buy car fax machines, note pads that clamp to a steering wheel, dictation machines linked to a transcription machine at the office, laptop computers, portable refrigerators and a book on commuter calisthenics. Campbell Soup predicts that by 2000, 25 percent of all cars will have microwave ovens.

Into this time-starved society trudges the old-fashioned printed word. Do people who have to brush their teeth in the car on the way to work have time to read a newspaper or magazine?

Some do, fortunately, because not everyone spends hours driving to and from work. But even those of us who don't commute long distances have other demands on our time. The primary reason people give for not subscribing to newspapers is that they don't have time to read them. So the pressure is on to make our products time-efficient and *useful*. Skimmers and scanners don't want to waste their time, especially with something that is not useful to them.

For those readers able and willing to devote more time to our products, we have described in previous chapters ways to engage and to entertain them. We are not asking that you abandon any of the principles of good writing. They always apply—though with different emphases.

Now we're taking another step beyond the inverted pyramid. It's an approach to presenting information that:

1. quickly shows the reader that the information is *useful;*
2. gives information to the reader in the most *usable* way; and
3. tells the reader how to take *action* or how to get more information.

In many cases, writers decide not only what article to write but also how the information will be presented on the page. You can decide or help decide the best way to inform readers—narration, sidebars, lists, photos or charts. These are the techniques of service journalism.

Service journalism has been around about as long as journalism has. Some even call advertising a form of service journalism. Advertisers show people what's new, what to do and how to do it better or with less effort. Don't ignore what advertisers have learned about readers. Don't ignore what free-lance writers have long known—that how-to articles on most anything are their bread and butter. In the '50s, the do-it-yourself era blossomed, and the bloom never withered. Advice columnists continue to be among the best-read writers in the press.

Nevertheless, the 1990s' thrust toward more service journalism articles and periodicals is unprecedented. The one word that best characterizes service journalism is "useful."

For example, a Woman's Day cover has the following blurbs:

"How to Pay Your Bills When You Can't"
"Create a New Wardrobe With Clothes You Own"
"Learn to Cook Low-Fat Recipes"
"Save $$ Hundreds on Housewares, Food, Drugs"

You'll find service articles not only in consumer magazines. They're in corporate, association, university and specialized business magazines as well. Newspapers are using them in style, food, travel and entertainment sections—and even in the news pages.

☐ WHAT IS SERVICE JOURNALISM?

A lot of the credit for the concept and spread of service journalism goes to James A. Autry and the Meredith Corporation of Des Moines, Iowa. Autry, who became president of the Meredith Magazine Group, was the first to try to define the term and the first to speak about the need for journalists and journalism schools to become familiar with and to employ the concept.

Autry, along with John Mack Carter, editor-in-chief of Good Housekeeping, and Dorothy Kalins, editor of Metropolitan Homes, was instrumental in getting the American Society of Magazine Editors to initiate a category of Personal Service in the annual American Magazine Awards. He spurred Meredith into funding programs to train college students in service journalism.

In a speech first delivered in 1979, Autry defined service journalism as "the delivery of ideas and information through words, illustrations, design and various mechanical formats, which is intended to produce on the part of the reader a positive action."

Service journalism, he said, was to go beyond the delivery of pure information and to include the expectation that the reader will *do* something as a result of the reading. Service journalism is "action journalism"—not action on the part of the journalist but expected action on the part of the reader.

Service journalism is the epitome of putting readers first. Think of your readers, find subjects they want to know about, and present those subjects simply, quickly and attractively.

The best piece of service journalism is one that the reader would tack on the refrigerator. The term "refrigerator journalism" captures the gist of service journalism. If you can digest useful information into a graph or chart or list that your reader hangs on the refrigerator or bulletin board or puts in the special save-to-do file, you have done your job well. You have done your job even better if the reader does something as a result of the information.

You can use service journalism techniques on most stories because it's not a separate category of writing. It's simply a different approach to writing.

☐ WORKING PRINCIPLES OF SERVICE JOURNALISM

Here are some working principles you can use to produce effective service journalism.

1. Save time. Because for most people the cliche "time is money" happens to be true, tell them how much time it will take to do something or how much time your advice will save them. The words "quickly," "immediately," "soon" and "easily" come to mind.

WORKING PRINCIPLES

1. Save the reader time.
   a. Be concise.
   b. Be clear.
2. Involve the reader.
3. Think usefulness.
4. Think new or news.
5. Think money.

You, too, must save readers time. They must be able to grasp the information you are giving them *quickly* and *easily*. This means you must:

a. Be concise. Remember, you can't always be brief, but you can always be concise. Don't waste a second of the reader's time.

b. Be clear. Remember when you bought that outdoor cooker and tried to follow the directions to put it together? Don't make readers read anything twice before they understand it.

2. Involve the reader. You have three ways to do this most effectively.

a. The "how-I" approach. You are the expert. The author speaks with authority and experience. Well-known experts have credibility. If you are a chef in a popular Cajun restaurant, your article on how to prepare crawfish etouffe will interest more readers than one by an amateur.

However, you don't have to be a long-time expert. Subjects such as "How I Creamed My Crabgrass," or "How I Saved $200 on Air Fare to Europe," may be based on a one-time experience.

b. The "how-you" approach. You do not have to be the expert. Talking directly to the reader works best for for most kinds of writing. A direct-marketing expert, Vic Schwab, compiled a list of "100 Good Headlines and Why They Were So Profitable." John Caples, another direct-mail advertising expert, took these 100 headlines and found that "you" appeared 31 times; "your," 14 times; "how," 12 times and "new" 10 times.

If you combine "you" and "your," the total of 45 mentions is almost as great as the combined scores of the other top eight words. Even Caples was surprised by the wide margin, but he was not surprised by the high score of "how." "This word," Caples writes, "and the combinations *how to* and *how you*, have been used in successful advertising for as long as I can remember."

What advertising has proved works will work editorially as well. Using "you" applies to more than the title. It's an entire approach to a piece. Here's an opening by John B. Thomas in Better Homes and Gardens:

> It's back-to-school season, and, once again, you've vowed to complete your college degree. Sounds good, but between work and family, where will you find the time? Here's an idea that really clicks: Finish the last two years of your bachelor's degree by watching cable TV in your own home.

The use of the second person and contraction (you've) makes the passage personal, conversational and engaging.

Even newspaper reporters are using "you" in their leads. Formerly a lead might read: "Last night by a 5–4 vote, the City Council raised the price of garbage pick-ups for Springfield residents." Now it might read: "You're going to be paying $2.22 a month more to get your garbage picked up beginning in July."

c. The "how-Jane Doe" approach. Here are three ways:

- Find the expert. When you are not the expert, find someone who is. If you are not a famous chef, find one who is. Get Martina Navratilova to tell you how to help others improve their backhand.

- Find a celebrity. People love celebrities. The celebrity need not be an expert on the topic of the article. Country America has a recipe column called "Celebrity Kitchen." Country humorist Jerry Clower loves the sugar cookies his mama bakes for him, and his fans loved the story and recipe for "Big Mama's Tea Cakes."

- Find an amateur. If stockbroker Miriam Stakes found an old barn in the country and turned it into a country estate, readers may well enjoy finding out how she did it. Where did she get help? How much did it cost? What advice does she have for others who would like to try it? What mistakes did she make?

4. Think usefulness. Try using words such as "handy," "practical," "versatile," "reusable," or "recyclable."

5. Think new or news. "New" is important to news and advertising. Advertising expert David Ogilvy says that copywriters who leave out the news in commercials should be boiled in oil. "Products, like human beings," Ogilvy writes, "attract most attention when they are first born."

"New" and "now" are also key to service journalism. What is the best and latest advice on how to avoid high cholesterol? Which software program provides the best grammar-checker? Even old things can be new. People are nostalgic. Look for new ways to use and enjoy old things.

6. Think money. One of the first questions readers ask is cost. Everyone likes to save money and to make money. Everyone likes a bargain. The only thing people like more than a bargain is something free. In "My First Sixty Years In Advertising," Max Sackheim writes: "Sixty years ago the best word in the English language for getting attention was the word FREE. And today, the best word for getting attention is still the word FREE."

☐ DEVICES AND TECHNIQUES OF SERVICE JOURNALISM

Because you want your articles to be read, you may want to use the devices and techniques that make service journalism quick and easy to use. Don't leave these important elements entirely to the designer. If you provide them, the designer will have more to work with to create more interest on the page. You can help draw readers in by using the following:

USE:

1. Lists.
2. Subheads.
3. Blurbs.
4. Sidebars and boxes.
5. Questions and answers.
6. Charts.

---

1. Lists. Whenever you can make a list, make a list. Sometimes a list is all you need. In a typical short piece in Woman's Day, Jenny Craig, president of more than 500 weight-loss centers that bear her name, gives some tips. Here are three examples, each starting with a bullet:

- Lose weight to please yourself, not someone else.
- A support network of people works better than diet books and such.
- Find an exercise that you really enjoy, and do it.

Bullets find their target every time; they get readers' attention. Craig uses sentences, but don't hesitate to use fragments in a list.

In a piece on "Lifesaving News About Strokes," Woman's Day uses sentence fragments to list symptoms you may not recognize:

- paralysis and loss of sensation down one side of the body
- dizziness
- problems with speech or vision
- clumsiness

You can summarize the key points of a service-journalism article with a "do" and "don't" or "advantages" and "disadvantages" list.

Magazines know the effectiveness of numbers in titles. Home Mechanix offered "12 Ways to Increase Gas Mileage." Ski wrote about "The 14 Best Ski-Better Tips of All Time." Reader's Digest used numbers as a subtitle to tell readers the benefit of reading the piece: "How I Survived a Tax Audit: Eight tips for the fearful, anxious and wary." The author numbers the lessons learned in the story.

This use of numbers builds structure. Because the story is organized clearly, logically and sequentially, readers can grasp and retain the information more readily.

2. Subheads. Subheads can do more than decorate the page or break up the copy. They can show the organization and structure of the article so that readers can scan the subheads and grasp the essence of the story. Subheads provide entry points for readers who need or want only certain parts of the article.

For example, an article in Consumer Reports "COPING WITH A RECESSION" presents ideas under these heads: AT THE SUPERMARKET; AT THE PHARMACY; IN THE GARAGE; AT THE BANK; AT HOME; IN THE AIR. Under each subhead, of course, the author lists what the reader should do to save money. Readers who don't have a car would not read the "IN THE GARAGE" segment, and those who don't fly would skip "IN THE AIR."

3. Blurbs. You may call them pullquotes, lifts, drop-outs or drop-ins, but they all mean the same thing. It is useful, however, to make two distinctions:

a. External blurb. This is a crisp, clear summary of what the article is about. Regard it as a contents blurb, a few words that give readers the benefit they will gain from reading the piece. As a matter of fact, this contents blurb may appear on the table of contents as well as on the opening spread of the article. Usually it appears directly below the title or headline.

Readers must learn the benefit—immediately.

Busy readers need to know immediately how they can benefit by reading the article. Tune them in to WIIFM—"What's In It For Me?"

b. Internal blurb. The internal blurb breaks up the copy, entices readers and offers useful information. For instance, an internal blurb in "Double Up on Trout and Reds" in Salt Water Sportsman reads: "Fisherman who work the shallows may catch fewer trout . . . but they'll take more trophies." That's good bait for fishermen, and it's useful information.

4. Sidebars and boxes. A sidebar contains information that complements or is related to the main story. Because sidebars are short, scanners are more likely to read them than they are to read the story itself. Also, if you get readers to read what's in the sidebar or box, they just might get interested in reading the story.

Look for ways to include some information in sidebars. If you use sidebars properly, you need not worry as much about having a story that is so long readers will be scared away. A long story that is broken into three shorter pieces gets more readers. It's all a matter of presentation. For every three pages of double-spaced copy, have at least one sidebar.

For example, a story on moving has a sidebar on what to do if you are only moving across town. Another sidebar lists the moving companies in town with their addresses and phone numbers. This is refrigerator journalism at its best. Readers can clip and save the information they need.

References. Always include information readers need to take action: a short bibliography, addresses and phone numbers. In travel articles always tell readers how to get where they want to go and what it costs.

Notes. Also consider a box that contains a summary of all the most important information in the article. Think of it this way: If you were taking notes on the article to prepare for an exam, what would you write down? Readers don't have time to take those notes. Why don't you do it for them?

A newspaper headline reads, "Risky Business: Entrepreneurs don't always succeed." Here are some notes the writer took for the reader:

Why they fail

These are among the major reasons small business fail, according to the Small Business Development Center:

1. Inadequate front-end planning.
2. Insufficient capital.
3. Inexperienced management.
4. The wrong location.
5. Inventory mismanagement.

That's good note-taking. If you're an entrepreneur, you could clip that.

Quizzes. Quizzes involve readers by asking them what they know about a topic. The quiz can include a scoring mechanism by which readers can rate themselves as "excellent," "good," etc. The quiz can use multiple choice or simple "yes" or "no" answers. For example, an article on "burnout" in Shape magazine asks readers whether they have a list of symptoms. The more often they say "yes," the closer they are to a serious emotional problem.

Glossaries. A box containing a glossary of technical terms used in an accompanying article is most useful. Rather than defining terms within the story and breaking the flow of the piece, put those words in a box. You need not worry about offending people; they like to increase their vocabulary. Also, if the words are difficult to pronounce, give the phonetic pronunciation.

For example, an article in the business section of the Birmingham Post-Herald about commodities contained a box with definitions of the words commodities, futures and futures transactions.

Biographies. In a profile story, you may want to box a brief biography of the subject of the story. The box could contain the person's name, title, date of birth, education, and places of employment. It's a good way to deliver that information without interrupting the flow of a story, and readers will pay attention to it. If the story has more than one key person, you may want to create a box for each one.

5. Questions and Answers. An excellent way to present useful information in a useful way is by using a question-and-answer format. The Q-and-A article or sidebar gets high readership because readers are able to jump to the questions and answers that interest them.

6. Charts. Writers often act as if the only way to give information is to write sentences and paragraphs. Some charts tell the story—or part of it—faster and clearer. Charts are the responsibility of the writer as well as of the designer and editor.

Think visually when you are doing service journalism. Try to envision what graphs and charts will best present the information. Then, in consultation with your editor, plan how the graphs and charts will appear on the page—in what order and in what juxtapositions—and how your writing will complement and enhance the message.

Sometimes the chart will simply supplement or complement what the article says. Or, it will present the same information in a visual way. But sometimes, the bulk of the story can and should be the chart.

You may want to talk to a designer about ways to make the chart itself reflect the subject matter of the chart. A chart showing the nutrients, calories, fat, etc. of breakfast cereals need not be just words and bars and lines. The chart may be constructed in such a way that cereal boxes or cereal bowls give the information. The graphic becomes more graphic.

Here's an example from the American Association of Retired Persons Bulletin. The drawing adds interest to the statistics on the decline of income as people get older.

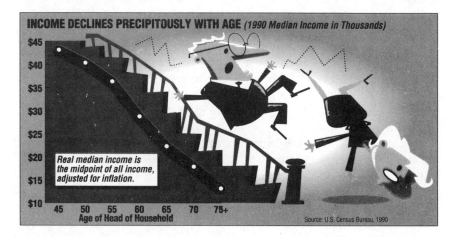

INCOME DECLINES PRECIPITOUSLY WITH AGE *(1990 Median Income in Thousands)*

$45
$40
$35
$30
$25
$20
$15
$10

Real median income is the midpoint of all income, adjusted for inflation.

45   50   55   60   65   70   75+
Age of Head of Household

Source: U.S. Census Bureau, 1990

Not every service journalism piece has to contain all of these elements. But the more you use, the more usable your information becomes.

Many stories, no matter how long, can use service journalism techniques. Investigative stories, for example, need a strong summary, lists, pullquotes, subheads, and information about whom to call or to write. When you think about it, which stories don't?

☐ QUESTIONS AND EXERCISES

1. Go to a magazine rack and find the magazine with the most service journalism titles on the cover. Read it, and then list the techniques and devices used to make the articles useful and usable. Indicate the article that is the best example of service journalism, and indicate why.

2. Discuss: Service journalism does not apply to news articles.

3. Compare your local newspaper to USA Today. Which is of more service to readers and in which ways? Be specific.

4. Find an article in a publication that is primarily one continuous text. Then redo the article using the techniques and devices of service journalism.

5. Discuss: The principles of service journalism are a fatal blow to good, creative writing.

12
Writing
for Organizations

Writing for business does not mean abandoning literary standards. Some of America's best prose is being published today by business communicators who adjust their style to accommodate their employers' concerns.—Downs Matthews, winner of 110 awards while editor of "Exxon USA."

The wind blows constantly over parts of the Texas Panhandle. Sweeping dust under dried brush, it hurries over the barren plain as if tidying up after the human intruders.

These intruders are the exploration companies who come to play a gambler's game. They don't roll dice, spin wheels or shuffle cards. They shake the ground and drill holes, hoping to find natural gas and oil deep below the earth's parched, yellow cover.

Despite all the fancy technology, from seismic studies to satellite pictures, the exploration and production business remains a game of chance. The stakes are high, and Mother Nature has shaved the dice. . . .

That's good writing. It didn't appear in a commercial newspaper or consumer magazine. It was written for a corporation publication.

Good writing is often found in organization publications—but not often enough.

We choose the term "organization publications" because we mean to include government at all levels, the trade press, associations, businesses, corporations, offices of public information of hospitals, universities and other institutions.

People who belong to an organization or work for a company want and need to be informed. Take advantage of their special interest, but don't waste their time. You are spending company dollars to buy time in today's hurry-up society. If your publication is sent to the homes of your readers, you are competing with the best writing and the best publications out there.

Because of the unique nature of organization publications, we'll begin by discussing their purposes and content. Your appeal is different from other publications people buy. If you want to be read, you need to know your audience's interests and to adapt your style and approach to its needs.

Organization editors must also be aware of their management's goals. The approval process can be and often is painful. Part of an organization writer's job will always be to enlighten management about the importance of open and honest communication. Organization writers must accept the fact that they are writing for a client. Therefore, while always insisting on the truth and open disclosure, they are bound to present the client in the best possible light.

However, as this chapter will demonstrate, writing for an organization is no excuse for bad or boring writing. We will apply the principles of good writing to organization writing. We'll urge you to tell your organization's story through people. Most of all, we'll show you how to be more creative by demonstrating that there are no dull subjects but only dull writing. Making copy more interesting is merely a bigger challenge for creative nonfiction writers, not millstones meant to drown you.

☐ PURPOSES AND CONTENT OF ORGANIZATION PUBLICATIONS

The first requirement is to know the organization for which you work. What does it do? Who makes it happen? To whom does it happen?

The second is to know your audience. What is their gender, age, income, education, reading level? What do they want and need to know to help make the organization better? You, like all magazine and newspaper editors, must conduct regular readership surveys. But you can learn a great deal just by speaking with members of the organization or by meeting with small groups of them. If possible, give your readers space in your publication for questions, gripes and suggestions.

Organization writers, perhaps more than others, can apply the principles of service journalism as outlined in Chapter 11. The question always confronting the organization writer is: How can I be of help?

The third requirement of the organization writer is to know the objectives of the publication. Write them down, and be sure to get management to sign off on them.

**EFFECTIVE WRITING FOR
ORGANIZATIONS**

1. Know your organization.
2. Know your audience.
3. Know the purpose or the objective of the publication and of
   the article you are writing.

A good place to learn the publication's objectives is from the audience. When Exxon asked employees what they wanted covered in the company's employee periodicals, the top seven subjects were:

1. Wage and salary administration policies

2. Career development opportunities

3. Compensation policies

4. Job performance appraisal system

5. Management's goals and objectives

6. Management's business philosophies

7. The company's plans for the future

Management may have different goals, such as increasing productivity, improving safety, reducing absenteeism, preventing waste, holding down medical costs and preventing insurance abuse. These management goals need not be in conflict with those stated by the employees. The challenge is to balance them with the employees' wishes and to write interesting and effective stories.

Increasing productivity is the goal of every organization though other goals differ from organization to organization. Also the purposes of informing people have not changed since Thomas Jefferson's time. Jefferson said that if people aren't told what is going on, only three possibilities exist: rumor, apathy or revolution.

Rumors are destructive. Rumors that a company is going bankrupt have caused it to go bankrupt. A wag once said most people aren't concerned about apathy, but productivity declines and organizations die, as a result of it. Revolution manifests itself in many ways. Violence and sabotage have occurred in factories and in mines, and associations have disintegrated when leaders failed to communicate.

Communication must meet the needs of people, and the needs of people everywhere are much the same most of the time. The philosopher Nietzsche wrote that what people need to be human is a sense of security, a sense of accomplishment and a sense of recognition. Organization editors and writers would do well to remember those needs when deciding upon the objectives and subject matter of their publications.

☐ A Sense of Security

What people most want to know about their work is how secure their jobs are. Company news is their chief interest because if the company is doing well, their jobs are secure, and the likelihood of raises and promotions is good.

For example, here's the lead in the story of a financial service corporation newsletter:

> December business resulted in the largest gain in consumer credit of any month in the company's history.

Nothing works like success, but success must be communicated if more is to come. News isn't always good, however, and just as certainly the organization editor must tell about financial problems and even impending layoffs and cutbacks. People may not like the truth, but they can deal with it much better than with rumor or uncertainty. And it's always better that they learn the truth from those with whom they are associated than from outside sources such as the daily newspaper.

When a rumor circulated in a steel company that because of cutbacks newsletters to the various plants would no longer be published, the company published this story that stopped the rumor cold:

> A rumor has been spreading that newsletters will be discontinued. "On the contrary, it's times like now that newsletters can and should be providing employees with information about the steel business," said Ron Pyke, director, Communications. "Employees are understandably concerned about their jobs, and they need to hear specific information pertaining to operations in their own departments."

Laying off workers is always bad news. Here's how one company handled it:

> Adopting the methods of a custom tailor, the Pipe Division last month was forced to take in its seams and cinch its waistband to fit a lean national economy.

A decision "reorganization" became effective at the beginning of October which meant that several staffs were trimmed. Fifty employees at WHQ and in the Pipe Division's sales force were affected.

The tailoring was necessary because, according to division general manager John Swenson, "with the economy the way it is, we had to reorganize to compete profitably in the market."

The story goes on to discuss specifics and how the company would help those who were laid off. Editors of association publications also must enhance the sense of security of the members. After all, security is the main reason people join associations in the first place.

☐ A Sense of Accomplishment

But there's more to life than security. Nietzsche also said people have to feel as if they're accomplishing something, as if they're doing something worthwhile. Organization publications can do that by reporting on the achievements of the organization and its members. These achievements must be related directly to the self-interest of the members or employees. Everyone wants to be a part of something, and usually a part of something that's doing things. You must learn what the organization is doing by cultivating sources and digging out the information.

☐ A Sense of Recognition

Individuals in the organization like to feel as if they, too, are accomplishing something. They need someone to recognize their worth and their contributions. Employees indicate in surveys that they rank personal news far below company news, yet they often turn to personal news first. Editors know that readers want to see names of people and what they have done. Most of all they want to see their own names in the news. They like and need recognition. Some communicators make fun of the birthday, bowling and baby news, but this news has a place in organization publications. Editors who say readers are bored with such news are kidding themselves. Only the editors are bored.

Readers look for names and pictures of people—especially their own. When Archie Bunker was locked in his basement, convinced he was going to die, his son-in-law, "the Meathead," asked him what he most regretted about his life. Without hesitation, Archie said, "I never got my picture in the paper."

With costs of paper, printing and postage being what they are, you have to decide whether you can afford to run Archie's picture. You have to decide how to communicate the organization's message in the most effective, efficient and economical way. Many organizations are choosing to cut costs and to cut reading time by publishing short, frequent newsletters. They are making a wise choice.

☐ THE NEWSLETTER

The newsletter contains, first of all, news. It says what's happening, and what's going to happen. If a newsletter is to have news, it must come out frequently. Members of an organization or employees of a corporation like to know what's going on, and they don't want to be the last to know. They also like frequent contact.

The newsletter is also a letter. It's short, friendly, conversational, informal. By being short, it says to the reader, "Read me now!" If the reader sets it aside for when there is time, chances are it will remain on that stack of good intentions until time for cleanup and the circular file. Too many newsletters are too long. In our big-is-better society, many editors have expanded their two- or four-page newsletters to eight or 12 pages. As a result, they have bigger publications but notably fewer readers.

Letters are personal and informal because you write them in the second person, and you use contractions. If you were writing a news story for a newspaper, you might write the lead this way:

> Employee Stock Ownership Plan (ESOP) participants will receive at least one extra card with their Sept. 29 paycheck.

Now the newsletter approach:

> If you're an Employee Stock Ownership Plan (ESOP) participant, you'll be receiving at least one extra card with your Sept. 29 paycheck.

Letters are written to individuals. A letter is not a mass medium. Don't write about employees in an employee newsletter; write to them. Instead of "Employees may apply for additional health benefits," write: "You may apply for additional health benefits."

If your budget is bigger and you have the luxury of writing for an organization magazine, you have more space for expanded writing. In the magazine, as in the newsletter, your style should be personal, friendly and informal. But you have more space to tell the organization story, to fill in the background, to talk about goals and plans, to write about people's accomplishments.

☐ TELLING YOUR STORY THROUGH PEOPLE

As you learned in Chapter 9, you write for people best by writing about people. Any organization's story is the story of people. In a magazine, seize the opportunity to tell us about those people.

For example, if you're writing about how well the city bus system can transport employees to work, look for a person who regularly rides the bus to work. That's better than calling the officials or simply printing a schedule. If you look around you may find a Mary Koenig:

> "We've had some of the best bus drivers in the world," says Mary Koenig, bond department. "They are more than just our drivers—they're our friends."
> And that to Mary is just one of the many benefits reaped after 30 years of bus riding from her home in East St. Louis. She never did learn to drive and uses the bus for shopping and visiting, as well as for transportation to and from her job.

Now you have an expert. You tell about the bus system in a human, interesting way, and you introduce Mary Koenig. Mary likes that, and so do the people who know her. Mary relates experiences she has had riding the bus, and before the story ends, you include the bus schedule.

You can tell the story about a hospital through the people who work there. Some of those people aren't often seen, and few people know what they do. But without them, the hospital could not function. One story on a two-page picture spread in a hospital publication starts this way:

> People depend on Bob Williams.
> For the past seven years, Bob has delivered supplies and linens to hospitals in Beaumont's Shared Services program. He makes daily runs to hospitals throughout Michigan's "thumb" area, and drives his 20-foot truck to Beaumont's warehouse in Traverse City.

The story accomplishes two things: It tells of an essential part of the hospital's operation, and it introduces us to one of the hospital's personnel.

Tell your story, whether that's selling a machine or selling a service, through the people who have used or experienced it. When a telephone company decided to write about its newest digital switchboard system, it looked for people already using it. It found them in Busch Gardens. The story began this way:

> You are expecting 6,000 hungry guests for lunch, and at 10 a.m. you realize 15,000 are coming.
>
> You pick up the phone and are told you have five minutes to take the chairman of the board on a tour of The Congo.
>
> You discover on a routine inspection of your 300-plus acre plain that one of your prize giraffes is delivering two weeks early.

The story goes on to say why, in this hectic environment that demands immediate action, Busch Gardens selected the digital switchboard system.

Sometimes you write about people in your organization because they are interesting, important people outside the organization. People are more than just employees or members; they have dignity and worth and are contributing members of their communities. Perhaps they have unusual hobbies or an exceptional skill. Here's the beginning of a story with the delightful heading, "Bottle cap king searches for crowns."

> John Meyer's dedication to bottle caps runs deep.
>
> So deep that he dug a Dr. Mutch's root beer bottle cap out of a hot tar parking lot in Hershey, Penn., when he was 9 years old.
>
> Meyer, 28, thought he would outgrow his hobby.
>
> Instead, the hobby has grown to 1,026 lids. He has even built a display case to accommodate the Dr. Mutch's lid and the rest of the collection. And he's catalogued each cap.

The writer tells readers the kind of person Meyer really is. At one point he says, "I'd like to think I'm an enterprising guy trying to preserve a moment in history." It's a good people story, and John Meyer undoubtedly felt good about it. His fellow employees talked to him about it, perhaps gave him extra copies, and he probably sent one to his brother in Albuquerque and to his mother in Keokuk. A story such as this helps people want to come to work and to be more productive, and it lets others outside the company know that the company cares about its people. It's good internal communications, and it's good public relations.

☐ GOOD WRITING

It also is good writing. Regardless of the medium, the writing is what counts. You must grab your readers and fight for every second of their time. Perhaps most of all in organization writing, you must write to be believed. Credibility is crucial. If you apply the characteristics of good writing as outlined in Chapter 8, you have a much better chance of being credible.

Start by being fanatically correct with facts, names, titles, grammar, spelling and everything else. Perhaps as important, be consistent. Far too many organization publications have not adopted a stylebook. Editors abbreviate states in one story and not in another. They write out numbers in one place and use Arabic numbers in others. They capitalize titles in one paragraph and lower-case them in another.

Titles of people present special problems for organization editors. Whom do you call "Mr."? Do you use the first or last names? Do you treat women's titles the same as men's? Do you use Miss, Mrs. or Ms? There is no way that you can please everyone in these matters. But you can be consistent if you follow a stylebook, and readers will understand your need to be consistent.

Because you regularly deal with and write for the commercial press, use The Associated Press Stylebook and Libel Manual. Don't risk the ire of newspaper copy editors by making them edit the copy to fit their style.

In addition, you'll need a set of guidelines to cover your own situation. You'll have to decide how to refer to the company or to the chairman of the board. If you have several members on you staff or if your organization is spread out over different locations, you need a stylebook even more. After all, being inconsistent makes you appear incorrect. Consistency helps credibility.

☐ Be Clear

So does being clear. Organization writers lose credibility with their audience and with the press when they are unclear—deliberately or otherwise.

There is also a tendency in organization writing, especially in government and academia, to try to impress readers with big, often manufactured words and long sentences. Writing expert Robert Gunning said it best: "Write to express, not to impress."

To write more clearly, you must know what you are trying to say. Before you write a story, write a summary or a contents blurb. You'll write a clearer story, and the contents blurb gives the reader the benefit of reading the story.

☐ Be Concrete

You are always more clear and credible when you are specific rather than general. Beware of adjectives and adverbs that don't work for you. As Mark Twain said, "As to the adjective, when in doubt, strike it out." How many is "many"? How far is "far"? How far is "very far"?

Being concrete means having the facts and examples to back up your story. For example, a beer company would have been more effective in its story about the effects of a container deposit ordinance in a Midwestern city had it bothered to gather and write the convincing details. Here are a few paragraphs:

> If there is anything remotely humorous in the situation, it is the number of people who are so used to tab tops and twist off caps that they must call local retailers to ask how to get the caps off returnable bottles. At present, there is also a severe shortage of bottle openers and "church keys" in the city.
> The increased costs of transportation, delivery, storage and handling are shared by the consumer, and the result is soaring beverage prices. This has caused consumers and forced deposit proponents to cry "foul" because they failed to realize that business and consumers are partners in the market place.
> Many beer buyers have responded by going outside the city limits to purchase beer where they can select from a full variety of brands and packages, at significantly lower prices . . .
> Grocery stores and liquor stores report a general loss of volume from people who are resistant to higher prices, housewives and older people who don't like to lug heavy cases of returnables, and beer drinkers who just prefer other packages and can get them outside the city.

The writer missed every opportunity to give concrete information, which would have been more convincing. In the first paragraph, he talks in generalities about "a number of people" and of a "severe shortage." In the second paragraph, he writes about "increased costs" and "soaring beverage prices" without ever mentioning a number. The second sentence of the second paragraph is an assumption: "The increased costs of transportation, delivery, storage and handling are shared by the consumer, and the result is soaring beverage prices." With some research the writer could have reported how many beer buyers were going outside the city limits to purchase beer, and surely he could have found out what "significantly lower prices" and "a general loss of volume" were. If the writer had gone to one beverage dealer and told the story specifically and in depth, readers would have been more interested and more inclined to believe the writer. Because the story is not concrete it is also less credible.

◻ Be Complete

So is an incomplete story. Telling the whole story is often a problem for organization writers. Sometimes you have to persuade management that it is better not to write a story at all than to write it without answering all the questions. Readers know when you are covering up something or when you are leaving out important details.

One corporate writer defended his incomplete story by saying: "The story is written the way it is written because we were being deliberately vague. We have reasons for doing it this way which we would rather not go into."

Because the story is vague and incomplete, it lacks credibility. If you are going to be of any real worth to your organization, you must be an advocate of getting out the news as soon as possible—at least before your readers hear it through rumor or from the daily press. For you, the communicator, the question is not *if* you're going to release the story, but *how* and *when*.

Building credibility with your internal and external publics takes time. Don't blow it with a single story.

◻ Be Creative

As important as a credible story is, it can still be boring. To compete for readers' time, your writing must be interesting. To be interesting, it must be creative—original in thought and original in expression.

Here's where the fun starts. Your publications can be more fun—for you and for your readers. Certainly you can't write about every subject lightly, but you can write about them brightly. One thing's for sure, if you don't have fun doing your publications, your audience won't have fun reading them. If you don't think they are exciting and interesting, neither will your readers.

Much of what you write about seems to be routine, humdrum stuff. For example, suppose you're assigned to write a story about a citation the Red Cross is giving your company. Boring stuff. Not the way Susan Melanson handled it:

It seemed a bright idea at the time.

The North York chapter of the Canadian Red Cross Society had announced plans to give IBM Canada a citation for holding 20 years of successful blood donor clinics in Toronto.

What better way to cover the story than by a firsthand account?

I looked about for a likely volunteer. The other staff members winked at each other slyly when approached. "Sorry, I'm below the acceptable weight limitations," said one.

"I've given plenty of times," said the other. "It needs a fresh approach."

Right.

Don't misunderstand me. Giving blood is a noble deed, and I have great respect for the countless IBMers who've done so over the years. But all those white cots, needles and rubber tubes have always made me highly nervous. Suppose I couldn't take it and collapsed from the effects?

"Nonsense," they said.

Mustering all the reporter bravado that flows through my veins I marched dutifully to the clinic that afternoon.

The first step is a snap. "Would you care for a glass of orange juice? We only take sweet blood," said a chuckling woman clad in the blue Red Cross volunteer garb.

The story is interesting, entertaining and informative. The writer spices up her copy with sentences like these:

Then she led me down the hallway to a converted board room that now looked like a scene from M.A.S.H. Unfortunately, Alan Alda was nowhere to be seen.

She ends the story this way:

Will I ever give blood again? Let's put it this way. Clinics are held here three times a year. And when the next one rolls around, barring the onslaught of some dreaded disease, or the overwhelming desire to have a tatoo planted on my person, I'll be there.

Why not? I lived to tell this tale.

The writer went that extra step. She did more than talk about a citation or about how and when to give blood.

You don't have to participate in an event to write a good story. Here's a paragraph from a profile about a man who has just become a bank president:

He's the all-American boy made good. A scrawny kid who grew up on an Aberdeen farm and dreamed of becoming a banker. He enjoys his work so much that his eyes sparkle whenever he speaks about his job.

In fact, if you didn't know he was 47 years old, you'd think he just got his first hit in a Little League game.

If you don't know the man, you want to get to know him.

Here's the opening of a retirement story—often a ho-hum story. This one's about the retirement of a vice-chairman of AT&T:

> An unopened Egg McMuffin sits on the corner of his desk. It's 10 a.m. Coat off. Collar unbuttoned. Chuck Marshall is a busy man.
>
> He listens and nods as his secretary, Linda Kasparian, gives a 30-second update of a half-dozen changes to his daily schedule: calls to make, places to be, things to do.
>
> Marshall leads an ordered life for the company that once told him 35 years ago in Chicago, "We don't have any reason to hire someone with a degree in agriculture."

Those opening words. That one detail—"an unopened Egg McMuffin." As David Ogilvy the advertising genius keeps saying, "God is in the details."

But profiles, stories about people are relatively easy to write. What do you do if you have to write the story about the company party? Here's how a corporate editor handled it:

> Cinderella's carriage turned into a pumpkin and her coachman and horses returned to their lives as mice, as the annual Triple C Club Christmas party ignored the stroke of midnight.
>
> Prince Charming didn't even notice Cinderella's rags through his blood-shot eyes. But then, frogs never did have excellent eyesight.
>
> The carriages began to arrive at the Centre Plaza Inn at 7 p.m. Friday, Dec. 4, though carriage parking was limited. Each dame and damsel was presented a long-stemmed rose as she entered the ball. Soon the hall was filled with 400 people.
>
> The buffet was fit for a king . . .

The writer tells about the menu and the guests. A different writer might have begun this story this way:

> The annual Triple C Club Christmas party was held on Dec. 4 at the Centre Plaza Inn. More than 400 attended.
>
> On the menu was. . . .

Even in technical writing you can be creative. Here's how a story in Beaumont Hospital's publication about an eye disease begins:

> A crisp, new dollar bill rests at the bottom of a pond. Beneath the rippling water the straight edges of the bill appear curved. George Washington's face is lost in a greyish blur.

For a person with an epiretinal membrane blocking his center of vision, the whole world looks as blurry and distorted as that waterlogged dollar bill.

The writer explains terms and procedures as the story moves along:

Epiretinal membranes grow like cobwebs across the inner rim of the eyeball. They cannot be seen from the outer surface of the eye.

The membranes are semi-transparent and, in many cases, so thin they're invisible. . . .

Clinging to the retina, the delicate inner lining of the eyeball, the membranes interfere with the work of the macula, a central spot behind the retina that is responsible for sharpness of vision.

To remove an epiretinal membrane, the surgeon must ever so carefully peel it off the retina with a hooked needle or retinal pick.

According to the steady-handed Dr. Margherio, trying to peel off the membrane is like trying to pluck fingernail polish off a nylon stocking without ripping the stocking.

If the needle should accidently tear the retina behind the membrane, the patient night lose all sight in the eye.

It's a careful, clear piece of writing. And it's done creatively. Good description is good writing. When Raytheon magazine did an article about the radar equipment it manufactures that is used on jet fighters, the story began this way:

It looks so easy there in the brittle, clear Nevada afternoon. The F-16 jet fighter seems almost to hover like a hummingbird as it flares for touchdown. The main wheels kiss the runway with a puff of rubber, the nosewheel plants itself on the centerline, and the sleek blue-gray arrow whistles past, decelerating smoothly, the engine's roar hushed to a whisper.

The pilot has just been "talked down" to one more safe arrival using a ground-controlled approach.

The writing is sensual. This awesome hunk of technology is made to be as soft and wondrous as a hummingbird.

When John M. Brooks wrote a piece for AT&T's Focus magazine about the 100th birthday of the pay phone, he did a little research and came up with this lead:

William Gray's wife lay critically ill. He needed a doctor. He needed a phone—but only the well to-do could afford subscription rates for new-fangled telephone service.

Gray eventually made his call—after running to a local factory where he convinced workers he had a genuine emergency. But the frustrating experience led him to invent the first pay phone, later installed in a Hartford, Conn., bank in 1889.

Gray's inventiveness turned local drug and grocery stores into the "neighborhood phone booth" and put daily phone service within reach of millions of Americans.

This year, the pay phone turns 100 years old, with an estimated 1.8 million pay phones in service nation-wide.

This anecdote is the perfect way to get into the story, which is filled with interesting historical facts and figures. The writer dares the reader to stop reading. Organizations ought to foster and promote more of that kind of writing. Unless they do, they are wasting time and money. No, not the readers' time. The readers will give them no time to waste.

☐ QUESTIONS AND EXERCISES

1. If you work for an organization, find out the objectives of the publications. Then study an issue or two of the publications to determine whether and how the objectives are being carried out. If you are studying at a college or university, do the same for its publications.

2. What are the advantages of the newsletter?

3. Discuss ways that you would put people into your organization's publications.

4. Your boss tells you that there is no room for creativity in your publication. What would you tell your boss?

13
Writing Project and Investigative Stories

Writing isn't hard: thinking is hard.—Pulitzer-Prize-winning writer Saul Pett, quoting from an otherwise-forgotten play.

Laura Sessions Stepp was editing a series on health hazards in the textile industry when she encountered a challenge common to all major projects. She had painstakingly trimmed from 80,000 words to 40,000. Now she was struggling in vain to craft the perfect lead.

Her boss asked, "What's the story about?"
She replied, "Cotton dust is killing people."
"Period. Paragraph. That's your lead."

The series won a Pulitzer Prize for the Charlotte Observer.

Not every difficult story wins a prize, and not every writing problem is so simply solved. But every long and complex story presents similar problems of bulk, complexity and focus. The solutions, though each must be unique to the story, usually also have a lot in common. Long stories all require planning and organization. All demand discipline. All force you to make that most painful of a writer's decisions: the decision to leave out much of the material you have so diligently accumulated. If your reporting has been good, you'll have a lot to leave out. All long stories require, most of all, focus.

This chapter will help you plan, organize, discipline and focus your work. One way to start doing all that is to return to the most basic questions of American journalism—the five W's and the H—and apply them in a new way to the problems of writing. Ask yourself:

WHAT is this story really about?
WHY should anybody read it?

WHO is affected and WHO is involved?
WHEN have I done enough reporting?
WHERE do I start writing?
HOW am I going to tell this story?

Find the answers, and you've found your story. Some of the answers, of course, come easier than others. Your reporting will tell you who's involved. Knowledge of your audience will help you understand who will be affected. You'll know you've done enough reporting when you can answer who, why and what. The question that holds the key to all the others is, What.

◻ WHAT'S THE STORY ABOUT?

The most fundamental principles of good writing, clarity and coherence, are the most often violated when you are writing at length. The sheer volume of your raw material—stacks of notes, tapes of interviews, copies of documents, books of background reading—can be overwhelming. The complexity of your subject can be paralyzing. The blank sheet of paper in your typewriter, the cursor blinking in the upper left-hand corner of an empty computer screen can drive you to consider seeking work as a school bus driver. But deadline approaches. What's an overburdened writer to do?

First, sit still. Then organize.

The hardest part and the most important part of writing any story, whether of five paragraphs or 5,000 words, is deciding its theme, figuring out just what the story really is. That decision guides all the writing that follows. The process of reaching that decision, and the accompanying process of organization, should begin long before you sit down at the keyboard.

In fact, your first version of the answer to what the story is emerges the first time you put into words your story idea. So it may be useful to draw a distinction that too many beginning writers overlook. A story topic isn't the same thing as a story idea. "I want to write about a small town," you might say to yourself or to your editor. Fine; that's a topic. But what's the idea? Write what about a small town? "Can the town survive?" Now that's an idea. It gives you a starting point. A topic is general, shapeless, without direction. An idea about that topic has at least the beginning of form, the suggestion of a direction your reporting can follow. The world is full of topics. Writers find in those topics ideas.

A story idea can be likened to the hypothesis or research question that guides the work of a social scientist. Its first version is usually based on previous knowledge gained from your own experience or the work of others. It can be stated as a question: "Can the town survive?" Or it can be a prediction of what you expect to find: "This town is dying." Either way, this hypothesis, this research question, this story idea is the essential first step in focusing your work.

Focus often changes, of course, as your reporting uncovers the unexpected. But each new discovery helps you refine and develop your hypothesis, your story idea. A good reporter is often compared to a vacuum cleaner, voraciously sucking facts from desk tops and dark corners. The analogy is not perfect. A reporter whose fact-gathering is simply suction will wind up with a bag full of junk, the useful information buried in debris. A vacuum cleaner is not concerned with relevance or story line. Reporters must define relevance broadly, trying to learn everything that may be of use and trying not to overlook any fruitful source. But the test of relevance must be applied.

This may not be easy. In the early stages of a major project, often it isn't clear what the story is going to be. Preliminary reporting may seem inefficient as you read material you'll soon forget and interview people who have little to contribute. Even this work is worthwhile, though, if you use it to define the edges of your idea and to gain an understanding of the context that surrounds your story. Experienced writers devise ways to organize and reorganize especially during this early stage of the reporting. Like a hiker in the wilderness who pauses from time to time with map and compass, experienced writers know the danger of wandering too far off the trail.

For a writer, the best map usually is an outline of some sort. The compass may be a theme paragraph, a brief summary of what you think the story is. The outline will need continuous revision, and the theme paragraph will be rewritten repeatedly as your reporting leads you deeper into the unknown. But both can serve you as guides. Without them, or something like them, you run the risk of wandering in circles.

☐ WRESTLING THE MONSTER

Ken Fuson, a writer for the Des Moines Register, regularly ventures far from the beaten path as he works on stories he has conceived. If you look over his shoulder, you can pick up some valuable tricks of the trade. You'll see that organization is Fuson's path to success.

His idea was . . . well, let him explain: "The idea was to spend one year in a typical Iowa small town and write a story for each of the four seasons. The farm depression of the early-and mid-1980s had crippled Main Street in rural America. First the businesses left, then the people, and it wasn't unusual to drive through an Iowa town and see half of the storefronts boarded. By 1988, the state economy had begun to show signs of life again . . . and we wanted to see if the gains were filtering down to those places that needed help the most."

It's a clear idea, with form enough to allow the work to begin. The town Fuson was to profile was State Center, Iowa, population 1,180. He began, he recalls, with a deliberate attempt to avoid preconceptions. "I didn't reread Our Town or Main Street or anything else. I wanted to approach this town with fresh eyes."

He approached like a sculptor. "Before sculptors can begin work, they need clay. They know they're not going to use it all, but they need it before they can start chiseling away. For reporters, facts serve as our clay. In the beginning of any major project, we collect as much information as we can and dump it on the pile. We know we'll only use a tenth of it, if that much, but we still have to collect it. It's the only way to know what's good and what isn't."

Fuson collected his clay, as many writers do, in his computer. Organizing as he reported, he divided those working notes into 15 categories—school, commerce, sports and other topics that seemed likely to be important. By the time he was ready to write his first story, he had thousands of inches of notes in the computer.

Now he was ready for what he calls "the wrestling-the-monster stage" of his project. This is the match that determines "whether you are going to control the material or the material is going to control you."

To win control, he used a two-step outlining process. In the first step, he sits down with his notes and a legal pad and just writes down the facts and themes he expects to use from among all those notes. This first step produced about 100 entries such as these:

1. Kindergarten roundup—future of town, fewer kids attend.
2. Eric Eckhard born on first day of spring.
3. Concern about Rose Festival—roses are dead.
4. New businesses open. . . .

That may strike you as dull, mechanical work, but it or something much like it is essential. And it doesn't have to be dull.

You can use the act of outlining—whether you are physically separating notebooks into piles, shuffling notes like cards, or drafting a formal outline as you were taught to do in elementary school—as part of the creative process.

For Fuson, once he had drafted his list of key ideas, the next step was to decide just what he wanted to accomplish with this first story. "State Center, it seemed to me, was struggling for a place—whether to compete for new businesses and jobs or to remain the cozy bedroom community that it always had been. But interwoven in the debate was a larger issue: Would the town survive?"

Clearly, that larger issue would be the theme of the entire project. Fuson again: "I had other goals for the first story. I wanted to introduce readers to the town and make them care about State Center and the people there. The best way to introduce them to State Center, I thought, would be to give the readers a tour, so I went up there about 6 a.m. one morning and stayed until the bar closed, writing down everything that happened. As it turned out, that's how I started the story."

☐ THE OUTLINE

Methodically but imaginatively, Fuson follows a working pattern he didn't invent in order to tell a story he will mold from thousands of facts. Starting with a general idea—to look in on life in a small town as the American Century draws to an end—he reports broadly and deeply. He sorts his facts into categories as he records his notes. Then he picks through his mass of information to identify the recurring themes and the most important bits of information supporting those themes. Then, having established his control over his material, he turns to crafting the story.

Here is Fuson's final outline:

Part 1—Introduction
Overall theme—will the town survive:
Introduce town with early morning tour.
Introduce Ralph Moody and the funeral home light.
Talk about spring.
New day—spring—hope but foreboding about future.

Part II—Struggling for a Place
Why we're doing this project.
Show how State Center is typical of problems being faced in all small towns.
Problems there—newspaper almost closed, homecoming queen's family lost their farm.

Part III—Heart of the Heartland
Go into specifics about State Center.

Continue the tour through town.

History of the town.

Pressures on the people who live there.

Part IV—Main Street

Most people work elsewhere.

Businesses struggle to keep going (brings back theme of survival).

Some townsfolk upset with bank.

Economic development—do they really want it?

Part V—The Rose Festival

How the festival splits the town.

Roses in the Rose Garden are mostly dead (brings back theme of survival).

Part VI—Weather

Use weather as metaphor for what the town went through during farm crisis.

Also use weather to remind readers that it's spring.

Part VII—Schools

School is the heart and soul of the town.

Kindergarten round-up—town's future.

How town protects each other—Alison Clark.

Part VIII—Sports

Youth—will they stay? (brings back theme of survival).

Use Wade Baker to show what happens to kids who don't fit in.

Part IX—Main Street Tap

Bar is a metaphor for town—people sit around and complain about problems.

Bar provides a nice contrast with school kids.

Reintroduce Ralph Moody.

Reintroduce funeral home light.

End of day—end of spring—but town survives. Brings story back full circle.

Notice the structure Fuson has created. Notice the literary devices he intends to employ: narrative, foreshadowing, metaphor. Notice the humanity, the specifics. Notice his frequent reminders—even to himself—of the story's theme.

An outline like Fuson's not only provides the skeleton of the story; it helps you decide which quotes and anecdotes you will use to put muscle on the skeleton. It helps you spot holes in your reporting. It brings you face-to-face with ambiguities or uncertainties that may still stand between you and a real understanding of some key point. Perhaps most important, outlining allows you to decide what to leave out.

The outline, for a writer, is the sculptor's rough model. With the outline, the writer begins to mold the lump of clay into shape. The unneeded clay is pinched off, left for the discard pile.

The painful decision to leave out a good quote, a delightful anecdote, a hard-earned fact is a decision that too many writers avoid. Their avoidance burdens either an editor, who is forced to make choices the writer should have made, or a reader, who is burdened with redundancy.

An outline, especially a formal outline, makes it much easier for you to see how much is too much. Three quotes that carry the same message or two anecdotes with similar points may each appear unique scattered through your notes. Their repetitiveness is revealed when they are clustered under the discipline of an outline.

As a reporter, like the sculptor accumulating clay, you have to collect every quote, anecdote or fact. You cannot know in advance which will contribute to your search for truth. As a writer, you risk obscuring the truth if you dump, unshaped and undisciplined, too much of your collection onto your readers.

☐ BREAKING UP STORIES INSTEAD OF READERS

Just as you break up your material into manageable chunks by outlining before you write, so you need to help your readers by breaking your long stories into readable chunks. Often the best way to do that is either to make the chunks of roughly equal substance and run them as a series or to tell the main story in one chunk and break off subsidiary elements into sidebars.

A series is usually best if:

- the amount of information you want to convey is too much for a single story of reasonable length;
- you have several elements of roughly equal importance to anchor each installment in the series;
- you want to keep your subject in the public eye for longer than just one reading.

Reasonable people, to say nothing of writers and editors, can disagree about what is a "reasonable length." The worst way to settle the argument is by the imposition of arbitrary limits. A reasonable length for one story may be 6 inches and for another 60 inches. One flexible but usable guideline is this: When a story looks long to you, think of the poor reader and look for ways to break it up. Good editors will welcome, though they won't always adopt, writers' suggestions on story treatment.

Once the decision is made to tell a story in multiple parts, the most important question is whether a series can be sustained. You should not start readers off with a blockbuster first story and follow with a string of firecrackers. Those should be treated as sidebars instead of chapters in a series. Each story in a good series has substance enough to stand on its own, while being clearly identified as part of a greater whole.

For example, Olive Talley led off her Dallas Morning News series "Care and Punishment: Medicine Behind Bars:" with several examples and then this paragraph that set the theme for the six parts:

> Criminologists and penal experts long have regarded the U.S. Bureau of Prisons—and its health care for inmates—as the Cadillac of the nation's network of state and federal prisons. But an investigation by The Dallas Morning News reveals a medical system plagued by severe overcrowding, critical shortages of doctors, nurses and physician's assistants, and life-threatening delays in transfers of inmate patients to major prison hospitals. . . ."

The next five chapters, each identified by the same "Care and Punishment" logo, elaborated on an element of the overall theme. The result was a long but readable story.

Let's take a closer look at another long story, Ken Fuson's portrait of State Center, Iowa. Reprinted below is Part 1: Spring. Read it twice, once for enjoyment and then again more critically. As you read, keep in mind what Fuson described as his idea for the story. How well is that idea realized? How closely does the finished work follow the early outline? Who won the wrestling match, Fuson or the monster?

> STATE CENTER, IA.—As the first light of a fresh spring dawn brushes the new water tower and the old grain elevator, a small town stirs to life.
> "I'm gonna die!" a boy groans at the high school, where track team members sprint in the morning chill, thick puffs of frosty air trailing them.
> Nearby, Leland Weuve, 74, heads for the Trojan Inn, where men with calloused hands, seed corn caps and bibbed overalls cram into wooden booths for a cup of coffee before they leave for the fields.

Along Main Street, at the elementary school, buses return from the six towns that feed the West Marshall School District. Alison Clark, a third-grader, hops from the Melbourne bus, ready for her spelling test.

Down the street, Olaf Klomsten sweeps the Main Street Tap. The regulars—Ralph Moody, Duwane Miller, Ubbe Rops and the rest—will straggle in soon for another day of playing cards, drinking beer and cursing friends.

Here comes Ralph Moody now, in his rusty green pickup truck with the cracked window (he hit a pheasant). Like most of the town, Moody, 65, rises before the sun, a habit acquired during 20 years of owning the garbage business. These days, he's either buying rounds at the Main Street Tap, feeding the 300 sheep he bought "just for something to do," or introducing his town to strangers.

There's much to see. Spring is a time for churning soil and planting corn, for mother-daughter banquets and school proms, for sitting on benches during the day and shooting free throws at night, for cooing at babies (Erik Eckhardt was born on the first day of spring) and wondering what the future holds for a town that 1,180 people call home.

"I love this town," Ralph Moody says "I'll die here."

He swings past the funeral home on Main Street and looks at the sign above the door. If the red light is shining, somebody has died during the night.

The light is dark.

Spring beckons in State Center.

Struggling for a place

This cooling morning, with skies the color of a swimming pool and clouds as plump as pastries, finds State Center neither thriving nor dying. It is, as its name and location suggest, somewhere in the middle, one of 832 towns in Iowa with fewer than 2,500 people that are struggling to find their place in a new era in rural America.

A year in an Iowa farm town is no different from a year in a Texas oil town or a West Virginia coal town or any other small town where economic forces have assaulted a way of life. It's the daily battle of proud people who believe they have a tradition worth protecting and a community worth saving—but don't know where to begin.

The backbone of the country, the rural towns were called, first as outposts for Western expansion, then as collection centers for the nation's food, always as custodians of the most cherished American values— hard work, fair play, respect for the land, service to the church. Places worth keeping. Home.

Then it changed.

"Everything's big business now," says Butch Horn, 39, who owns the Steak Center restaurant in State Center. "That's where our country's going, whether we like it or not. I hate it. I loved it when it was all small towns. That's what made this country."

Today, grain prices and land values are rising, thanks to government farm payments. Mike Eckhardt, Erik's father, says the tax returns he prepared in April for area farmers were some of the healthiest in years.

Yet apprehension reigns, scars still tender from the farm crisis. State Center has lost 10 percent of its population since 1980. Selling a home takes an average of six months. School enrollment will decline by 30 students next fall. One of four people in town is a senior citizen.

Those are only numbers.

They don't tell how the State Center Garden Club was forced to cancel its flower show because members are too old to lug the heavy displays.

They don't tell how Kristin Robinson, graduating senior, star athlete and homecoming queen, got so sick she couldn't eat when her parents lost their farm two years ago.

And they don't tell how Nelda Grage waits for customers to visit her year-old crafts store, Aunt Jane's Attic. When she and her partner held an open house, three people came.

No longer master of its own universe, the town is wrapped in a straitjacket of confusion and indecision. "To be honest with you, I don't think we have any planning for the future in this community," says Mayor Larry Bohnsack, 39.

In the season of rebirth, does State Center have the energy to recover?

Inne Taylor and Roxanne Goecke publish the State Center Enterprise and the Melbourne Record—"the only newspapers in the world that really care about the West Marshall area," the mastheads read.

Taylor, 39, writes the stories. Goecke, 36, sells the ads. Each earns about $150 a week.

Two years ago, they came within hours of locking the door on the 120-year-old Enterprise and the 90-year-old Record.

"You think, 'If it folds, it's my fault,'" Taylor says. "It's up to me. I think people feel that way about the town. There's a pressure you feel all the time. How much can you give before it crushes you?"

Heart of the heartland

From a distance, State Center's new water tower stands as a beacon of progress, the most visible symbol of the town.

The old tower was shaped like the Tin Man's head; the new tower, built last year, looks like a bloated egg plopped atop a giant golf tee, gleaming white, as slick as porcelain.

But somebody goofed. The logo on the tower—a rose surrounded by the words State Center, Rose Capital of Iowa—is too small to read from the highway. No matter. Few people happen upon State Center by accident.

Boxed in on all sides by some of the world's richest farmland, the town sits along U.S. Highway 30 between Ames and Marshalltown, 45 miles from Des Moines, 30 miles from the nearest interstate highway and 13 miles from the nearest McDonald's. If Iowa were a dart board, State Center would be the bull's-eye.

The town is small enough that no presidential candidates campaigned here last winter, but large enough that residents can rent R-rated movies from the Gutekunst Library (although the most popular rental is "Grease").

State Center has produced few notable sons or daughters in its 121-year history. Oh, Debbie Sue (Weuve) Rohrer was crowned Miss Iowa in 1975. Larry Poling, a city councilman, portrayed Nikita Khrushchev in "Miles From Home," the movie filmed in Iowa. And Bob and Dennis Baker smashed the state record for average soy-bean yields last year. But that's about it.

"I wouldn't call it a progressive town, but it's not as dead-set against new ideas as some small towns," says the Rev. Ken Stuber of the First United Presbyterian Church.

When he arrived three years ago, Stuber's sermons tackled sensitive issues: foreign policy, racism, gossip.

"I had some people very upset with me," he says. "I've learned to be more diplomatic."

Word travels fast. When Roger Evans, the high school guidance counselor, rented an apartment one night, the first person he saw at school the next morning asked him about it. Melissa Billman, 12, says she enjoys small-town living, "because you get to hear stuff you're not supposed to know."

Ask the people in State Center to describe their town and they haul out the familiar traits: safe, clean, friendly. Sure, petty jealousies exist, but there's an understanding, as in any family, that what you hear stays here. As more people and businesses leave, small towns grasp even tighter to their image of pastoral wholesomeness. It's their one drawing card.

Moderation is king. Don't make too much money, or get into too much trouble, or act too different, and everything will be just fine. Evans says the first boy who wore an earring to school nearly had it yanked from his head by another student.

"The problem is our kids aren't tolerant of differences," he says. "There isn't a good appreciation of people who look different or dress different or think differently."

State Center is white, mostly Republican and of predominately German heritage, the telephone book filled with Henzes, Hillemans and Riemenschneiders.

The railroad gave birth to the town—even now, some 50 times a day, freight trains rumble through without stopping—but farming supplies the lifeblood. When President Reagan needed to mend relations with farmers in 1982, he chose the Dee Brothers farm outside State Center. He said he particularly enjoyed the homemade peach ice cream.

There are six churches, one for every 200 people, but you still can find a dice game at night if you know where to look and promise not to tell.

Three of the churches are Lutheran. A fire on New Year's Day in 1945 destroyed St. John's Lutheran Church. Half the congregation wanted to rebuild in the country, half wanted to rebuild in town. So each side built its own.

Fires have played a major role in State Center's history. Much of Main Street burned in 1895. Perhaps that explains why the town has such a strong volunteer fire department, capturing the state championship 10 times, finishing second the past four years.

Many of the fire department members belong to other civic groups. As small towns lose population, and those who remain get older, the demands pile on the people who are left.

Margaret Hemphill, 65, a librarian, watched the seniors leave town when her late husband was the school superintendent. Most of them, she knew, were gone for good.

Earlier this month, her son, Jim, 27, who had been living at home while he worked at a Marshalltown television station, left for a magazine job in San Diego.

"You know how mothers are," Hemphill says. "I went in and cleaned up his room and cried the whole time."

For every Jim Hemphill who leaves, a Jim Maish must pick up the slack or watch the town slide.

Maish, 63, who owns a plumbing and heating business, belongs to the Lions Club, the Commerce Club, the Methodist Church Board, the Marshall County Conservation Board and helps his wife, Dorothy, with the Welcome Wagon. He also prepared the lemon chicken dish for the church's mother-daughter banquet this spring.

"You think about a laid-back, rural community and it isn't like that at all," Maish says. "You're stressed and pulled in so many different directions, trying to do the right thing.

"There's a feeling that everybody has to take their turn."

Reinforcements are needed. Boyd Van Metre, the real estate agent, says enough vacant housing exists for 20 families.

But where would they work?

Main Street

In April, the City Council postponed Roger Yeager's request to put a billboard along the highway, lamented drag racing on Main Street and approved a new toilet for the City Hall restroom.

Then Mayor Larry Bohnsack dropped a bombshell. He had talked with a businessman who expressed interest in building a manufacturing plant in town, he said. Maybe 40 jobs. He declined to say more.

Like most in Iowa, the town is desperate for new business. When the Des Moines City Council rejected a loan for a condom factory, Irma Henze, 50, who owns a clothing store, and other business leaders joked that State Center should offer a site. It was just as well they didn't. The last thing a town whose school nickname is the Trojans needs is a condom factory.

If State Center were an Army camp, Henze would be its sergeant—cajoling, pushing and begging people to open businesses, support civic groups and promote the town. But even she is wary of the mystery factory.

"I'm always hopeful, but I'll believe it when I see it," she says.

One reason for the town's lack of enthusiasm is that hopes have been squashed before. Another is that State Center hasn't decided how much development it wants.

Probably half the town, including Bohnsack and three of the five councilmen, works in Marshalltown, Ames or Nevada.

"People don't come here to find a job," says Don Goodman, who owns Goodman Milling, the grain elevator. "They come to live."

The debate is an old one. Years ago, the town spurned advances by Maytag and Fisher Controls to build plants in State Center.

"Maytag begged to get in here," says Ernie Westphal, 78. "The people running this town wouldn't let them. They said niggers would come to town, that's just what they said."

Today, State Center pays for that attitude. Only five new homes have been built since 1979. Last year's retail sales were the lowest in 11 years.

"I'm fearful of what the next 10 to 20 years will bring to Main Street," says Jim Jorgensen, president of the Central State Bank.

But some say Jorgensen's bank stifles progress by not investing enough in local business. Mayor Bohnsack banks in Melbourne. So do the newspaper publishers and several store owners.

"We had many business opportunities that we turned down for what we considered to be strong economic reasons," Jorgensen says. "If that's a deterrent to economic development, I guess I have to look at our business first. It's more important to this town to keep the bank open."

As a result, the Central State Bank reported troubled debts of only 11 percent last year; the Melbourne bank's ratio was 152 percent. That bank was sold this spring.

Economic efforts sputter. One group, State Center Development Inc., was formed years ago to loan money to promising ventures, but the $9,000 account sits largely untapped. Bohnsack organized another development group last year, but it fizzled. Only the Commerce Club, representing the town's 41 businesses, shows signs of life.

At the April club meeting, members discussed whether to build a float for the summer's Rose Festival parade. The vote was three yes, with 13 abstaining.

Nothing stretches the limits of town and business cooperation more than the event for which State Center is best known, if it is known at all: the Rose Festival.

Thirty years of roses

Bill Haesemeyer was hot.

"It's not supposed to look like this," he says, pointing to the dandelions and brown stems that littered the beds in the town's rose garden.

"This one's dead. That one's dead. This one. This one. Over here. Here. Here."

Haesemeyer, 74, the bank owner, played a major role 30 years ago in State Center's coronation as the Rose Capital of Iowa.

This June, as it does every summer, the town will be the host to about 10,000 people for the three-day festival.

The trouble is, the people who started the event want the young adults to take over. The young adults say they're busy—and they're still bitter.

Years ago, a swimming pool was planned for the area where the rose garden now sits. "We still want a swimming pool," says Deb Horn, 35.

A handful of volunteers keep the Rose Festival afloat, with the responsibility for cleaning the garden and planting fresh roses passed like a virus among the City Council, the Jaycees and the Rose Board.

The great rose crisis of 1988 was short-lived. City workers mowed the grass, volunteers transplanted fresh rose bushes and, says Irma Henze, who serves on the Rose Board, "the good Lord gave us sunshine."

Sure could use some rain

Of all the seasons, spring is the most unpredictable, nature's 2-year-old. Three examples:

March 22—Alison Clark and her third-grade friends toss their jackets in a pile on the school playground. Eighty-two degrees. Branches rock gently, leaves dance in the street.

At the Gutekunst Library, 4-year-old Anthony McGrew breaks from his mother's hand and races for the twisting slide.

Across town, Leland Weuve, the Trojan Inn regular, pushes a tiller along a patch in his front yard. The blades spit chunks of soil the color and size of coal.

Weuve sold his 700-acre farm to his son-in-law and daughter years ago, but he returns each spring to help.

"I like to see things grow," he says. "I like being out there. I just like the smell of it."

In the country, grass stands in ditches like hair on a punk rocker's head, its color changing slightly each day, from yellow to greenish yellow to green. Broken stalks of corn, last year's soldiers, await the disc.

Farmland values have rebounded. Soybean prices are higher. It's time to plant.

March 24—A bruise-colored mange spreads across the sky. The radio warns of tornadoes.

Blackbirds hide on the ground. Grass ripples in nervous shudders. Quick as a lizard's tongue, the storm strikes with a burst of rain and hail.

Just as quickly, the rain and hail stop, the blue skies return and the sun bathes the town in a soft butterscotch light.

The economic storm of the farm crisis also has abated in State Center, but the victims are easy to find.

In town, Jackie Henchal, 48, works as a deputy city clerk. She and her husband, Larry, 50, lost their 600-acre farm two years ago.

"The economy's got to get a lot better before it can heal all the wounds," she says. "Your dreams are broken. Your hearts are broken. Your spirit is broken. You're just broke."

May 4—Soil crumbles in the hand. Rainfall during April was four inches below normal.

"We need rain just to know it can rain," Don Goodman says at the elevator.

As each dry day ends, the plea becomes a mantra. Rain. We need rain. Wish it would rain.

"There's just fewer farmers to do business with," says Goodman, 48. "It was nice for everybody when there were lots of farms and lots of people."

By the end of the week, the skies open with a vengeance, unleashing almost an inch of rain and some hail.

"That was a lifesaver," Leland Weuve says. "The hail gave the corn a haircut, but it'll be all right."

Future of State Center

The largest buildings on Main Street are occupied by Goodman Milling and the schools, appropriate given the importance of agriculture and education. But Don Goodman, elevator owner and school board president, knows which comes first.

"The school's what keeps this town," he says.

In that case, the future of State Center gathered on an April afternoon to color ducks, sing about eensy-weensy spiders and practice standing in line for recess.

Kindergarten round-up was a success. A total of 69 children attended, more than Superintendent Jerry Nichols had expected.

Nichols, 54, who watches enrollment trends as closely as Goodman monitors grain prices, has seen the number of West Marshall students decrease from 1,300 in 1969 to the 780 expected for next fall.

The impact is seen in everything from the high school chapter of the Fellowship of Christian Athletes, which has three members, to sporting events. West Marshall will compete in a new sports conference next fall with smaller schools.

Nichols worries that if Iowa legislators force school districts to maintain a minimum enrollment of, say, 1,000 students, State Center could lose its high school.

"Ultimately, we're probably going to have to restructure," he says.

Right now, Tyler Dose, a freckle-faced, tow-headed 5-year-old, only cares about the duck he's coloring during kindergarten round-up.

"I know what color their feets are supposed to be," he says. "Orange. Because that's what color the baby chicks' feets are."

Upstairs, the 17 students in Dolores Horn's third-grade class also are discussing birds. Alison Clark, a pixie-faced 8-year-old, says her brother saw an owl holding a snake. Gross, the kids say.

The class protects Alison. In March, her father, Dan Clark of rural Melbourne, was killed in a truck accident near Tama.

Horn, a teacher for 31 years, took doughnuts and a plant to the house. Several students brought presents for Alison.

"The whole class was real sweet," Horn says. "They still are. Everything she does, they pull for her."

In music class, when Alison misread the song Old Dan Tucker as Old Dan Trucker and began to cry, several students hugged her.

And sometimes, Horn will find a note at the bottom of Alison's spelling test, such as, "I hope my Dad is all right."

"I'm sure he is, honey," Horn writes back.

The tie that binds

West Marshall High School enjoyed a productive spring. Gita Nason's trumpet-playing won an outstanding performance award at the state solo and ensemble contest. The mixed chorus received a top rating at state. And both performances of "The Music Man"—whose cast included townsfolk to supplement the students—received standing ovations.

But sports is the tie that binds the school district.

On the west side of the elementary school, Brian Winkler and his eighth-grade friends shoot baskets far into the night, their silhouettes outlined on the pavement.

Winkler, 14, who was born with cerebral palsy but stars on the basketball team, jumps and dangles from the chain net.

"We're talkin' serious hang time now," he says.

Winkler's father, Ken, has coached the football team to the state playoffs the past four years. This spring, the boys' track team won four first-place trophies and set several school records.

Wade Baker was a member of the relay team that broke one of those records. But the 17-year-old junior is best known as one of two boys who broke into the high school two years ago, causing about $50,000 in damage and outraging the town and students.

Baker returned to school last fall after spending 11 months in a Fort Dodge boys home. "I noticed some of the teachers looked at me like, 'Oh boy, he's back.' But I think it had mostly been forgotten or forgiven," he says.

With brown hair, braces and a winning smile, Baker says he's trying to behave better, but trouble seems to find him. If it finds him too often, he risks violating his probation.

He and his classmates minded their manners prom night, the boys sharp in their black and gray tuxedos, the girls elegant in their satin strapless gowns and puffy bubble dresses.

At the dance, Principal John Dotson, 31, stood sentry in the door, with the slightly uncomfortable look of a man whose sole goal in life was to last until dawn without hearing from the county sheriff.

For the 89 seniors, the last of the large West Marshall classes, prom represented the final rite of high school before graduation ceremonies this afternoon. College or trade school await most of the graduates. Few will find jobs in State Center.

"They have to leave," Don Goodman says. "There's nothing for them here."

Cards, beer, friends

The Main Street Tap is a dank, dark sanctuary, a place to belch, scratch and solve the world's problems, but mostly a place to play cards and drink a few beers. Or a lot.

"Drink, Vince?" Ralph Moody asks.

No answer.

"Drink, Vince?" Moody asks louder.

"Why, sure."

"Need a draw, Kenny?" Moody asks.

He does.

There's Moody, 65, war veteran, former boxer and baseball catcher, who started the town's garbage business 20 years ago with three customers and sold it last fall.

There's Ernie Westphal, 78 and ornery, who played billiards there when he was a kid, dropping the pool cue through a hole in the floor when his father walked in.

There's Duwane Miller, 53, who everyone calls Cooter, a retired Navy veteran. He has blood and kidney problems, but that doesn't stop him from drinking shots of brandy, which he orders with a glass of water, or smoking Chesterfield cigarettes, which he places atop a package of Vicks cough drops.

"This used to be quite a town, by God," Westphal says. "We had four implement dealers at one time, and two or three car dealers and three or four grocery stores. There were two movie houses in town. We used to sneak into the Princess Theater. You could always tell when the train was coming through because the screen would shake."

All day long, the regulars sit in front of the only window in the bar and play Queens, an incomprehensible card game in which diamonds are trump, tens beat kings and queens are better than everything. The men keep score by trading kernels of corn and cuss worse than prison inmates. The constant dealing of cards has worn a white cross in the table top.

"It could be a pretty good town if people wanted to change it," Miller says. "But they don't want to change it. They want it to be like it was 25 years ago."

"This town has to change in order to get disparity—whatever they call that word, disparity, diversity. Improve, improve, improve."

Later, at night, after a full day of cards and beer, Ralph Moody leans close, showing pale blue eyes, flushed cheeks and hair parted almost in the middle, the style in old movies.

"I'm proud of State Center," he says. "This is a good little town. I'm so satisfied here."

When the bar closes, Moody swings past the funeral home for one last look above the door.

The light is still dark.

State Center has survived another day.

This is good stuff, isn't it? Look at the imagery, the narrative thread, the pacing, the people, the tone, the structure. Take a few minutes to measure Fuson's work against the standards and techniques we discussed in Chapters 8–11. This measures up, doesn't it? Look closely, and you'll see that Fuson also has done what he sketched in his outline. The sections are easy to identify by the subheads, which also help readers follow a story this long. But even without the subheads, Fuson's writing is as clear as his organization.

Compare, for example, Fuson's outline summary of Part II—Struggling for a Place with the section under that subhead. He delivers what he planned. You can perform the same analysis of each section of the outline and the fleshed-out version in the published story. The story is the payoff for the planning.

Now here's the writer's self-analysis. "As it turned out, I think this is the weakest of the four stories," Fuson concludes. "Here's why:

1. What I had envisioned as a tour through town in the beginning becomes a leisurely stroll. It simply takes too long to get to the point of what the series is going to be about. I don't like editor's notes, but it might not have hurt to use one at the beginning of this series to tell people what's in store.

2. There's too much telling and not enough showing, particularly in the second and third sections.

3. I'm stuffing too many names and places in there. It would have been more effective to focus on one person or event—Ralph Moody, say, or the homecoming queen—and explored them a little more. I started doing that in the third and fourth parts, and they were much more effective as a result. In other words, I was trying to say too much here.

What do you think? Is Fuson being too hard on his own work? Is his 11-paragraph introduction a "leisurely stroll" or an enticing preview of scenes and characters who will reappear again and again? Would an editor's note have been this compelling? Apply your own analysis to Fuson's second and third points. Some readers will agree with the self-criticism. Others, like the authors of this book, will conclude that a little tightening might have moved the story along, but that the richness of this writing rewards a reader for time well spent.

☐ WRITING THE INVESTIGATIVE STORY

The challenge of writing an investigative piece has much in common with any writing at length. The same problems of organization, discipline, structure and helping the reader along must be overcome whether your story is investigative, analytical or descriptive. But the writer of investigative stories faces some complications that are less common, and sometimes unknown, in other forms of journalism.

- The substance of an investigation is often heavy going. Many important investigative stories are based on contract specifications, computer analyses, travel vouchers, telephone records and other details with little intrinsic reader interest.
- The threat of challenges, by lawsuit or by public relations counterattack, is always present. The prose of a feature writer is seldom scrutinized by the company lawyer; the investigative reporter's writing must be able to sustain such scrutiny.
- The burdens of fairness and balance are never heavier than when your story will damage reputations or careers.

The final requirement of any story is that it be read. If you are to expose an evil, right a wrong or accomplish any other worthy end, you have to get the customers into your tent and keep them there. That's why the best investigative reporters and editors today bring to their work the same sharp-eyed observation, the same precise crafting of the language that all good writers employ.

Rick Tulsky of The Philadelphia Inquirer is one of the best. He investigated bad maintenance and bad management in the Philadelphia mass transit system. This is a subject that has the potential for a story as deadly dull as the system was deadly. Tulsky relied on a classic approach to lure readers into his tent. He told his story in human terms:

> Melvin Young lost his life boarding a train. With his foot caught in the door of a crowded subway car, he was dragged down the 15th Street station platform into the tunnel and killed.
>
> William McDowell lost his right eye driving a bus. The brake pedal fell off and lay like a broken toy on the floorboard while McDowell's bus, unable to stop, rearended an Audi and then a Chrysler on City Line Avenue, then jumped a curb and rammed a tree.
>
> Bertha Pressley was luckier. All she lost was several months' pay after being injured when the bus she was riding collided with a car. But as a

result, Mrs. Pressley fell behind on her house payments and other bills and couldn't send her teenage children to the prom.

These three people are victims of the Southeastern Pennsylvania Transportation Authority (SEPTA), the nation's third largest transit system. They are three among thousands. . . .

Notice the ominously alliterative cadence of the last line. It hints of even greater horror to come. Notice the specifics, the details. Good reporting is being put to the service of good writing.

Tulsky's is an anecdotal lead. It works. Usually, this kind of story-telling approach is the best lure into a story that is hard and heavy. Readers aren't bass, though. You can't just set the hook and reel them in. The writer's lure must be an integral part of the story, not a deceptive adornment.

Tulsky's story of neglect, decay and danger is packed with vivid imagery and full of people all the way through. Riders complain that subway stations "are dreary and reek with the smell of urine." Readers meet trolley driver Ken Tomczuk, whose brakes failed on a hill. "Result: 21 people taken to hospitals, one of them unconscious." And 74-year-old Helen Creedon, a bus passenger in another crash. "Result: five people taken to the hospital, including Mrs. Creedon and her 72-year-old husband, Francis."

This is detail that enlivens and advances the story rather than encumbering it.

Sometimes, more rarely, your material will lend itself to a hard, summary-lead approach. Most investigative reporters and editors probably would agree with the late editor and teacher Paul Williams' criteria for deciding when the hard lead is best. Use a hard lead, he advised, only if:

- There is a single, overwhelming revelation to be made;
- The context is already familiar to the average reader;
- The evidence supporting the lead is unequivocal;
- The story is simple enough to have few subplots and to need no chronology.

Remember Laura Stepp's lead? "Cotton dust is killing people." You will seldom have a single more overwhelming revelation. The project was long and complex, but the theme was clear.

Norman Sinclair and Fred Girard of the Detroit News exposed laxity and wrongdoing in Michigan's system of appeals from criminal convictions. Their finished product was massive (the reprint filled 16 tabloid pages) and loaded with detail. Their lead was straightforward: "Publicly paid lawyers, through carelessness or incompetence, are undermining the constitutional right of appeal of needy defendants in Michigan."

That is about as clearly and strongly as you could start a story. The lead is what those lawyers would call libel per se. That is, its unequivocal accusation is damaging to the reputations of the lawyers, many of whom are named later in the story. It is not a paragraph to be written if you harbor the slightest doubt that you could defend it in court. If you have the goods, though, as Sinclair and Girard did, this lead delivers them on the spot.

Tom Braden spent six months investigating mismanagement in the public housing agency. His report in The Columbia Missourian began with a simple sentence: "The city's biggest landlord also may be the worst." Then Braden goes on to perform another service for his readers. He tells them, in a five-paragraph theme section before the page one story jumps to an inside page, what it all means:

> . . . Housing Authority administrators admit they do not even know how much money they have because the agency's accounting is in shambles. When Housing Authority workers and contractors have made repairs, they have wasted thousands of dollars on incompetent workmanship.
>
> Federal officials responsible for overseeing public housing have long known that the city's housing program has been one of the worst-run of its size in the Midwest, according to interviews and documents.
>
> Tenants also have known that. They have been forced to live with rotting floors, peeling paint, broken windows and dripping faucets.
>
> Even the Housing Authority's own housing inspector described the agency as riddled with waste and mismanagement.
>
> "What we've had in the past is just wholesale incompetence and neglect," said inspector Rick Monroe. "That's why we spent all this money and have nothing to show for it."

Too many investigative reporters are content to marshal their findings and parade them across a page without ever summing up, without taking the step of making clear the significance of those findings. This failure to get to the point—usually defended as "letting the readers draw their own conclusions"—is really an abdication of the writer's first duty: to be clear.

Detail must be used to support the point of an investigative story, not allowed to obscure it. The point sometimes will be that the situation itself is confused and unclear. An important part of the reporter's craft is the ability to write clearly about confusion. Every investigative story worth publishing has a point, maybe more than one. Your job as a writer is to distill them.

Distillation demands simplicity of language as well as clarity of thought. The best way to write about a complicated subject is as simply as possible. You'll notice in the examples in this chapter everyday words and uncluttered sentences. You won't find technical jargon or rhetorical flourishes.

Some projects are so complex and the topics so important that writers and editors go to even greater pains to achieve clarity. The Lexington (Ky.) Herald-Leader, for example, used a readability formula and went through multiple rewrites to ensure that a massive series on the woes of the state's education system could be read by anyone with an eighth-grade literacy level. The series was so successful that seven other newspapers across Kentucky distributed it to their readers. And the state legislature initiated reforms.

Clarity requires, in investigative or other long stories, a theme paragraph or section such as Tom Braden's that answers for readers two central questions: What does all this mean? Why should I read it? Increasingly, as journalists strive to make their publications easy and inviting to read, they are telling stories with the aid of such graphic devices as subheads, highlight boxes, charts and graphs. Verbally and visually, the significance and relevance of complicated stories must be made clear before your readers wander away.

One other benefit of graphics is that they can substitute for paragraphs and shorten stories that seem to go on forever. Sometimes, of course, the material demands great length. When it does, a series or multiple sidebars is usually the best format. But in many cases, investigative pieces run on and on and on because the writer, the editor or the company lawyer feels compelled to display every shred of evidence and use every quote from every witness. The compulsion is understandable, but you should resist it.

Your obligation as a writer is to tell the readers what you've found and what it means. Then you should provide enough evidence to show that your conclusions are well-founded, but no more. If, as is often the case, you have 10 examples, use two and just tell the readers you have more. If the two really show what you say they do, readers will believe you. And they probably will thank you for your restraint. Similarly, if you have three or four human sources saying essentially the same things, print only the best. Save the rest.

Especially in these litigation-happy times, it will be a great comfort to you and your lawyer to know there's more where the examples you've printed came from. Being able to demonstrate that you've shown restraint should also be helpful when an opposing lawyer starts inquiring into your state of mind, as the courts now allow. It will be much more difficult for the other side to show malice if you can truthfully point out that you dug up even more evidence than you published.

The appearance and reality of fairness, of balance, are just as important in establishing credibility with readers as they are in protecting yourself against lawsuits.

"Harsh stories turn off readers," says veteran investigative reporter Gaylord Shaw. Avoiding harshness is particularly desirable in stories that have the effect of accusing someone of wrongdoing. That's why Shaw, after establishing in a story that his target is a rotten crook, often includes a "to be sure" paragraph, as in, "To be sure, the world is full of rotten crooks." The impact of a strong story is heightened, not diminished, by a demonstration of balance and fairness.

Fairness requires not only that you give your target a chance to respond to your findings but that you include any findings that are in the target's favor. The Detroit News report on the state criminal justice system showed rampant injustice. But writers Sinclair and Girard took pains to be fair:

> Of nearly 200 prisoners interviewed by The News, a few did feel the system had protected their rights.
>
> "I did the crime," one Jackson inmate said. "I copped (pleaded guilty); and the only reason I appealed was they told me I had a free one coming. I thought maybe they'd find some technicality or something."
>
> And a woman imprisoned at Huron Valley Women's Facility for second-degree murder said, "I got no complaints about my (appeals) lawyer. She tried hard, but there wasn't much she could do. I'm only doing 5½ years, and I deserve it. That's not much for taking a life."

The writers note the exceptions to the overall pattern, and they make clear that these are exceptions. It is clear, and it is fair. Readers expect no less.

As these examples show, investigative writing can be good writing. You may have to work a little harder because of the special demands of investigative stories, but the principles of good writing apply universally.

☐ QUESTIONS AND EXERCISES

1. Pick a long story in your favorite newspaper or magazine. Analyze it by using the "Five W's and H" model outlined in this chapter. How clear and compelling is it? Using these analytical questions as a guide, how might it be improved?

2. Do the same with your most recent piece of substantial length.

3. Take a piece of your own or a friend's writing and outline it. What flaws in organization or gaps in information do you find? Now create a formal outline for your next story. Is outlining a helpful part of the writing process?

4. Re-read the Ken Fuson article reproduced in this chapter. Critique it using the criteria in this chapter. How does your critique compare to his? Remember that good writers usually are their own harshest critics.

5. Choose an article in the current issue of The New Yorker and perform the same kind of critique. Compare this article to the Fuson article. Which strikes you as better writing? Why? What can you tell from the writing about the audiences the two writers are trying to reach?

6. Find a good piece of investigative reporting (perhaps the most recent winner of the Pulitzer Prize or a winner in the annual competition of Investigative Reporters and Editors). Analyze its style and structure by the criteria in this chapter. Now compare it to the Fuson article or some other well-written example of non-investigative prose. Which makes better reading? What, if any, writing lessons might the investigative journalist learn from the feature writer? What reporting lessons might the feature writer learn from the investigative reporter?

7. As you tackle your next substantial writing project, try consciously to follow the guidelines in this chapter.

14

Writing Opinion and Persuasion

Where there is much desire to learn, there of necessity will be much arguing, much writing, many opinions; for opinion in good men is but knowledge in the making. —John Milton, 1608–1674

Here's USA Today columnist Barbara Reynolds expressing an opinion:

> During a lull at the 1984 Republican National Convention, near the set of the "Dallas" TV series, I remember dueling with Clarence Thomas over Ronald Reagan. He thought he was a savior; I argued he was wrecking black America.
>
> Thomas, then chief of the Equal Employment Opportunity Commission, had the last word that day.
>
> "You haven't seen anything yet," he roared, blowing a few rings of smoke from his cigar. Then he laughed. It was a gleeful laugh, deep, eerie and unforgettable.
>
> I recoiled, muttering to myself: "Thank God he's only a little fish in a little pond."
>
> Today, he is a Big Fish. By next month, as Justice Thomas, if he has a mind to, he can turn into a shark. He could swim in the big pond and help take big hunks out of the hides of women and minorities.

This is opinion writing, and it's done well. Notice the unmistakable presence of the writer. Columnists have opinions, and they don't hide them.

Opinion is the heart of the essay, the column and the editorial. You find it on the editorial pages of newspapers, magazines and publications of all kinds. Although you apply the same techniques of good writing to this genre as you do to any other kind of writing, opinion writing has its own characteristics and techniques.

☐ WHAT IS OPINION?

Opinion is just short of fact. If you can prove an opinion, it no longer exists. You base an opinion on facts and on experience. Politics is rife with opinion because politics deals with ever-changing particulars in a never-the-same world. Seldom is there only one correct way to do something or one solution to a problem.

Thus, when the U.S. senators voted themselves a pay raise, columnist James Kilpatrick argued:

> There is nothing honorable about honoraria. It is simply a way for special interests to gain access to senators and, in doing so, the special interests hope—hope—to influence senators.

Then Kilpatrick quotes Sen. Robert Byrd, D-W.Va.:

> "The perception that members are beholden to the special interests is reinforced by the system. The senator who receives the honoraria may indeed, not be influenced thereby, but the perception is to the contrary and the damage is done, and it is done to the institution."

Kilpatrick continues:

> Not a senator rose to deny it. Under the system that now will be abolished, senators could pick up $2,000 for merely having breakfast with a special interest group and answering a few questions. This was not outright bribery, but it was the next thing to it. The speaking fees were directly personal. They were subtly different from the campaign contributions from political action committees.

Columnist William Buckley had a different opinion:

> The design of the current reform is to remove this temptation. It is an idle enterprise. The reason is that it is unimaginable that a senator or a member of Congress is going to be suborned by the price of a speaking fee. Such fees are small potatoes up against the larger picture. The representative who votes for farm subsidies, or for tariffs on fabrics, or for a limitation on Japanese car imports, or for minimum wage increases or Social Security immunities, is being manipulated by pressures that don't express themselves in the mini-coin tips for public speeches. . . .
>
> It isn't a matter of the speaking fee that dominates the thinking of a senator when the time comes to cast a vote. It is his feeling for the power of the special interests. And they make their power felt by organizing the voters, by contributing to political action committees and by letting the senator know that unless he votes their special interest, he will be jobless after the next election.

Who is right? Kilpatrick or Buckley? As with most opinions, probably both have a handle on some truth.

Notice the presence of the columnists in their writing. Both have a voice, a persona, that readers have come to recognize and respect. Kilpatrick—the master stylist, the wordsmith, simple and direct, candid, often barbed, no holds barred. In the beginning of the column, he quotes Sen. Byrd, " 'This is a great issue to demagogue,' he said, and he went on to prove it."

Later, Kilpatrick acknowledges:

> The only rational criticism that may be offered, of course, is that members of Congress, as a body, haven't earned a raise and don't deserve it. On their record of performance, members are an irresponsible and incompetent lot.

Notice also the simple but elegant line, "There is nothing honorable about honoraria."

Then there's Buckley, only sometimes simple but just as direct, always erudite. Kilpatrick often chides Buckley for sentences with words like these: "The challenge to a functioning democracy has to do not with the little temptations, but with the large ones. The idea of the commonweal is very nearly lost in the particularizations of pressure politics." Note these words, "functioning," "commonweal," "particularizations." Vintage Buckley—you love him or you hate him, but you always know where he stands. His opinions are well-founded and well-expressed.

☐ WHY OPINION?

Why bother with writing about opinion? Or why should you do opinion writing? Here are three reasons:

1. To have an opinion is to be human. Human beings can reflect on what they do; they can learn from the past. Without opinions, people would not advance; they would not explore; they would not improve.

2. Opinions, like ideas, are essential to finding the truth. Our democracy is founded on the opinion that the best way to arrive at truth is to allow ideas to conflict in the open marketplace.

Essayists perform an important function in any society or organization. Expressing opinions leads to discussion, discussion can lead to consensus, and consensus can lead to new and better ways of doing things.

3. Opinion is fun to write and fun to read. Advice columns are full of opinions, and few forms of writing are read more. Newspapers have op-ed pages—pages opposite the editorial page that are filled

with readers' opinions. Publications of all kinds have letters columns, often among the most-read sections of the publications. Others have a forum. Forum is the Latin word for "marketplace." In the marketplace, people barter and exchange goods. In the marketplace of ideas, people barter and exchange opinions. The place where the Roman senators debated issues was called the Forum.

☐ REQUIREMENTS OF THE OPINION WRITER

Essay, then, is a broad term. It encompasses all forms of opinion writing. How you execute it depends upon your purpose. If it is explanatory or interpretative, you marshal facts. If it is argumentative, you draw general conclusions from specific instances (inductive reasoning), or you apply a general truth to a specific instance (deductive reasoning). If it is descriptive, you recreate scenes, events, encounters, in the same way you would set up a situation lead for a story. All the variations of essays have this in common, though: they require a clear theme statement, evidence to support it and a conclusion.

Note how columnist William Raspberry recreates a scene, establishes a theme, goes on to support it and reaches a conclusion:

> (Setting the scene) Urie Bronfenbrenner, the celebrated child-development expert, looking for all the world like an exaggerated portrayal of the absent-minded professor, forgets to use his microphone, loses his train of thought and misplaces the transparencies containing his statistical charts.
>
> Nobody in his small audience, convened by the National Council for Families and Television, seems to mind. All remain focused on his unsettling message.
>
> (Theme statement) U.S. children—perhaps the children in all English-speaking countries—are in trouble: too poor, too likely to grow up in single-parent households, too little supported by their government and too low a priority for the society at large. . . .
>
> (Support) Bronfenbrenner details those difficulties. Virtually all industrial countries, except the United States, provide a universal child or family allowance. American children are disproportionately products of broken or never-formed marriages. The United States even has more poverty than other industrialized societies, and its children constitute the single biggest element of that poverty. . . .
>
> (Conclusion) But it does seem clear to me that we cannot have a work force that equalizes opportunities for fathers and mothers—that eliminates the career costs of parenthood—and still do what we need to do for children.

The column is longer, of course, but this excerpt illustrates the structure.

Because the essayist often does not set out to persuade people to agree with a point of view or a course of action, it really doesn't matter whether the copy amuses, outrages, cajoles, insults or pleases the readers. Researchers have demonstrated that most readers read material that agrees with their point of view.

For example, readers of columnist Mike Royko generally know his view of the world and how he will respond to people and events. His millions of readers love him because he says better what they would like to say. His outrageous conversations with Slats Grobnik delight his followers and outrage his detractors—if and when his critics read him at all.

Here's Royko using Grobnik:

> "You think we're gonna get in a real shootin' war with Japan again?" asked Slats Grobnik.
> What a ridiculous question.
> "Whadaya mean, ridiculous? I read in your paper that some egghead professor wrote a book that says it's a cinch to happen because of the way we're bashin' them and they're startin' to bash us."

Grobnik knows why Japan might start a war with the United States: "If they ever start a war with us, it's because they don't have enough land for golf courses of their own."

Columnists don't hide their feelings. Note this opening in a column by Susan Estrich, professor of law at the University of Southern California, from the OP-ED page of The New York Times:

> Earlier this week, NBC News jumped off the Empire State Building. So The New York Times, like any thoughtful toddler, decided it had to follow suit. The woman who filed a complaint of rape against William Kennedy Smith has been "outed" after a week in which repeated questions have been raised in print about her actions and character. The Times's explanation for its decision to publish her name was that NBC News had done it the night before. My 5-year-old nephew couldn't have put it better.

The stage is set. Then she crafts the theme clearly.

> Rape may be the most underreported serious crime in America. The practice of not publishing rape victims' names is intended to encourage more women to come forward . . .

Sometimes columnists just play to their audience. A sports columnist in St. Louis expects his audience to love the Cardinals and to hate the Cubs. Bernie Miklasz of the St. Louis Post-Dispatch knows how to please them. In yet another bad year for the Cubs and yet another Cub losing streak, Miklasz reports that the manager canceled batting practice to hold "one of those don't-worry-be-happy team meetings."

Miklasz wonders: "Would this man-to-man chat become a turning point in the Cubs' lost season? Would the depressed, zombie-eyed Cubs spring to life? . . . Inspired, the Cubs went out and lost to the Cardinals."

Using facts, not opinion, Miklasz gives his readers some evidence that the Cubs were "zombie-eyed." He writes:

> In the second inning, the Cubs developed a sudden, allergic reaction to a harmless pop foul. If you are looking for one incredibly stupid play, the one, wacky moment that best defines the Cubs' bizarre attempts to play this game in 1991, it was this one:
>
> With the Cubs trailing 1–0, starting pitcher Bob Scanlan had two outs and two strikes on Cardinals pitcher Omar Olivares. The bases were empty. Olivares hacked at a pitch. His slice floated to the right, drifting like a hot air balloon.
>
> And this is how those alert Cubs responded:
>
> The catcher, Rick Wilkins, did not move.
>
> The first baseman, Mark Grace, did not move.
>
> The pitcher, Scanlan, did not move.
>
> Ozzie Smith moved, to avoid being struck atop the noggin. The unclaimed ball plopped down in the middle of the Cardinals' on-deck circle.
>
> Olivares then walked. The Cardinals then scored four runs. The rout was on.

Miklasz was having fun. Many times you will want to do more than let people know your opinion. You may want them to agree with you. To do that you will have to use the techniques of persuasion.

To persuade people, you have to reason with them, and it doesn't hurt to appeal to their emotions. Aristotle argues in his "Rhetoric" that persuasion is necessary if several persons are to agree on one of several good means to get something done.

☐ KEY ELEMENTS OF PERSUASION

For people to be persuaded, Aristotle says, they must recognize three qualities in the persuader: intelligence, character and good will. Without these, credibility is impossible, and without credibility, persuasion is impossible.

KEY ELEMENTS OF PERSUASION

1. Intelligence
2. Character
3. Good will

---

1. *Intelligence.* The persuader must demonstrate intelligence. The more facts you have at your command, the more easily will you be able to make your point.

In an essay in Time magazine, Barbara Ehrenreich argues that "real patriots speak their minds." To make her point, she cites the early patriots of our country:

> To these, our first patriots, freedom of speech, even jarring, unpopular speech, was a right worth dying for. Paine upheld "the right of every man to his opinion, however different that opinion may be to mine." Franklin said, "Without freedom of thought there can be no such thing as . . . publick liberty." Jefferson believed "uniformity of opinion" was no more desirable than uniformity "of face and stature." Staid George Washington warned against "the impostures of pretended patriotism."

By demonstrating her knowledge of history and by using patriots whom everyone recognizes and accepts, Ehrenreich is more persuasive.

2. *Character.* Persuaders are also believed because they are perceived as people of character. Aristotle tells us that "The character of the persuader is the most important element of persuasion." If you are trustworthy, people are much more likely to believe what you are saying. Hence, not only must what you say be true, but you must have a history, a reputation for telling the truth.

Your background, education and position also help establish credibility. If you have experience, if you have recognized degrees in the subject, if you are the president of a company or a U.S. senator, you may use these facts to establish your character.

You might remember media theorist Marshall McLuhan's famous (and oversimplified) dictum, "The medium is the message." People often tend to believe people not because of what they say but because of who they are. Readers are more likely to believe a person writing in a respected publication such as Commentary than a person writing in the National Enquirer.

If readers think that you are attempting to deceive or to mislead or that you have done that in the past, persuasion is most difficult. An old German proverb says that once a person lies, people tend to disbelieve that person even when he or she tells the truth. Perhaps it is unfair, but most people believe that once a con, always a con.

Good character embodies more than just telling the truth. Some people won't believe anything you say if they know you have cheated on your income tax or on your spouse. Presidential candidate Gary Hart discovered how important character is in the 1988 campaign when voters rejected him because he first lied about, then admitted his association with a woman other than his wife.

To establish good character you must demonstrate that you are fair. Fairness demands that you know the arguments against the position that you are promoting. Not only should you know the arguments, but you should state them accurately and in context. When possible, state opposing views in the words of those who hold them. No one can argue a position as well as the person who deeply holds it. Your rewording and paraphrasing often diminishes the impact of a person's argument. John Stuart Mill said it best:

> Nor is it enough that he should hear the arguments of adversaries from his own teachers, presented as they state them, and accompanied by what they offer as refutations. That is not the way to do justice to the arguments, or bring them into real contact with his own mind. He must be able to hear them from persons who actually believe them, who defend them in earnest, and do their very utmost for them.

For example, on the OP-ED page of The New York Times, Jonathan Sherman argued against videotaping and rebroadcasting a gas-chamber execution. Nevertheless, Sherman quoted Pat Clark, director of Death Penalty Focus, a California anti-death penalty group, who said that if such executions were televised, "People will ultimately realize it's a human being murdered in a premeditated, calculated way by the state in our names."

By quoting Clark's strongest argument, Sherman demonstrated his fairness. He later argues: "I strongly oppose capital punishment, but its steadfast supporters know that violence is the price of vengeance— and they accept that price."

Never be tempted to pass over the strongest arguments of the opposition. When you do, your readers know that either you are being unfair or that you are not able to answer the opposition's case. Worse, they may think you are ignorant of the opposition's arguments.

3. *Good Will.* The best way to establish good character is to demonstrate to your readers that you have good will. This means simply that you want what is best for them and society, that you sincerely have others' interest at heart. Although at times persuasion may be self-serving, it is never exclusively so.

You must establish more than rapport for persuasion. You must establish an air of friendly confidence. Friendliness is the key. You do not persuade people by saying that those who disagree with you are ignorant or evil or by calling them names or insulting them. Attacking a person's character is called an *ad hominem* argument, and readers recognize that you are avoiding the issue at hand. Though wit and humor can be great tools, beware of sarcasm because it's often misunderstood or thought to be rude and unfriendly.

Unfortunately, a great deal of what porports to be persuasive writing appeals only to those who already agree with the writer. Granted, there may be some purpose in strengthening the resolve of the believers, but there is little point in preaching to the saved. Persuasion's purpose is to win over those who disagree.

You establish good will when you demonstrate that you believe your readers are intelligent, good and changeable.

Good Will Assumes That Readers Are:

1. Intelligent
2. Good
3. Changeable

---

1. *Intelligent.* Readers may be ignorant of some of the facts that you have, but they are not stupid. Remember, never underestimate the intelligence of your readers; never overestimate what they know. Most of all, you must believe that people are educable. If you have not educated your audience, don't blame your audience. Blame yourself.

2. *Good.* Don't assume that people are basically selfish, greedy and generally evil creatures. With that attitude you appear self-righteous, condescending and generally obnoxious.

3. *Changeable.* Don't bother attempting persuasive writing if you believe that people can't or won't change. People do change, and what they read can sometimes be a catalyst for change. Some people do stop smoking, begin exercising, think differently about abortion, gun laws and the death penalty. You have changed; you hold some opinions now that you used to consider foolish or erroneous.

As a persuasive writer, you must have confidence in your ability to help people to change. This means that you must understand the principles of rhetoric.

An editorial in The Gainesville Sun after the mutilation-murders of five young people at the University of Florida demonstrates that the editorialists considered the readers intelligent, good and changeable.

First the editorial praised the University of Florida for coping well with the fear and panic of the community. "Under the leadership of John Lombardi, the university coped marvelously." Then there was praise for the police:

> Likewise, there is much to admire about the speed and efficiency with which the community's law enforcement establishment mobilized, and of the dispatch with which reinforcements were sent from Talla-hassee and Washington. Many of us felt safer sleeping Tuesday night with Gainesville Police Chief Wayland Clifton's promise that we would "see more police coverage than any city you've ever been in."
> Given the macabre nature of the crimes, even the most hardened police investigators might be hard pressed to perform in the most expedient manner. And a top priority of the police must always be to muster the evidence necessary to track down and apprehend the killer.
> Performing basic police work could not have been easy in the face of the community's rising tide of fear—not to mention the distraction of the media circus that descended on Gainesville.

After demonstrating the intelligence and goodness of the police, the editorial then gently makes its point:

> Nonetheless, when the immediate crisis is over, when police officials have time to review and critique the way in which law enforcement responded to the unfolding crisis, they would do well to ask themselves whether their initial refusal to disclose very many details of the killings actually contributed to the panic—whether their silence helped to feed the rumor mill.

A couple of paragraphs then described that at a press conference on Tuesday, questions came not from the press but from frightened students. Then the editorial showed more understanding and good will:

> We don't want to be overly critical on this point. There is a fine line between divulging critical evidence or releasing gruesome details and providing enough information to help other potential victims see to their personal safety. In the chaos that followed the discovery of the bodies, that line must have seemed very blurry indeed. And by Wednesday, police were being much more helpful in releasing such details.

The editorial concludes, confident that the police have learned and will change their behavior:

> Nonetheless, it is clear that the events on Tuesday constituted something of a learning experience for law enforcement as well. No one knows if this living nightmare is over yet, but whether it is or not, we trust that the police will be more candid in the future with a very frightened community.

☐ THE TECHNIQUES OF PERSUASION

Aristotle defines rhetoric as the ability to discover in the particular case all the available means of persuasion. He says that rhetoric is an art. You can study the efforts of successful speakers, he says, and the principles of success can be used as a method. In short, you must learn the tools of persuasion.

☐ The Argument

The essential tool of persuasion is the argument. Aristotle discusses 28 valid lines of argument. You'll find eight of them particularly useful:

1. The inductive argument
2. The deductive argument
3. The enthymeme
4. The rhetorical example
5. The analogy
6. The maxim
7. The a fortiori argument
8. The reductio ad absurdum argument

When you argue, you usually need a premise and a conclusion. For example, if the premise is true that Betty received all "A's" her first semester, it may be inferred that Betty is a superior student.

Of course, not all statements are related as premise and conclusion. For example, if the premise is that rookie Jack Smith is batting .350, you may conclude that he might be rookie of the year. But if the premise is that Jack Smith is batting .350, it is not a conclusion to say that he is a rookie.

The better you are at making inferences, the better you will be at argumentation and persuasion. You must always begin with a solid premise. The best premise is a verifiable fact, but you may quote an expert. St. Thomas Aquinas says argument from authority is the weakest of all arguments. Quoting Aquinas here assumes that he is a recognized expert on this subject and that he speaks without bias about it. If arguments from authority are weak, why use them? Because it is usually stronger to quote a known authority than for you to make the statement yourself.

1. *The inductive argument.* When you use a number of particulars and draw a general conclusion from those particulars, you are using the inductive method. The best you hope for by using the inductive method is a high degree of probability. Obviously, this method invites people to draw invalid conclusions or to over-generalize or to stereotype individuals or classes of people. This leads some to say that all generalizations are false. Certainly, that generalization is false. There are valid and useful generalizations, and our survival demands that we make use of them.

If five people swimming in Lake Bruno were bitten by water moccasins this summer, it's logical to conclude that you should not swim there.

However, if you are wondering about how people feel about the president, you can't just ask five people. To reach a conclusion, you must know the rules of sampling. You must know the size of the population you are sampling; you must do random sampling (for example, every tenth name in a directory); you must know what percentage of response is necessary to acquire valid information.

Fortunately, you don't have to do a lot of this research yourself. Pollsters and researchers such as Gallup and Roper do a lot of this for you. But be careful how you use the data they offer.

Editorial writers make heavy use of the inductive method. In a July 4 editorial, the St. Louis Post-Dispatch wrote that U.S. citizens were losing their civil liberties. Here are some of the particulars the writer cites to make the case that "the power of the state has grown" (asterisks added):

* Prison conditions may be horrendous, so long as they are not the result of "deliberate indifference."
* A confession that was coerced from a defendant is admissible in court, so long as it resulted from a "harmless error."
* First-time offenders, convicted of nonviolent crimes, may be thrown in prison for life with no chance for parole.
* Police may board buses and ask to search luggage, even if they have no reason to suspect any criminal activity.

* Someone arrested without a warrant may be held for up to 48 hours while authorities determine if the arrest was proper.

Although some might argue that these are oversimplifications of the Supreme Court's decisions, nevertheless, they are verifiable facts. From them, the writer can make a valid generalization or conclusion.

2. *The deductive argument.* With inductive arguments you begin with particular statements and conclude with a generalization. With deductive arguments you begin with a generalization and end with a particular statement. An argument with a major premise, a minor premise and a conclusion is called a syllogism.

Syllogisms are often used in persuasion, even though such proofs, says Aristotle, belong to logic and to science, and not to the world of opinion and rhetoric. It is important to understand syllogisms if only because your opposition may attempt to use them and often do so incorrectly.

A valid syllogism draws a conclusion from what is implied in the premises. For example:

Major premise: All persons born in the United States are U.S. citizens.

Minor premise: Jane Dobson was born in the United States.

Conclusion: Jane Dobson is a U.S. citizen.

Such a syllogism is categorical. It is valid and true because the major and minor premises are true.

A valid syllogism is not true if the major or minor premise is not true. For example:

Major premise: All labor unions are controlled by the mafia.

Minor premise: The Union of Electrical Workers is a labor union.

Conclusion: The Union of Electrical Workers is controlled by the Mafia.

Because the major premise is untrue, the conclusion and the syllogism are untrue, even though the syllogism is valid.

Look how William Buckley ends his column on the pay-raise of senators:

Our senators are for sale for speaking fees. Therefore, we shan't have speaking fees. Therefore, our senators will no longer be for sale.

Buckley concludes: "The syllogism is very leaky."

You may want to study the syllogism further to recognize common fallacies. Logic is your strongest tool.

· 3. *The enthymeme.* However, Aristotle believes the enthymeme is a better tool for persuasion than the syllogism. The enthymeme has been described as the "logical shortcut." It is a rhetorical syllogism in which one or more elements are not expressed. With the enthymeme you assume that the audience will supply the missing element or elements, that one or two parts of the rhetorical syllogism are already in the minds of the readers.

It is precisely because the enthymeme allows readers to make judgments about the missing elements that you'll find it is a powerful tool of persuasion. With the enthymeme you assume people are intelligent, reasonable and free. You don't hit them over the head with what portends to be absolute proofs. Don't risk the appearance of saying that if readers do not agree, they must be ignorant or unreasonable.

The enthymeme is not so certain in its premises. It deals more with probabilities in human affairs, not with scientific proofs. Also, the enthymeme assumes that the audience has certain knowledge and beliefs.

Columnist Lewis Grizzard assumed that readers believe that highly paid baseball players don't win pennants. When he listed the 10 reasons Atlanta would finish ahead of Los Angeles, his 10th reason was: "Our guys don't have a lot of big fat contracts like their guys. So their guys aren't as hungry as our guys." It's not a formal syllogism; it's an enthymeme, and it works.

4. *The rhetorical example.* Another shortcut is the rhetorical example. Examples are a great tool for writers of all kinds, including the persuasive writer. However, note the distinction between the expository example and the rhetorical example.

An expository example is merely an instance of what the person is writing about. If you are talking about buildings, you may use a house for an example.

A rhetorical example is similar to induction, but it argues from the particular to the particular, not from the particular to the general. It argues from like to like or from one or more parallel cases.

For example, an editorial in the St. Louis Post-Dispatch begins: "Peru's military has an ignominious human rights record, the most atrocious in South America, according to some human rights groups." Arguing against aid to Peru by way of millions of dollars and advisors, ostensibly to fight the drug war, the editorial uses U.S. aid to El Salvador as a rhetorical example:

> The Peruvian military is reminiscent of another beneficiary of U.S. generosity, the Salvadoran military. As followers of that ongoing conflict

know, U.S. military aid has not prevented the Salvadoran army from engaging in torture and murder.

5. *The analogy.* Similarly, you can use analogy, which tries to demonstrate that if two things are similar in some respect, they may also be similar in certain other respects.

Columnist Ellen Goodman uses analogy when she argues against all-male African-American schools in Detroit being an effective educational reform. She writes:

> Reading the manuscript for Jonathan Kozol's upcoming book, *Savage Inequalities*, I am struck by the pernicious and profound effects of racial segregation in today's city schools. If racial segregation is a cause of vast inequalities in school, how can sexual segregation be the cure?

6. *The maxim.* You can take another shortcut with the maxim, a statement that everyone accepts as true. For example, an article in "The Talk of the Town," in the New Yorker begins: "It is an axiom of governance that power, once acquired, is seldom freely relinquished." The article uses this accepted wisdom to make the point that in spite of the end of the Cold War, "our government has shown little eagerness to surrender the powers it claimed under cover of the shadow."

Beware the tired cliche and the overused truism, but at times the maxim is the foundation for further reasoning.

7. *The a fortiori argument.* Simply stated, this argument says that if something is true in one case, it is all the more true in the case in question.

Columnist Tom Bethell argues that Democrats and Republicans more and more resemble a one-party system. He writes: "In the 50 states, the two major parties collude with one another to restrict access to the ballot, making it difficult for other political parties to be listed without time-consuming and costly petition drives."

He then argues: "If two dominant corporations were to restrict competitors' access to the market in this way, they would certainly be charged with antitrust violations."

What he is saying, of course, is that if we have laws forbidding corporations to collude, all the more reason why we should not allow political parties to collude.

8. *The reductio ad absurdum.* Sometimes further reasoning can lead down a path to the absurd. This argument pushes an argument to an extreme in an attempt to show that the entire line of thinking is flawed. Mike Royko is a master of the reductio ad absurdum argument.

So is columnist Russell Baker. Baker cites some statistics from his Committee on the Pace of Life on time consumed by humanity's most vital activities in the 1990s: War, 100 hours; Coup, 60 hours; Baseball, three hours. Baker says that his committee warned that this lengthening of the time it takes to play a baseball game is alarming. He writes:

> Some people will say, 'But the average game consumes only a silly 3 percent of the time needed for a war, so why get excited?' Here's why: World War II lasted nearly six years. That's about 2,190 days, or 52,560 hours, 3 percent of which is about 1,577 hours. Imagine World War II Americans sitting through a simple baseball game 1,577 hours long. That's 65 days if nobody ever pauses to sleep. It would take an entire season to play three games! America wouldn't have had time left over to whip Germany and Japan into shape to run the world economy.

☐ Good Writing

Using good argumentation is essential to persuasive writing. But the best arguments will not persuade unless they are written well. Remember the audience. Aristotle says this about persuasion:

> These are the reasons why uneducated men are more effective than the educated in speaking to the masses—as the poets say that the unlearned "have a finer charm . . . for the ear of the mob." Educated men lay down abstract principles and draw general conclusions; the uneducated argue from their everyday knowledge and base their conclusions upon immediate facts.

Remember, too, that Aristotle does not rule out appealing to the emotions, which he defines as those states that are attended by pain or pleasure. Even though persuasion appeals primarily to reason, you may put your readers in a certain state of mind by arousing their emotions.

To do that, write to people about things that touch their lives, that go to the core of what they believe and hold of value. Often it means writing about what will come out of their pocketbooks.

That means be specific; use literary devices such as similes, metaphors, allusions and even alliteration. Use devices such as repetition, parallelisms and lists. Cite classical references and historical data. Columnist James Kilpatrick says that you must write sentences "that ripple, or soothe, or smash, or do anything but lie in the columns and flop their limp participles on a beach of type."

Writer William David Sloan, in an introduction to a collection of more than 50 years of Pulitzer Prize editorials, said that what best characterizes many of them is "ordinariness." With most of them he found two common problems: dullness of writing and lack of unity. In a survey of editorial writers in the early 1980s, Ernest C. Hynds found that "blandness and poor writing" was a principal concern.

Add poor or little use of persuasive techniques to poor writing and there's little wonder that editorial pages get little attention. Bill Hall, an editorial writer for the Lewiston Morning Tribune, says that "a paper that riles people is a paper that sells." Hall says the most important elements are great headlines and strong leads.

Indeed, to write persuasive articles, read the masters such as George Will, Mary McGrory and Anthony Lewis. Then find a topic you care deeply about, research it carefully, find an audience to read it, and write it well.

□ QUESTIONS AND EXERCISES

1. What is essential to good opinion writing?

2. Find an example of your favorite writer's opinion piece. Then analyze it carefully, and indicate why you think it is good.

3. Find examples of editorials that indicate good character and good will.

4. Discuss: Editorials today speak only to those who agree with them. They do not attempt to persuade those who don't.

5. Read editorials and find an example of all eight lines of arguments. Write them down, and discuss them.

6. Write an editorial that employs at least five lines of argument.

15

Writing Humor

From the moment I picked your book up until I laid it down I was convulsed with laughter. Someday I intend reading it.— Groucho Marx, on S.J. Perelman's first book

Here's something funny. At least, we think so.

> Any right-thinking boy would have sold his little brother for a dog like that.
>
> She was obedient, patient and loving, and barked only if you were about to die.
>
> She was fluent in dog, human, bear, cat, cow, timber wolf and woodchuck. She could fetch a stick, open a door, snatch babies from a burning barn, do your homework and stop a runaway tractor. And she never, ever, had an "accident," even if you locked her in the house for a year.
>
> Let's face it. Lassie was one hell of a dog.

Tim Fish wrote that. The New York Times published it. Surprised? You shouldn't be. Even the good, gray Times has come to appreciate the value of a chuckle in a newspaper—and a world—where life often seems grim. And how better to begin a story about a new television series based on the life of the dog America loved most until Snoopy came along.

If variety is the spice of life, humor is the honey of journalism, sweetening the usually dry and often bitter fare served up by most newspapers and magazines most of the time. Humor can serve a writer well:

- Humor can bring a person or a story to life.
- Humor can convey even serious messages more palatably than can straight exposition.
- Humor can provide a few minutes of plain, uncomplicated fun.

A light touch can be the right touch even in stories in which you wouldn't expect it. An obituary, for instance. When Henry Milander, a local legend who was the mayor of suburban Hialeah, died, The Miami Herald wrote in its front-page obituary:

> Once, in about the 29th year of his reign over Hialeah, several politicians were discussing Milander's remarkable hold on the mayor's office.
> Councilman Jack Weaver said, "He won't be around forever, but when he goes, he'll probably take the city with him."
> Henry himself told a reporter visiting City Hall, "The only way they'll get me out of here is shoot me."
> They didn't shoot him and he didn't take the city with him when he went Sunday, but the death of Henry Milander leaves a considerable void in the politics and the folklore of South Florida. . . .

Lightly but not flippantly written, the anecdote captures something of the style and the substance of its subject. That's just what a good obituary, or a good profile, should do. Another improbable locale for humor is the parking lot of an art museum. Dick Pothier of The Philadelphia Inquirer stumbled across an intriguing bit of Americana on the asphalt:

> It's one of the last parking bargains in the city—the 145-car parking lot at Eakins Oval in front of the Philadelphia Museum of Art.
> Unless Eugene Harris is on duty. Then it's a ripoff.
> And Harris says he may be on duty again this weekend, if he can avoid the undercover police officers who keep a close eye on him.
> Harris doesn't work for the city, or the museum, or for anybody but himself.
> He has made thousands of dollars in the past year or so by charging people $3 to $5 to park in the free lot. He's got his "job" down to a science. He even carries a supply of ticket stubs that he picks up from Center City parking lots to give his "customers."
> "It's an art. Let's see . . . I've made up to $60 in 10 minutes and I guess a couple of thousand dollars over the past year or so," Harris said in a parkbench interview near the parking lot Thursday after he was kicked off museum grounds for panhandling.
> To Harris, who is 27 and says he sleeps in 30th Street Station, this is the free-enterprise system that made America great—and has given him a tidy income in recent months.
> To Philadelphia police officers who have arrested Harris three times in the last month and then released him for lack of prosecution complainants and other reasons, this is theft, fraud and larceny.
> And to officials of the Art Museum, this is an outrage. Harris has even charged brand-new security guards $5 to park in the lot before they discovered that parking was free. . . .

Pothier, who has covered science and higher education for the Inquirer—and even has written about his own heart transplant—says, "This is my favorite story." It was, he says, "a quick and easy Sunday page one hit." Humor is a hit with editors because it is a hit with readers.

Here's one more example, from another seemingly unlikely source, The Wall Street Journal. In fact, the Journal regularly leavens its daily diet of corporate reports and serious reportage with humor, often on the front page. Here, writer Dennis Farney entertains while he educates readers on the role of the political maverick in Congress:

> WASHINGTON—One dreary afternoon, as the House of Representatives debated plant patents for hybrid okra, the tousle-haired figure of Rep. John Burton materialized to transform boredom into chaos.
>
> The San Francisco-area Democrat seized the microphone with a question—a serious one, he insisted. Might not the proposed changes in plant patent law lead to bureaucratic meddling in human reproduction?
>
> Not "unless the gentleman can extract a fetus from okra, celery, peppers, tomatoes, carrots or cucumbers," answered a nonplused Rep. E. "Kika" de la Garza, the Texas Democrat who managed the legislation.
>
> "I could do that," Mr. Burton replied airily. "In fact, I have seen it done. It was in the gentleman's district."
>
> A fleeting expression crossed Mr. de la Garza's face. It was the expression of a man who stumbles into a nightclub and, inexplicably, finds himself playing straight man in a comedy act. The irrepressible Mr. Burton moved on to a discussion of genetics. . . .

☐ BEING FUNNY ON PURPOSE

These stories have several things in common. First the humor in each emerges from the writer's applying the universal principles of good reporting. In each case, the key was close observation that yielded detail and anecdote. In the Milander obit, for example, direct quotes are the key. Paraphrase would have been far less effective. In the story of the free-lance parking attendant, attention to specifics makes the bizarre believable, and therefore funnier. In the politics story, a keen eye aided a good ear. John Burton is a "tousle-headed figure" speaking "airily." Rep. de la Garza appears "nonplused" and wears a bemused expression that most readers will be able to imagine. In all three stories, the images are sharp, the description precise. Readers are given ample material from which to build the mental pictures that are essential to written humor.

Another important characteristic is that each excerpt is under-written. The writers have avoided the common trap of trying to be cute. There is no fakery; no quotation marks used to call attention to "special" uses of words; no exclamation points; no stretching of the usual conventions of reporting and writing.

The lesson of these examples is probably the single most impor-tant—and maybe the only—rule of effective humor writing in journal-ism: Find good material and under-write it. Slapstick seldom works in print. If the substance is not funny, no typographical tricks, no verbal gymnastics will persuade a reader that it is. Print is a straight-faced medium. If you fail to respect its limitations, you risk being laughed at rather than laughed with.

There's another warning implied by the examples, too. At least some of you will not find them amusing. Humor is intensely individ-ualistic. An anecdote that moves you to laughter may leave the person at the next desk stoically unmoved. Humor writing is risky. That is another reason for writing humor with restraint. Those who agree with you that this is indeed funny will appreciate your subtlety. Those who disagree are likely to be at least less offended than if you had beaten them over the head with it.

◻ BEING FUNNY JUST TO BE FUNNY

Here are two more examples. The styles are sharply different, but both are funny. We think they are, anyway.

> MOTLEY, Minn. (AP)—Sunflower seed shells are too light. Metal shot, accidentally swallowed, might cause gout. Olive pits are football-shaped and could dent spittoons.
>
> So members of Sit'N'Spit International will again use cherry pits when they participate in the club's spitting classic during its annual con-vention next weekend.
>
> Omar McGuire, president of the 300-member organization, said members will discuss whether to build a domed stadium in downtown Motley in case the City Hall isn't large enough for future spitting con-tests. The club also will take its annual tour of Morey's Fish Market, "just to have something else on the agenda. We believe there should be more foolishness in life," McGuire said.

That's it, the complete story. Ridiculous facts are straightforwardly reported. The humor lies in the situation, which is stripped of super-fluous information and laid out in traditional wire service style. The writer has resisted every temptation to go too far. The result is a tiny gem. Then there is Dave Barry, who lives by hyperbole, capitalizes wildly, punctuates playfully and violates every guideline. But is he funny? Judge for yourself.

I'm going to start my own airline. Hey, why not? This is America, right? Anybody can have an airline. They even let Donald Trump have one, which he immediately renamed after himself, his usual, classy practice despite the fact that "Trump" sounds like the noise emitted by livestock with gastric disorders: "Stand back, Earl! That cow's starting to Trump!"

Well if he can do it, I can do it. My airline will be called: "Air Dave." All the planes in the Air Dave fleet will utilize state-of-the-art U.S. Department of Defense technology, thus rendering them—this is the key selling point—*invisible to radar.* That's right; I'm talking about a Stealth airline.

Think about it. If you're a frequent flier, you know that the big problem with commercial aviation today is that the planes can be easily detected by air traffic control, which is run by severely overstressed people sitting in gloomy rooms drinking coffee from Styrofoam cups and staring at little radar-screen dots, each one representing several hundred carefree people drinking Bloody Marys at 35,000 feet. Naturally the air-traffic controllers become resentful, which is why they routinely order your Boston-to-Pittsburgh flight to circle Mexico City.

They won't be able to do that stuff to Air Dave. They won't even be aware that an Air Dave flight is in the vicinity until it screams past the control tower at Mach 2, clearly displaying its laser-guided, air-to-tower missiles, and requests permission to land *immediately.*

Air Dave planes will not park at a gate. Air Dave planes will taxi directly to the rental-car counter.

The official Air Dave spokesperson will be Sean Penn.

There will be no mutant in-flight "food" served on Air Dave. At mealtime, the pilot will simply land—on an interstate, if necessary—and take everybody to a decent restaurant.

Air Dave will do everything possible to live up to its motto: "Hey, you only go around once." There will be no in-flight movies. There will be live bands. Air Dave will also boast the aviation industry's finest in-flight pranks. For example, just after takeoff, the door to the cockpit might "accidentally" swing open, revealing to the passengers that the sole occupant up there, cheerfully sniffing the altimeter, is a Labrador retriever named "Boomer."

All Air Dave planes will have skywriting capability.

Air Dave pilots will be chosen strictly on the basis of how entertaining their names sound over the public-address system, as in first officer LaGrange Weevil, or ideally, Capt. Deltoid P. Hamsterlicker. Pilots will be encouraged to share their thoughts and feelings with the passengers via regular announcements such as: "What the heck does this thing do?" and "Uh-oh!"

In the event of an emergency, a ceiling panel will open over each seat and out will pop: Tony Perkins.

I've given a lot of thought to the flight attendants. My original idea was to use mimes, who would go around pretending to serve beverages, etc. But then I got to thinking about an opinion voiced a few months back by Al Neuharth, the brain cell behind USA Today, "The Nation's Weather Map."

You may remember this: Neuharth wrote a column in which he was highly critical of today's flight attendants, whom he described as "aging women" and "flighty young men." And quite frankly, I think he has a point, which is why all the flight attendants on Air Dave will be hired on the basis of looking as much as possible like the ultimate human physical specimen: Al Neuharth. Assuming we can find anybody that short.

The preflight safety lecture on Air Dave will consist of five minutes of intensive harmonica instruction. Passengers will also be notified that under Federal Aviation Administration regulations, anyone requesting a "light" beer must be ejected over Utah.

Air Dave pilots will have standing orders to moon the Concorde.

That's the Air Dave master plan. On behalf of Capt. Hamsterlicker and the entire crew of Neuharths, let me say that it's been a real pleasure having you read the column today. And remember: Under the Air Dave Frequent Flier program, if you log just 25,000 miles, we'll let you off the plane.

To many people, this is the rarest kind of journalism—really belly-laugh writing. It's the kind of work that won for Barry a "best writing" award from the American Society of Newspaper Editors. In an interview for the ASNE annual "Best Newspaper Writing" book, Barry describes, sort of, his secrets to success. One secret is an understanding editor.

"It's just wonderful when you have an editor who'll let you bring out your absolutely most childish impulse and call somebody a really bad, stupid name right in the column. And I just enjoy that freedom so much that I abuse it immensely."

Reread what he did to Donald Trump and Al Neuharth. Is that abuse? Or is it classic parody, deliberate exaggeration of well-known characteristics of famous people?

Another secret: "I'm not into symbolic writing, or writing on a bunch of different levels, or anything like that. I usually just say it, whatever it is. I'm a very obvious writer. Maybe people like that: seeing something simple and clear, stated simply." So people get from Barry outrageous observations, solidly based on widely shared experiences, overstated simply.

Another secret: "I can lie, because I'm a humor columnist." Barry's lies, though, often approach a kind of truth, as in his description of air traffic controllers or his summary of "mutant in-flight 'food'." And isn't Air Dave a reasonable facsimile of every frequent flier's fantasy?

☐ WRITING HUMOR IF YOU'RE NOT DAVE BARRY

The real answer to how Dave Barry does it may be that he is a comic genius. Genius can't be taught. But for all the would-be humor writers who aren't Dave Barry, here are a few guidelines that should be useful.

- Look closely and listen well to capture the nuances of description and phrasing that will permit you to show your readers something funny instead of having to try to persuade them that it is funny.

- Strip your material of superfluous detail and unnecessary information. Focus on the point—the contrast, the absurdity, whatever it is that makes this funny. Provide just enough context to make the point clear.

- Under-write. Avoid tricky constructions, fake names, dialect or any other device that violates the conventions of the language. The humor must come from the material, from your ideas, from the use of legitimate literary devices such as metaphor and simile.

- Finally, violate any of these guidelines if you can do so and still be funny. True comic genius can make its own rules. These guidelines are just that—guides for any who need them. Those who don't are bound only by the ultimate rule: The reader must think it's funny.

And now a few last words from the founder of Air Dave:

"If you decide you're going to write humor, don't hold back. Too many people try too hard to be dry or ironic or reserved or British almost in their humor, instead of really letting go and saying what they really think is funny. And don't try to write humor like anyone else. People try to copy the humor styles of other people, but it just never works, any more than a standup comic doing somebody else's bits looks real. All the people who are funny are funny because they're funny."

☐ QUESTIONS AND EXERCISES

1. What do you think? Is Dave Barry's column funny? Why do you think that?

2. What makes a piece of writing funny?

3. Write a funny paragraph. Put it aside for at least 24 hours. Now read it again. Is it still funny? If you think so, show it to a friend and get the friend's reaction. Your friend is your audience. Keep at it until your friend laughs out loud. How easy was it to earn that laugh?

4. Find three examples of humor in the news columns of your local newspaper. How do they employ the principles outlined in this chapter?

5. Some people think Mad magazine is funny. Some prefer the jokes in The Reader's Digest. Still others fall out of their chairs over the humor in The New Yorker. After surveying these, or a similar range of efforts to be funny, assign yourself a free-lance humor piece for any magazine. Write it and submit.

Epilogue: Have Fun

Good writers are those who care and those who dare.

They care about people, about their readers, about their subject matter, about their work, about themselves. They take pride in what they do.

Effective writing isn't easy. Few like to write; many like to have written. After they stuff themselves with information, successful writers not only write, but they rewrite—and they rewrite. They polish, trim, sketch in a detail, create a metaphor, take one out. If, and only if, they are stuffed full of information and have worked and reworked the copy, they sometimes have moments of inspiration. Inspiration is what keeps writers writing and readers reading.

It doesn't come easily. Write a draft and then put it away for a while. When you come back to it, the real writing begins. As journalist-author Stephen Crane once told novelist Willa Cather, "The detail of a thing has to filter through my blood, and then it comes out like a native product, but it takes forever." You don't have forever, but putting away your copy for a few hours is better than for no time at all. Too often stories are in print just when the writing should begin.

You must care enough to write bright, creative copy. Again, not all subjects can be written about lightly, but you can write about them brightly. Messages, like food, can be bland or ambrosial. "If you have anything to say," director Billy Wilder advised, "wrap it in chocolate."

Ideas, after all, are entertaining. Watch the smile on a child's face at the moment of discovery, at that split second when the miracle of understanding happens. It's that "aha" moment of recognition, that sigh of intense pleasure that reassures us that communicating gives pleasure.

When communication happens, ideas we have are changed, shifted about, recreated. That's why communication is recreation, both for the writer and for the reader. The moments of inspiration and of recognition are moments of pleasure.

It's not that pleasure is the only thing to live for. It's just that people seek pleasure, and that people are at their best when they are at play. You need to work with your copy, yes, but you also need to play with it, to brighten it. Have fun with it. Good writing is a great playground; good writing gives pleasure even when the news is bad.

It's a matter of caring—and of daring. You need to be challenged and to be pushed. If there's no one around to do that, push yourself. Beginning writers on their first job often complain that no one, not even their editors, criticizes the copy. First drafts are too easily accepted, or copy is changed or deleted without any discussion with the writer. Students may find it difficult to believe, but most editors are not demanding enough. Professors won't be there to grade your work; you will have to grade yourself.

Most experienced writers, especially staff writers, tend to be energy savers. Many fall into patterns and formulas and suffer various degrees of burnout. They have been edited and cut and edited some more. They have been battered and bruised and bounced around, and they have learned to play the company game—whether that company is a newspaper, magazine, house organ or whatever. If they ever risked being creative, they have long since stopped. They tried being creative once, or a dozen times, and someone always told them they were being too cute. They tried something new, and someone stopped them, or worse, no one noticed. The fun has oozed out of their writing—for themselves and for their readers.

If any of this has happened to you, no one can help you except yourself. If you're not getting a kick out of you writing, no one else is getting pleasure from reading you.

Nothing comes from nothing. Quality writing is done by people of quality. Robert Pirsig, in "Zen and the Art of Motorcycle Maintenance," says quality depends on three things: self-reliance, integrity and gumption. If you are self-reliant, you will not blame your boss, or your mother, or your journalism teacher for the kind of writing you do. Second, you have to like who you are and what you do. If you feel good about what you write, it will show. Third, no matter how many prizes you have won or how much criticism you have received, you have to have the gumption to give it your best, one more time. When Frank Lloyd Wright was 76, someone asked him what his best-designed building was. Without hesitation he replied, "My next one."

Make your next story your best one. And have fun.

APPENDIX A

Getting Your Article into Print

You probably don't write just for the fun of it. You want to see your article published, and you want to get paid for what you write. Here's some advice.

☐ THE MARKET

Don't just write something and then look for a place to send it. Here are some reference books to help you know what's out there:

Editor and Publisher International Yearbook. Updated annually, this directory of newspapers includes department-head names and newspaper circulations. You'll find help for placing stories with local angles.

Encyclopedia of Associations. Most of the 20,000 associations listed here produce publications. These publications are briefly described. It's updated periodically.

Gale Directory of Publications and Broadcast Media. Formerly called the Ayer Directory of Publications, this directory contains thousands of listings for trade publications, newspapers and magazines. It's updated periodically, and it'll help you target a market for local or special-interest pieces.

Directory of Little Magazines and Small Presses. Updated periodically, this directory lists thousands of publishers by subject and location.

Magazine Industry Market Place. Updated annually, this directory includes 3,500 publication listings, as well as information on organizations, awards and syndicates.

Newsletters in Print. Updated periodically, this directory lists more than 10,000 newsletters.

Readers' Guide to Periodical Literature. Updated semi-monthly, this guide contains subject listings of articles in 200 magazines. You'll learn what articles have been published when by which publications. In addition to being a research tool for your article, it will keep you from sending an article to a publication that has just published something on that topic.

The Standard Periodical Directory. More than 75,000 U.S. and Canadian publications are listed by category and by title. You'll find corporation publications listed under "House Organs." It's updated periodically.

The Writer's Handbook: What to Write, How to Write, Where to Sell. In addition to a listing of 2,500 markets, this handbook contains more than 100 articles by established writers designed to help free-lancers. It's updated periodically.

Ulrich's International Periodicals Directory. Publications are listed by category in these volumes that are supplemented quarterly by Ulrich's Update.

Writer's Market. Considered the free-lancer's bible, this annotated listing of 4,000 markets is updated annually. It tells you what kinds of articles each periodical publishes, how long they should be, what they pay, etc.

In addition, get familiar with these periodicals:

Folio: The Magazine for Magazine Management. Skim this magazine to keep abreast of trends and of the health of individual magazines. You'll also learn about new magazines that might be a potential market.

Freelance. This monthly newsletter provides information about article writing and events of interest to writers. It also contains free-lance directories.

Poets & Writers Magazine. Formerly Coda: Poets & Writers Newsletter. This bimonthly provides articles on writing and information on writers' conferences and grants.

Publishers Weekly. Although this magazine is devoted mainly to books, it also announces start-ups of new magazines you may wish to target.

The Writer. This no-frills monthly (it calls itself "The Oldest Magazine For Literary Workers"—founded in 1887) features how-to articles by established writers and listings of special markets.

Writer's Digest. How-to articles by known writers fill this monthly that is especially helpful to beginners. Each issue contains market listings.

After you choose a magazine because you know what it wants—what length, what form, at what fee—study the magazine. Read a copy. If possible, read several back copies. Not only does this make you familiar with the publication and its style, but it also tells you whether the magazine has published an article in recent issues that is similar to the one you are proposing.

☐ WHETHER TO QUERY

To query a publication means simply that you ask the editors whether they are interested in reviewing your article. Most writers and most publications say that you should always query a publication before sending an article. This is not a rigid rule.

Query before writing if you are an experienced, published writer. Why waste time on an article if the publication isn't interested in it? Also, query if the article is going to cost you much to research. You may even be able to get some expense money up front.

If you are not a known writer or don't have a publishing record, you may wish to save yourself and the editor time by sending the article without querying. This is especially true if you have already completed the article or if it is topical. If you have previously sent it to a publication and had it rejected, send it out again as soon as you can.

☐ HOW TO QUERY

There are three types of queries: the simple query, the query with a pitch and the query with a sample. Examples of each type can be found at the end of this Appendix.

1. The *simple query* presents the story idea, tells how long it will be, states whether photos, charts or illustrations will come with it and includes a brief statement about the author.

Query 1 (see page 220) is a simple "bare-bones" query. Like most queries, it will do the job if the proposed article meets the needs of the publication at that time.

2. The *query with a pitch* tells why this publication should want this article and why you are qualified to write it. Query 2 (see page 221) does that, and it also indicates the author will quote other experts.

3. The *query with a sample* might include the introduction to the article or a key part of it. In addition, the query may contain a somewhat detailed outline of the piece.

Query 3 (see page 222) demonstrates the writing style of the proposed article.

The type of query is up to you and to the publication to which you are sending it. Some editors want more than Query 1 has; others find it sufficient. Some prefer an enthusiastic sales pitch; others want an example of your writing and more information about how you will treat the topic. After a while, you will learn what works best for you. Querying gets easier once you are published a few times, especially if you have been published by the periodical you are querying.

☐ WHERE TO SEND IT

Whether it's a query or the article itself, address it to the right person. Sometimes it is difficult to know who that is. It may be the editor, the managing editor or the feature editor. If you are submitting an article to a department of a publication, send it to the person in charge of that department. In most cases, the article will eventually get into the right hands, but do all you can to expedite that.

☐ HOW TO PREPARE
THE MANUSCRIPT

First, be sure to send a perfectly clean manuscript—no errors whatsoever. Double-space the copy, and leave margins of at least an inch and a half. On the first page, put your name, address and phone number on the left-hand side. On the right, indicate the approximate number of words in the article. Also, on the first page, put your title about a third of the way down, and then begin the manuscript. Space allows editors to write on the top. Put your name and a page number on the top of each succeeding page.

Don't hesitate to suggest a title or two. You might also write a summary or contents blurb under the title. In the piece, you might use some of the techniques of service journalism described in Chapter 11. By suggesting how the editor may present the piece with blurbs and sidebars, you may have a better chance of having it accepted.

Some publications may ask you to submit articles on a floppy disk. If you do not know the software program your publication uses, you can send it on an ASCII (American Standardized Code For Information Interchange) file that can be converted.

Photos, charts and illustrations increase your chances for publication in many publications. Be sure to attach informative captions.

When you send the article, write a simple cover letter saying that you are submitting the article for first rights only at the publication's usual rates.

Always include an addressed, stamped envelope for the publication to return your article to you. If you don't, you might never see it again.

☐ RULES FOR FREE-LANCERS

Here's what you need to know and do to become a successful free-lancer:

Have confidence. You have to believe that you write well and that you have something to say. Unless some of the information is out-of-date, don't change your manuscript until you have had it rejected by at least five publications. You may have hit the publications at the wrong time, or the piece may have fallen into the hands of the wrong people.

Persevere. Good authors have had articles and books rejected 20 or more times. After you send the article out, research immediately where you will send it next. Address the envelope, and have the article back out in the next mail.

Be patient. Publications are notoriously slow to get back to you. Most don't even let you know when they receive your article. For most articles, wait at least a month. Then when you inquire, be gentle. Threats, sarcasm, anger do not work—even though they might be justified.

Cultivate editors; work with them. Get to know them, and get them to know you. Remember, if you want to play, they deal the cards.

Be ethical. Be fastidious about presenting only your own work. Quote and attribute properly. Do not send an article to more than one publication at a time. Even if you tell publications that you are doing this, most of them will reject your article immediately because they do not want to waste a minute on something that might not be theirs. As always, there are exceptions. Some periodicals and most newspapers, for example, are local, and you can tell them that the article is exclusive to their geographical area.

You may be tempted to take your published article, give it a new slant and send it elsewhere. Be careful. Be sure the article is unique or that the two publications are not at all similar. Of course, you may send an article that has been published if you tell the publication this. Some authors are highly successful using their second rights to get articles published again and again. Some in-house and association publications reprint articles. Of course, be sure to tell these publications where the articles have been published previously.

You may wish to draw a form of contract with your publication for each article. Experienced writers have done this successfully. Get things in writing as much as you can, including permissions when you cite other copyrighted sources.

In some instances you may be able to negotiate to keep the copyright to your article. Having the copyright leaves you free to publish the material again or to use it in a film or TV. In most cases, the publication will insist on first rights at least. If they have first rights only, you have a right with their permission to do something more with your article.

Take risks. You win some, and you lose some. But free-lancing does keep life interesting. And who knows, it may even make you rich.

☐ QUERY 1

John Alex Floyd Jr.
Editor
Southern Living
Box 523
2100 Lakeshore Drive
Birmingham, AL 35201

Dear Mr. Floyd:

I would like to propose a 1,500-word story about Elephant Rocks State Park in southern Missouri. The park is on Missouri State Route 21 at the northeast edge of Graniteville in Iron County. I can include pictures of the huge 1.2 billion-year-old rocks.

Currently I am a journalism student at Southern Illinois University. Several of my articles have been published in the campus newspaper.

Thank you for your attention.

Sincerely,

☐ QUERY 2

John Alex Floyd Jr.
Editor
Southern Living
Box 523
2100 Lakeshore Drive
Birmingham, AL 35201

Dear Mr. Floyd:

You have to see them to believe them. Rocks, seemingly out of nowhere, everywhere, larger than elephants.

As a long-time reader of your magazine, I know Southern Living readers will love reading about them, and the next time they get near southern Missouri, they will want to visit Elephant Rocks State Park.

The park is on Missouri State Route 21 at the northeast edge of Graniteville in Iron County. Even the visually handicapped can explore the wonders of these 1.2 billion-year-old boulders because of 22 Braille-English signs describing the natural features of the rocks. The park also features picnicking and fishing.

My article will be between 1,500 and 2,000 words, and I can supply black-and-white or colored photos if you wish.

I have a special interest in the park because I minored in geology in college. My articles have appeared in Woman's Day and Redbook, and the wire services have picked up several of my stories. I hope you agree that my article will interest your readers and that I'm the person to do it.

Sincerely,

◻ **QUERY 3**

John Alex Floyd Jr.
Editor
Southern Living
Box 523
2100 Lakeshore Drive
Birmingham, AL 35201

Dear Mr. Floyd:

Would you be interested in a 1,500- to 2,000-word article about Elephant Rocks State Park in southeastern Missouri?
Here's my opening for the piece:

At first, you're unimpressed. You start up the path, and you see some barrel-sized rocks. Hardly elephants, you say. And then they start to appear. A big one, and then elephants, indeed! How in the world did they get here? But here they are, and here they have been for 1.2 billion years.

Elephant Rocks State Park is on Missouri State Route 21 at the northeast edge of Graniteville in Iron County. Even the visually handicapped can explore the wonders of these monsters because of 22 Braille-English signs describing the natural features of the rocks.
I have been published in Woman's Day and Redbook, and several of my articles have been picked up by the wire services. I am especially interested in the park because I minored in geology in college. I will quote well-known geologists, such as Dr. Herman Witt, and I will write a sidebar about the history of the park itself.
I can include colored or black-and-white photos.
Shall I send the piece?

Sincerely,

APPENDIX B

The Joy
of Grammar

The rules of grammar are not a burden to the writer or to readers. Used correctly and consistently, they are a joy to both. If you are like most writers, you probably need a refresher on grammar from time to time.

This appendix has two purposes: To whet your appetite for grammar and to help you avoid some of the most common errors. It deals with:

1. Sentences
2. Verbs and their voices, tenses and moods
3. Verbals and dangling modifiers
4. Pronouns and their cases
5. Subject and verb agreement, subject and pronoun agreement
6. Commas, semicolons, hyphens and dashes

☐ SENTENCES

Sentences or independent clauses express complete thoughts. Readers can grasp our meaning most easily when we give them one complete idea at a time. A sentence has a subject and a predicate. The least a sentence can have is a noun (a person, place or thing) or a pronoun (a word that takes the place of a noun) and a verb (a word that expresses action, being or state of being). Sentences can carry much more than that, but if you want to be understood, keep most of your sentences short.

However, if you write only short, clipped sentences, your story will not flow. You must vary the length of your sentences unless you want a staccato, machine-gun effect. The average sentence should be 16 to 20 words.

You can vary the length of sentences by varying the types of sentences you write. Sentences can be simple, complex, compound or compound-complex.

a. Simple sentences. A simple sentence consists of one independent clause. An independent clause expresses a complete thought and can stand by itself. For example:

This is a complete sentence.

b. Complex sentences. A complex sentence has one independent and one or more dependent clauses. A dependent clause begins with a subordinating conjunction (e.g., *if, because, although, until,* etc.) or a relative pronoun (*who, what, which* and *that*). The dependent clause usually has little meaning when it stands by itself. The dependent clause is subordinate to or relative to the main thought. For example:

Although it was raining.

As part of a complex sentence, the dependent clause makes sense:

Although it was raining, the couple strolled along slowly.

c. Compound sentences. Compound sentences have at least two independent clauses. When you wish to show that two complete thoughts are related and of equal value, use a compound sentence. Both of the following sentences are compound. (The subjects are underlined once and the verbs twice.)

There is abundant evidence of a plethora of potential writing talent, but publishers lack material. The system has broken down, and the breakdown is not confined to writers.

In each sentence, two complete thoughts are joined by coordinating (meaning "making equal") conjunctions or connecting words. A coordinating conjunction (*and, but, for, or, nor, yet, so*) in a compound sentence always has a comma preceding it.

If the two complete thoughts are closely related, the semicolon may take the place of the conjunction. For example:

In Laos, I believe there is less fear of death; it is not something that is a no-no, a taboo.

Though the semicolon links two independent clauses, the comma never can do so without help from the coordinating conjunction. When the comma is used by itself, the error is called a comma splice or a run-on sentence. For example:

Phil likes to play football, he's a good passer.

Avoid run-on sentences even when the two sentences are short. Also, avoid them in direct quotations. Some writers try to justify run-ons in quotations by saying that the person's words and sentences run on together. No speaker, except Victor Borge, inserts periods or commas into the conversations. That's the writer's job.

Although you should never separate two independent clauses with commas, you may join a series of short sentences with commas. Semicolons in the following series of sentences are too heavy; they break the flow of the copy:

It rained yesterday; it is raining today; and probably it will rain tomorrow.

Sometimes you may even want to use a fragment, a group of words resembling a clause but lacking either a subject or a predicate. Because readers are accustomed to complete sentences that give them a complete idea, fragments jolt them. Here's an example (fragments are in italic):

What makes a young man with a coffin-shaped case under his arm spring from the pack so dramatically that the Russians take notice? *Energy mainly. Energy, drive, ambition, stamina.* Eugene Fodor is a sawed-off shotgun in a room full of bottle rockets.

☐ VERBS AND THEIR VOICES, TENSES AND MOODS

Verbs express action, being or state of being. Action is more interesting than merely being. Action verbs do something, and they usually do something to something or someone else. Verbs that require objects to complete their meaning are called *transitive* verbs. Verbs that do not require an object to complete their meaning are *intransitive* verbs. Transitive verbs have a momentum of their own. They pull the reader from the subject to the object.

Depending how you use it in a sentence, the same verb can be either transitive or intransitive. Verbs that refer to the senses are such verbs. Some call them linking verbs. For example:

He felt good. (*Felt* is an intransitive verb. *Good* is a predicate adjective, not an object.)

He felt the softness of her lips. (*Felt* is a transitive verb, and *softness* is its direct object.)

The quiche tasted great. (*Tasted* is an intransitive verb, and *great* is a predicate adjective, not an object.)

He tasted the quiche. (*Tasted* is a transitive verb, and *quiche* is its direct object.)

Knowing that some verbs are intransitive will help keep you from using them incorrectly. For example, the verb "to lie," meaning "to recline," is always intransitive. Therefore, you can *lie* down, and the book can be *lying* on the table. The verb "to lay," meaning "to put or place in a horizontal position," is always a transitive verb. Therefore, the book is *lying* on the table because someone bothered to *lay* it there.

These verbs are difficult because the past tense of the verb "to lie" is "lay." It is correct to say: Yesterday, I *lay* down for an hour. The past tense of "to lay" is "laid." So it is correct to say: I *laid* the book on the table.

Note these verbs and their principal parts:

Present Tense	Past Tense	Past Participle
lie	lied	lied
(to tell a falsehood)		
(intransitive)		
lie	lay	lain
(to recline)		
(intransitive)		
lay	laid	laid
(to put or place in a horizontal position)		
(transitive)		
sit	sat	sat
(to be seated)		
(intransitive)		
set	set	set
(to place)		
(transitive)		
rise	rose	risen
(to get up from a lying, sitting or kneeling position)		
(intransitive)		
raise	raised	raised
(to move to a higher position)		
(transitive)		

Another verb that is always intransitive is "to be." It is sometimes called a linking verb or the copulative and never takes an object. For this reason, the more often you avoid the verb "to be," the more movement and action your writing will have. Transitive verbs pull the reader to the object. Instead of saying, "It was raining hard," pick an action verb: "The rain *pummeled* the windshield." The verb, "pummeled," makes the reader ask, "Pummeled what?" Study the transitive verbs in this news story:

Two years after Proposition 13 *rocked* California, Massachusetts *registered* a powerful aftershock: Last month voters overwhelmingly *approved* a measure that *will slash* property taxes by an average of 41 percent and *drain* $1.3 billion from local coffers next year.

The lead refers, of course, to California's propensity for earthquakes. The lead is more powerful than if the writer had said:

Proposition 13 has been a law for two years in California, and now Massachusetts is in the same situation.

Another reason to avoid the verb "to be" is that it is wordy, as in these verb-adjective combinations that have no action:

He *is hopeful* of an easy win.

He *is needful* of more practice.

Make them:

He *hopes* to win easily.

He *needs* more practice.

Also, avoid the verb "to be" with the expletive (words such as *it*, *here* and *there* when they have no special meaning of their own). Instead of:

It is his wish to remain here for an hour.

Make it:

He wishes to remain here for an hour.

Especially avoid the expletive with a verb in the passive voice:

It was estimated by police that the accident occurred about midnight.

The sentence is punchier and shorter this way:

Police estimated that the accident occurred about midnight.

Even without the expletive, you should usually avoid the passive voice.

PROPERTIES OF VERBS

1. Voices
   a. Active—subject does the acting.
   b. Passive—subject is being acted upon.
2. Tenses
   a. Present—I do.
   b. Past—I did.
   c. Future—I shall do.
   d. Present perfect—I have done.
   e. Past perfect—I had done.
   f. Future perfect—I shall have done.
3. Moods
   a. Indicative—a statement of fact.
   b. Subjunctive—a statement not a fact.
   c. Imperative—a statement of command.

---

a. The voices of verbs.   Verbs can be in the active or the passive voice. A verb is in the active voice if the subject of the sentence is doing the acting:

In the third inning, George Brett *drove* the ball over the centerfield wall.

Drove is in the active voice. *Brett*, the subject of the sentence, did the driving. When a verb is in the passive voice, the subject of the sentence is being acted upon rather than doing the acting:

In the third inning, the ball *was driven* over the wall by George Brett.

In this sentence, *ball*, the subject of the sentence, was acted upon. The ball *was driven*. The verb is in the passive voice. Here's how to recognize it:

First, the form of the verb "to be" is always present: *"was driven."*

Second, the past participle is always present: "was *driven.*"

Third, the preposition "by" is always there or understood: "*by* George Brett."

That's how to recognize the passive voice. Here's why you should avoid using it:

First, it's wordy. The added word "to be" is always there, and the preposition "by" is usually there.

Second, the past participle makes the verb sound past, even when the present is intended. "It is suggested by experts" sounds past. "Experts suggest" sounds present, and it is.

Third, readers usually want to know who or what is doing the acting. Sometimes, the doer of the action does not want to take responsibility, or the writer does not wish to assign responsibility. Look at this sentence:

> Politicians, government writers, corporation writers and academicians often *are accused* of writing in the passive voice in order to avoid clearly assigning responsibility.

The verb, *are accused,* is in the passive voice, and the preposition "by" is missing. As a result, the reader never learns who did the accusing. The writer neither takes the responsibility for the statement nor assigns it to someone else.

Fourth, the passive voice isn't as dynamic as the active. These two sentences illustrate the difference.

> With three seconds to go, the winning field goal *was kicked* by Chip Lohmiller.
>
> With three seconds to go, Chip Lohmiller *kicked* the winning field goal.

The second sentence has action. The doer is doing something. The sentence has more punch.

In spite of all the reasons for using the active voice, the passive should not be avoided altogether. Sometimes the subject being acted upon is more important than the actor and therefore should come first in the sentence. For example:

> Southern Italy *was devastated* today by a massive earthquake.

Earthquakes are common; where this one happened is what's important. The active voice de-emphasizes the location:

> A massive earthquake today *devastated* southern Italy.

When you do not know the doer of the action, the passive voice is useful.

The car *was stolen* sometime between midnight and 1 a.m.

You would hardly want to write:

Some thief stole the car sometime between midnight and 1 a.m.

You may even wish to use the passive voice for a change of pace or variation in your writing. But use it sparingly.

b. The tenses of verbs. Reporters writing about past events usually put the verbs in the past tense. But many, if not most, of the features and profiles you write would be improved if you used the present tense. The present tense indicates that what happened or what was said continues into the present. If you write, " 'I like my job,' he *said*," it sounds as if he no longer likes it. If you write, " 'I like my job,' he *says*," you are saying that he still does. Note this paragraph, from Ambassador magazine:

> Without a "common ground" of rules that *are understood* and *obeyed*, people *can* no longer use language to communicate, (Edwin) Newman *says*. When the language *fills* with gas, people can no longer examine what they *are being told*, and they *run* the risk of *being deceived*. Pompous language *is* simply boring; Newman *says* that most people will never take an interest in politics until politicians *begin* to speak plainer.

You can be sure from this paragraph and the use of the present tense that Edwin Newman continues his battle against the abusers of language. The verbs in the present tense indicate that what Newman said at the time of the interview he would say today.

The present tense can be used then to indicate what is happening now and what always, repeatedly or habitually occurs:

She *rides* the bus every morning.

They often *walk* to school.

You can also use the present to indicate future time:

The plane *leaves* in one hour.

Smith *flies* to California on Thursday.

The historical present refers to events completed in the past. It is more often used in headlines, but it is useful also in many types of stories. The headline, "Smith *leaves* for California," means, of course, that Smith has already left. In a story, the historical present describes more vividly what took place in past time:

It *is* 6:30 a.m. on a spring Monday morning. Bill Middleton *wakes* up at his home in the Roland Park section of Baltimore. He *eats* a toasted muffin, *drinks* a cup of grapefruit juice, and then *takes* his English bulldog, Darwin, for a walk around the neighborhood. He has done the same thing each morning for the past seven years. Only one thing is different. Now he *is* the president of Equitable Trust Company.

The story continues to follow the new bank president for a day. The historical present works here, and you should try to use it as often as you can. Of course, the past tense has its place, especially in the straight news story. You would ordinarily use the past tense in a story telling of a past event like a meeting, press conference, accident, and such.

The past tense indicates that the action is completed. The past tense of most verbs is formed by adding "ed" to the stem of the verb. The past participle is formed the same way. Such verbs are called "regular." "Irregular" verbs have different forms for the past tense and the past participle. For example, the past tense of "go" is "went," and the past participle is "gone."

The past participle, preceded by a form of the helping verb "to have" is used to form the perfect tenses. You should pay special attention to the present perfect tense because it denotes an action that continues into the present. The difference between the past and present perfect tenses is illustrated in these two sentences:

Sarah Jacobsen *lived* in Crown Point for more than one year. (past tense)

Sarah Jacobsen *has lived* in Crown Point for more than one year. (present perfect tense)

In the first sentence, the verb indicates completed action: Sarah no longer lives there. The second sentence clearly means that Sarah continues to live there.

The present perfect tense can also indicate completed action at the present:

The House *has voted* overwhelmingly to block a shipment of uranium fuel to India.

Notice that the verb here indicates more immediacy than the simple past:

The Houses *voted* overwhelmingly to block a shipment of uranium fuel to India.

Many times the immediacy of the present perfect is preferable to the past. Broadcast writers, for example, prefer the present and the present perfect tense. They want their news to have the sound of immediacy and continuation. Print journalists can capitalize on the same strengths.

The progressive form of the verb also helps denote immediacy. The progressive indicates that the action is continuing at the time noted. You form the progressive by placing some form of the verb "to be" before the present participle. The present participle is formed by adding "ing" to the stem of the verb. Note these verbs in the past progressive:

Interest rates *were approaching* the record levels set last spring, inflation was going on the boil and the economy *was teetering* on the brink of another slump—the second scoop in a "double dip" that economists *were coming* to accept as inevitable.

Even though all of these events occurred in the past, the use of the progressive conveys a sense of action and immediacy. Use it when your story permits it.

c. The moods of verbs. In addition to voices and tenses, verbs have moods or modes. The mood of the verb is determined by the attitude the speaker or writer has toward the sentence. When you make a simple statement of fact, use the indicative mood. For example:

She *is* my friend.

When you make a request or a command, use the imperative mood:

Always *write* grammatically.

Put the verb in the subjunctive mood:
   1. when the statement is not a fact or a command,
   2. when the verb follows the subordinating conjunction "that" after verbs of wishing, demanding, suggesting, supposing, resolving, doubting, requiring, questioning, etc.
   Here are two examples:

I demand that he *leave* at once.

He wishes that it *stop* immediately.

Notice that the verb in the subjunctive drops the "s" off the third person singular in the present tense. That's the only change from the indicative in all the tenses of all the verbs—except the verb "to be." Here are the changes in the verb "to be" in the present and past tense of the subjunctive mood:

(present tense)	I be	we be
	you be	you be
	he (she, it) be	they be
(past tense)	I were	we were
	you were	you were
	he (she, it) were	they were

Use the present subjunctive for conditions that express a doubt or a possibility.

If he *be* guilty, he should be punished.

If you wish to express a condition contrary to fact, you must use the past subjunctive:

If I *were* you, I would learn the subjunctive.

In the second case, I am not you, and I never can be you. It is a condition contrary to fact. However, not every "if" is followed by a verb in the subjunctive. Consider the difference between these two statements:

If I *was* there, I don't remember. (past tense, indicative mood)

If I *were* there, I would be fishing. (past tense, subjunctive mood)

In the first sentence, the verb is in the past tense, indicative mood. The speaker is indicating that he believes he was not there. The verb in the second sentence is in the past tense, subjunctive mood. The speaker knows that he is not there. He is expressing a condition contrary to fact.

Verbals and dangling modifiers. Verbals are forms of the verb that are used as other parts of speech. The verbals are the participle, the gerund and the infinitive.

☐ THE VERBALS

1. The participle—verbal adjective
   a. present—add "ing" to the root stem of the verb
   b. past—add "ed" to the root stem of the regular verb
2. The gerund—verbal noun—add "ing" to the root stem of the verb
3. The infinitive—verbal noun, adjective or adverb—place the word "to" in front of the root stem of the verb

☐ A. The Participle

We have discussed how the present and past participles are formed and how they are used in the progressive and perfect tenses:

She is *going* home. (present participle)

She has *gone* home. (past participle)

We also use participles as verbal adjectives; that is, participles have some of the properties of a verb and some of the properties of an adjective. They can modify a noun (the *sleeping* child, the *required* amount), or they can take an object (the man *wearing* the hat).

When you begin a sentence with a participial phrase, be sure that the understood subject of the participle is the same as the subject of the main clause. If it isn't, you have a dangling participle:

Sitting in the driver's seat, the car was obviously too small for her.

The participial phrase modifies *car*, but it should modify the person in the driver's seat. The sentence could be rewritten this way:

Sitting in the driver's seat, she became aware that the car was too small for her.

The principle is the same when you use the past participle:

Denied a raise or a promotion, the job became tedious and boring.

Again, the job was not denied a raise or a promotion. The sentence must be rewritten:

Denied a raise or a promotion, he found the job tedious and boring.

❏ B. The Gerund

Now let's look at the gerund, which is a verbal noun. The gerund is formed in the same way as the present participle and is sometimes called a participial noun. The gerund may take an object (she likes *playing* chess), and it may be modified by an adjective or by an adverb (tiresome *droning; swimming* vigorously). As you do with a participial phrase, be careful when you begin a sentence with a gerund phrase. Make sure the understood subject of the gerund is the same as that of the main clause. Here's an example of a dangling gerund phrase:

After *swimming* in the cold water, the warm sand felt good on our toes.

Swimming is a gerund, the object of the preposition *after*. But the warm sand didn't swim. Rewrite it:

After swimming in the cold water, we enjoyed the warm sand on our toes.

❏ C. The Infinitive

The infinitive can be a verbal noun, adjective or adverb. It is formed by placing the preposition "to" before the stem of the verb, as in "to jog." Because the infinitive is one grammatical unit, ordinarily you should *not* place an adverb between "to" and the verb, as in "to easily do." Don't dangle an infinitive phrase either:

To break a record, the race must be run in three minutes.

The race cannot break a record. Rewrite it:

To break a record, you must run the race in three minutes.

❏ PRONOUNS AND THEIR CASES

To use the pronoun correctly, you must understand the grammatical cases. Cases indicate the relationship of nouns and pronouns to other words in a sentence. Only nouns and pronouns have cases. In English, nouns change their form only in the possessive case. Most pronouns change their form for each case. You choose the form of the pronoun by how you use it in a sentence.

For all practical purposes, English has only three cases: the subjective (or nominative), objective and possessive. Let's look at the declensions (the inflections according to case) of the pronouns:

PERSONAL PRONOUNS			CASES			
Gender	Number	Person	Subjective	Objective	Possessive Short form	Long form
		1st	I	me	my	mine
	singular	2nd	you	you	your	yours
masculine			he	him	his	his
feminine		3rd	she	her	her	hers
neuter			it	it	its	its
		1st	we	us	our	ours
	plural	2nd	you	you	your	yours
		3rd	they	them	their	theirs
RELATIVE AND INTERROGATIVE PRONOUNS						
	singular and plural	1st 2nd 3rd	who	whom	whose	whose

Now let's look at how and when they are used.

a. The subjective case. Use the subjective case when the pronoun is the subject of the sentence.

He and *I* are going.

You would not say:

Me and *him* are going.

You also use the subjective case after the verb "to be." For example:

It is *I.*

This is *she.*

These are *they.*

Grammarians call this construction (a noun or a pronoun following the verb "to be") the predicate nominative. In ordinary conversation, you will often hear, "It's me," or, "That's us." But when you are writing, ordinarily you should be grammatically correct.

b. The objective case. The objective case is used in the following instances:

First, the pronoun is in the objective case when it is the direct object of a verb. Here are some examples:

Wrong: I hit *he.*

Right: I hit *him.*

Wrong: She dislikes *he* and *I.*

Right: She dislikes *him* and *me.*

Wrong: They took my *husband* and *I* to dinner.

Right: They took my *husband* and *me* to dinner.

Second, use the objective case when the pronoun is the indirect object of a verb. The indirect object either has the preposition "to" in front of it or "to" is understood. For example:

Throw the ball to *me.*

Throw *me* the ball.

In both examples, *me* is in the objective case because it is the indirect object. The word *ball* is the direct object. You would not write:

He spoke to *I* about it.

Or:

He spoke to *he* and *I* about it.

Neither should you write:

He spoke to my wife and *I* about it.

Instead, be correct:

He spoke to my wife and *me* about it.

Third, use the objective case when the pronoun is the object of a preposition. A preposition shows the relation between its object and some other word or part of a sentence. For example:

He walked behind *her.*

Behind is a preposition, and *her* is the object in the objective case. Again, note the compound:

Just between *you* and *me,* this is an important example.

Fourth, use the objective case when the pronoun is the subject of an infinitive:

They begged *me* (not *I*) to go.

This is true also in the compound:

They begged *John* and *me* to go.

John and *me* are subjects of the infinitive.

Fifth, use the objective case as the subject and the object of the infinitive "to be":

She thought *him* to be *me.*

Both the subject and the object of the infinitive are in the objective case, even when the infinitive is "to be."

Similarly, when gerunds have objects, the objects must be in the objective case.

Helping Phyllis and *me* was most kind of you.

c. The possessive case. The possessive case is used to show possession. You form the possessive case of most nouns by adding an apostrophe and an "s" to the noun, as in "Bill's." Or you may show possession by using the preposition "of" in front of the noun:

This is the house *of* John.

Or you may use the preposition "of" and the noun in the possessive case:

He is a friend *of John's.*

Unlike the noun, some pronouns in the possessive case never take an apostrophe. The possessive case of some pronouns have their own form:

This is *my* house. This is *mine.*
This is *your* house. This is *yours.*

This is *his* house. This is *his*.

This is *her* house. This is *hers*.

This is *their* house. This is *theirs*.

This is *its* place.

Note especially the possessive case of the pronoun "it." When you write "it's," you are writing the contraction for "it is." You never write "its'."

You may also form the possessive of the pronoun by using the preposition "of" along with the pronoun in the possessive case. For example:

This is one *of hers*.

Pay special attention to the pronoun "who." It is either an interrogative pronoun or a relative pronoun. Interrogative pronouns (*who, whom, whose, which* and *what*) introduce questions. Relative pronouns (*who, whom, whose, which* and *that*) connect a dependent clause to an antecedent in another clause. Look at these uses:

Who is going? (Interrogative pronoun)

Did you say *who* is going? (relative pronoun)

I don't know *who* it is. (Relative pronoun)

In all the examples, *who* is in the subjective case. In the second example, *who is going* is the direct object of the verb *say*, but *who* is the subject of *is going*.

In the third example, the clause is inverted. *Who* is the predicate nominative: *it is who*.

The same is true in this example:

Who did you say was going?

Who is the subject of *was going*, although *who was going* is the object of *say*.

Another difficult case:

The Cardinals, *who* they said wouldn't come close to winning, lost by one point.

In this example, *who* is the subject of *wouldn't come close to winning*.

And one more:

To the question of *who* was going, he had no reply.

Even though *who* looks like the object of a preposition, it must be in the subjective case because it is the subject of *was going*.

The objective case of "who" is "whom." In the sentence, "Whom did he choose?" *whom* is the direct object of the verb *choose*. The same is true in this sentence:

He didn't say *whom* he would choose.

Note also the use of "whom" as the object of a preposition: "To *whom* are you speaking?"

In conversation you might say, "*Who* are you speaking to?" But you are not grammatically correct.

The possessive case of "who" is "whose" and not "who's," which is a contraction of "who is." Hence:

Whose is this?

Bill, *who's* (*who is*) a natural leader, handled it well.

Before we leave the pronoun, let's look at the intensive and reflexive forms. They have the same forms (*myself, yourself, himself, herself, itself, ourselves, themselves*) but are used differently. The intensive is used to add emphasis:

I *myself* don't feel that way.

The reflexive pronoun refers an action to the subject of the sentence:

I hurt *myself.*

The intensive and reflexive pronouns are seldom used wrong in these situations, but often they are used incorrectly as the subject of a sentence:

The chancellor and *myself* agree.

The correct use, of course, is: The chancellor and *I* agree.

As is the case of the verb, this treatment of the pronoun in no way exhausts most common errors. You may wish to explore the subject further.

❑ SUBJECT AND VERB AGREEMENT/ SUBJECT AND PRONOUN AGREEMENT

Let's look first at subjects and their verbs.

Plural subjects *require* a plural verb.

A singular subject *requires* a singular verb.

In the following sentence, the verb is singular when it should be plural:

Attempts by the Synanon Foundation to improve its public image *was* thwarted here when officials refused to appear before members of the press.

When a sentence has more than one subject (a compound subject), the verb must be plural:

Mary and I *are studying* grammar.

When the compound subject is more complicated, remember to use the plural verb:

One passenger, who is on her way to Japan, and another, who is headed for Hong Kong, *are* without boarding passes.

Are is correct because there are two passengers. You must be careful when a prepositional phrase follows the subject. If the subject of the sentence is singular, it takes a singular verb, even when it is followed by a plural object of a preposition:

One of the passengers *is* a Korean.

Despite the plural object of the preposition, *passengers*, the verb is determined by the singular subject *one*. Look at the verb in this relative clause:

One of the passengers *who are* en route to Japan is Korean.

In this sentence, *who* refers to *the passengers*. It is therefore plural and needs a plural verb.

Another vexing problem you often face is determining whether a collective noun should have a singular or a plural verb. Grammarians have a simple rule, but unfortunately, it is not easy to apply: If you consider the people represented by the collective noun as individuals, you need a plural verb. Both of these usages could be correct:

The faculty (as a group) *is* meeting.

The faculty (as individuals) *are* incompetent.

Generally, however, you will use the singular verb because you will consider the collective noun as a unit. Also, common usage makes the singular verb sound better to our ears: The group *is* waiting. Because the noun appears to be singular, the verb sounds better in the singular. In "The board *have* reached a decision," the plural verb jars the ear. If you wish to emphasize strongly that you are referring to the individuals in the collective noun, use the plural verb.

Indefinite pronouns such as *each, every, none, everybody, everyone, anybody, nobody, neither,* and *either* are all singular and take a singular verb. These words present a problem with the pronoun. If the verb is singular, then the pronoun is singular. Do not write:

The company *is* dividing *their* stock.

Everyone *is* doing *their* thing.

In the first example, "company" has a singular verb "is." The pronoun "their" is plural. Because the verb is singular, the pronoun must be "its."

When you can, avoid using "his/her."

Look at this sentence:

A reporter must not form his/her judgment of a person's gender from the use of a generic noun.

You have at least four ways to get rid of the "his/her."

First: Make the subject plural. "Reporters must not form their judgments . . ."

Second: Drop the "his" and replace it with an article. "A reporter must not form a judgment . . ."

Third: Do some rewriting. "A reporter must not judge . . ."

Fourth: When possible, write the sentence in the second person. "You must not form your judgment . . ."

Here as elsewhere, the important thing is that you at least are grammatical and consistent. Solve problems of sexist language with that in mind.

☐ COMMAS, SEMICOLONS, HYPHENS AND DASHES

Like the precise choice of words, correct punctuation helps the reader grasp the meaning of a sentence. Careful writers do not regard punctuation lightly or consider it peripheral to the writing process. Some rules of punctuation are arbitrary. Unlike grammar rules, some punctuation rules are dependent upon the medium. Book and magazine punctuation is usually more formal than punctuation in newspapers. Thus, where formal punctuation rules require a comma after items in a series, newspapers dispense with the last one:

Commas, semicolons, hyphens and dashes are often misused.

Newspaper style of punctuation, as suggested by the AP stylebook, is austere. Punctuation marks are left out unless clarity demands them. You would do well to adopt these stylebooks because your style would then conform to most newspapers and to a large number of magazines and newsletters.

Rules of punctuation often go hand in hand with grammatical rules. Knowledge of grammar will enable you to punctuate correctly and with confidence.

a. The comma. Particularly vexing is the comma. Some say commas have no rules, but they are wrong.

Commas generally separate or mark the boundaries of certain structures. We also tend to pause at the boundaries of these structures. In most instances, if a comma causes readers to pause and keeps them from having to reread the sentence, by all means use one. Introductory clauses almost always require a comma. Short introductory phrases ordinarily do not.

Wrong: A child without a real home Charles had nowhere to turn.

Correct: A child without a real home, Charles had nowhere to turn.

Wrong: After the meal was served he stood up to leave.

Correct: After the meal was served, he stood up to leave.

When the dependent clause follows the independent clause, usually a comma is not required: *He stood up to leave after the meal was served.*

A comma rule more easily applied deals with apposition. A word, phrase or clause is said to be in apposition when what it says merely adds to the meaning of the sentence and is not essential to the meaning:

The student, *who is not very bright,* missed the point entirely.

The clause *who is not very bright* is non-essential information. In grammatical terms, it is non-restrictive. The test is whether the clause changes the meaning of the sentence. Look at this sentence:

The boy who is wearing the green shirt should be watched.

The clause *who is wearing the green shirt* is essential because it designates which boy should be watched. Because the clause is essential for the identification of the boy, it is restrictive. By not using commas you make clear the meaning of the sentence. Here's another example:

Tom's daughter Mary is 16, and his son, Tom, is 9.

This sentence indicates that Tom has more than one daughter, but only one son. Because *Mary* is essential to know which daughter, no commas are used. On the other hand, *Tom* is set off by commas because it is non-essential information.

The relative pronoun "which" is most often used in an appositional clause. "Which" indicates that the clause is merely additional information.

The house, *which* badly needs repairs, is for sale.

Notice how the meaning of the sentence changes when you use the word "that."

The house *that* badly needs repairs is for sale.

Here the "that" clause is essential to the identification of the house. Always use "that" instead of "which" when you wish to write an essential, restrictive clause. A "that" clause never needs a comma before or after it; a "which" clause always does.

We must become which-hunters, Strunk and White say. Too often, "which" is used when writers mean "that." An additional reason for knowing the difference is to help you know when to use commas.

One more word about apposition. One comma of apposition always demands another one, unless the sentence ends with the apposition. Note the following:

The third house, which has green shutters is George's.

The sentence needs a comma after *shutters.* Another example:

The third house that has green shutters, is George's.

This sentence should not have a comma after *shutters.* Also note the difference between the meanings of the sentences. In the sentence with "which," you would simply count the houses to find George's. In the "that" sentence, you would have to count the houses with green shutters to find George's. The meaning of the two sentences is quite different and important—if you want to find George's house. Correct usage and correct punctuation make the difference.

Another comma rule deals with coordinate adjectives. Coordinate adjectives are adjectives of equal rank. In the following example, both adjectives modify the noun equally:

The *tall, narrow* skyscraper reached for the sun.

If the adjectives are coordinate, they can be interchanged without changing the meaning.

The *narrow, tall* skyscraper reached for the sun.

Also, if they are coordinate, you can use the conjunction "and" between them.

The tall *and* narrow skyscraper reached for the sun.

Coordinate adjectives always need a comma between them. Not all adjectives do:

The *tired old* man needed a drink.

You would not write:

The *old, tired* man needed a drink.

The adjective *old* outweighs the adjective *tired. Old* needs to go with man. The adjectives are not coordinate. They should not have a comma between them.

As noted earlier, remember to put a comma before a coordinating conjunction in a compound sentence.

Punctuating for Consistency

***Always* place a comma:**

1. After words in a series, but *not* before "and" or "or" unless the meaning is unclear.
   Example: Mary, Tom and Bill were there.
2. After an introductory dependent clause in a complex sentence.
   Example: Until he came, the party was quiet.
3. After an introductory independent clause in a compound sentence, before the coordinating conjunction.
   Example: The gang soon left, but Jeff stayed.
4. Around non-essential, non-restrictive words, phrases, and clauses. ("Which" always introduces a non-restrictive clause; "that" always introduces a restrictive clause.)
   Example: The third house that has green shutters is his.
5. After introductory participial phrases.
   Example: Waiting in the bar, Tom grew restless.
6. After a second introductory prepositional phrase.
   Example: In May of last year, profits were up.
7. After an introductory interjection, an independent element, a direct address.
   Examples: Oh, so that's it. Yes, I'm certain. Harry, come here.
8. Between coordinate adjectives. (Adjectives are coordinate if they can be reversed and if you can insert "and" between them.)
   Example: The gaunt, lonely creature was also afraid.

You *may* place a comma:

1. After introductory adverbs.
   Example: Suddenly, it's summer.
2. After an introductory prepositional phrase.
   Example: In his later years, he grew even more conservative.
3. After short sentences in a series (three or more).
   Example: It was cold yesterday, it was cold today, and it will be cold tomorrow.

Use semicolons:

1. After elements in a series when the elements have commas.
   Example: The list included the following: Bill Corrigan, 31, of 445 N. Main St.; Sheila Smith, 28, of 333 Elm St.; and Shawn Taylor, 36, of 789 S. Edgewood Ave.

2. Between independent clauses to show that they are closely related when no coordinating conjunction is present.
Example: She had an inquiring mind; she read a great deal.

Use a colon:
1. To introduce more than one item.
2. After an attribution that introduces a direct quotation of more than one sentence.

Use a dash:
—to show dramatic contrast or emphasis.
Example: The killer whale raced across the pool toward its trainer—then kissed her on the cheek.

Use a hyphen:
1. Between compound adjectives. (Adjectives are compound when both or several adjectives can't stand independently with the noun.)
Examples: light-green house; 4-year-old girl.
2. Between compound nouns.
Example: animal-lovers.
3. Between adverbs and adjectives unless the adverb ends in "ly."
Examples: well-constructed, badly burned.
Note: Periods and commas always go inside quotation marks.

b. The semicolon. For all practical purposes, the semicolon has only two purposes. First, it breaks up major divisions in a series that already has commas.

The list included the following: Phil Able, 29, of 145 E. Elm St.; Jeremy Wilks, 31, of 432 W. Ash; and Jim Blaney, 19, of 371 N. Main.

The second use of the semicolon shows a close relationship between the two independent clauses of a compound sentence. As was noted earlier, the semicolon in this instance takes the place of the coordinating conjunction:

Talese writes that "Bullaro would sometimes peddle alone for fifteen miles." But Bullaro is not selling something; he is a man peddling a bicycle.

The last two sentences are closely connected; hence, the semicolon.

c. The hyphen. When you have a doubt about whether an individual word has a hyphen, you have little choice but to look it up in a good dictionary or in your stylebook. The trend today is to remove the hyphen whenever possible. Hence, you write "nonapplicable," rather than "non-applicable." Note this example:

Middle-class families seem hardest hit by the recession.

Middle does not modify *families*. Class does not describe *families* adequately. The families are *middle-class*. *Middle-class* is a compound modifier.

Notice the non-use and the use of the hyphen in the following:

She was *8 years old*. (*8 years old* stands on its own; *8 years* modifies *old*, and *old* is a predicate adjective)

She acted like an *8-year-old* child. (*8-year-old* modifies "child"; it is a compound modifier)

She acted like an *8-year-old*. (*child* is understood; again, *8-year-old* is a compound modifier)

Knowing grammar also will help you know when not to hyphenate. For example, because you know that an adverb can never modify a noun, you know that you should not hyphenate an adverb. Note this incorrect example:

His *badly-damaged* car was near the house.

Badly does not and cannot modify the noun *car*. *Badly* modifies the past participle *damaged*. Hence, *badly damaged* cannot be a compound modifier and should not be hyphenated. The same is true of all adverbs. Nevertheless, to simplify and to be consistent, both AP and UPI hyphenate all adverbs except those ending in "ly" and the adverb "very."

d. The dash. Don't be a dasher. A dash should be used for emphasis or for a dramatic break in the sentence. Some grammarians allow the dash to substitute for simple apposition or for parenthetical expressions. Apposition takes commas, and parenthetical expressions need parentheses. Like the exclamation point, use the dash sparingly. If you emphasize everything, nothing is emphasized. On the other hand, you can use the dash effectively:

If you're thinking this is unimportant—forget it!

Most of all, don't use the dash just because you have written yourself into a hole and can't get out. Too many times we tack on afterthoughts by using a dash and end up with long, incoherent sentences:

The product was of little use to the company, although some expressed satisfaction—even if they didn't do so aloud.

The sentence would be better:

The product was of little use to the company, although some tacitly expressed satisfaction.

Don't underplay the importance of punctuation. Precision here is as important as the precise choice of words and the correct use of grammar. All will make your meaning clearer to readers, and that's what good writing is all about.

Learning grammar and punctuation rules begins with the will to learn them. With practice, they become part of you, and then, like any artist, you can break them occasionally to create the effect you want. But you will break them because you want to and not because you don't know them. It is then that you will experience, as wordsmith Edwin Newman says, the "pleasure and amusement and satisfaction" of using the language well.

☐ QUESTIONS AND EXERCISES

1. Discuss: Grammar is rigid and boring and stifles creativity.

2. Discuss the importance of understanding and using the subjunctive mood correctly.

3. Explain the difference between restrictive and non-restrictive. Then explain the difference between "which" and "that."

4. Discuss: Commas merely slow down the reader—the fewer of them the better.

5. Parse the following passage. Then list the verbs and verbals separately, and where appropriate, indicate their person, number, tense, voice and mood.

Being grammatical is not easy. But if one were to

make a living as an editor, one would benefit from

a thorough knowledge of grammatical principles.
Knowing the parts of speech is essential if one is to
understand syntax. Knowing syntax is crucial to writing
clearly.

Some publishers demand that an editor know
grammar. They have been known to fire those who
don't.

APPENDIX C

The Lessons
of General Semantics

" 'When I use a word,' Humpty Dumpty said, in rather a scornful tone, 'it means just what I choose it to mean—neither more nor less.'

" 'The question is,' said Alice, 'whether you can make words mean so many different things.'

" 'The question is,' said Humpty Dumpty, 'which is to be master—that's all.' "—Lewis Carroll, *Through the Looking Glass*

By now, you know good writing when you see it. You know how to achieve it. But do you know why it's good? Many writers don't really know why one word is preferable to another, why one description is clearer than another, why one sentence communicates more effectively than another. You'll be a better writer if you know.

This appendix will help. It will help by showing you what words do to people and vice versa. Research has shown that the nature of language itself dictates what effective writing is. To find out why some uses of language communicate better than others, you need to look more closely than most writers do at the words you use.

General semantics does that. By studying its principles, you can develop a deeper appreciation of language and its effects. You can come to understand something of the theory that underlies the practice of good writing. If, in addition to knowing *what* works, you know *why* it works, you can choose your words more carefully.

This appendix won't make you an expert in general semantics, but it will introduce you to principles you may find helpful. You may be surprised to discover that such a seemingly esoteric subject has intensely practical applications.

General semantics is the study of how language affects human behavior. We are using the phrase general semantics for a purpose. Semantics, the study of words and what they mean, is related to linguistics. It studies how words come to be what they are and how they came to mean what they mean to various people at various times.

General semantics is neither the study of words nor the study of meaning. It does not concern itself with the correct meanings of words. In one sense, it teaches you just the opposite. General semantics demonstrates that words have many meanings, or more precisely, that people have or bring many meanings to words.

This is not to say that words are unimportant. On the contrary, words are so important that we must constantly evaluate what they do to us. Spoken and written words have a physical reality, and they have a physiological effect on us, not just a psychological effect. Words affect our nervous systems physically. They can trigger joy, fear, anger, even violence.

Because words are so important, Alfred Korzybski, the founder of general semantics, hoped to train people to use and to evaluate language more effectively. Effective communication, he wrote, is necessary for human cooperation, human survival and human sanity. Korzybski taught not only to use words carefully but also to avoid reacting to them automatically. He urged us to delay our reaction to words. He called for a calm, mature, reflective approach to language.

His advice is particularly valuable to the reporter, and every writer must first be a reporter. We must pay attention to what people say, yes, but we must go beyond that. We must ask, what did the person mean by those words? Korzybski wanted us to realize that how people use words is often as important to communication as what words they use.

What he was asking for was a scientific approach to the sane use of language. Toward that end, he published "Science and Sanity" in 1933. It is the scientific approach to language outlined in this book that is so important to the writer.

☐ THE WRITER AS SCIENTIST

The methods of science are useful long before you choose the words you are going to write. First, look at the world the way the scientist does. The scientist recognizes that everything is in the process of change. The world of moving molecules and atoms only confirms what the Greek philosopher Heraclitus said long ago: You never step into the same river twice.

Scientists hold that no two things are the same, that no one thing is ever the same twice, that everything is in a state of flux. As an observer gathering information, you would do well to recognize the same principle.

Don't be one of those who say that if you've seen one, you've seen them all. Scientists do not begin by looking for what is the same in things; they look for differences. Only when they can find no differences do they categorize, classify or make general laws. To an untrained or inobservant person, things look the same when they are actually different. Sometimes, of course, when things look different, you should pay attention to their similarities.

Look for similarity among differences and for the differences among things that look the same. Look for the new, for the different, for what others do not see, because what is new and different is also usually interesting.

The semanticist Wendell Johnson writes that the scientist is a "master of discrimination." Scientists are adaptable; they test everything, expect things to change; they are expert at changing their minds. Imitate their approach. Dissect and assemble; analyze with synthesis. Set aside what is insignificant, and get to the core of things. Ernest Hemingway once said that the most essential gift for a good writer is a built-in, shock-proof crap detector.

If you want your writing to be interesting, start by being a careful, flexible, interested observer. The scientist, writes Johnson, "has a nose for the new, the exceptional, the fine shades of variation in the world about him and in himself and his social relationships." He could have written the same about the writer. The scientist is skeptical, cautious, not easily taken in, distrustful. The scientist looks twice. "The children of science," Johnson writes, "are from Missouri."

Missourians say, "Show me." You should do that, first, in your observation and preparation, and then in your writing. Perhaps the best advice ever given to writers is this simple sentence: "Don't tell me—show me!" But you cannot show your readers unless you have the information, unless you have observed, unless you have asked the right questions.

The scientific method begins by asking clear and answerable questions. That means that scientists must have some idea of what they are looking for. They continually refine their questions because they cannot find clear answers to vague, general questions.

Before you write, find a clear, answerable question. If you do not, your story will lack focus. Just as clear questions direct the scientists' observations, so will they direct yours. Scientists observe calmly and without prejudice. Their observations must be reported as accurately and objectively as possible so as to answer the original questions. Any preconceptions or assumptions must be revised in light of new observations.

Another semanticist, Kenneth Johnson, says the writer must imitate the anthropologist. Stand apart, stand back, observe, question and record.

The process, of course, does not stop. The scientific method is continuous. The reporting and the revising go on and on. Reporters, like scientists, are forever changing their minds.

Even so, always proceed with clarity. In the scientific method, clarity is paramount because without clarity there is no validity. Clarity comes by means of words. As Korzybski wrote, all science is ultimately verbal.

General semantics, then, urges a scientific approach, first of all, to the universe. This approach will help you to gather information for your stories. General semantics also teaches a scientific approach to the words you use to describe that universe.

☐ THE BASIC PRINCIPLES OF GENERAL SEMANTICS

Scientists see everything as changing. We must look at words the same way. Korzybski says we must never think that words can be identified with what they represent. He states three versions of one principle:

1. The symbol is not the thing symbolized.
2. The map is not the territory.
3. The word is not the thing.

A symbol is something that represents something else. It has an existence and an identity of its own, but its purpose is to signify something. A country's flag, for example, reminds people of their country and of all that their country stands for. Treating the flag with respect is a sign of one's respect for his or her country. Many have tried to make it a crime to burn the flag, so closely is the symbol tied to the thing symbolized.

For many during the 1960s, the peace sign was a warm, human symbol of an international movement for peace. That same sign for many others was a symbol of an unpatriotic, un-American acceptance of defeat in the Vietnam War, perhaps even representing a leaning toward communism.

Some signs, such as the Nazi swastika or the cross, are so closely identified with what they symbolize that just displaying them can cause strong emotional reaction. West Germany has had a law for many years banning the display of the swastika. The American Jewish Congress has been urging U.S. toy makers to halt production and sale of war toys bearing Nazi insignia. Interestingly, the leader of one motorcycle gang said members wore swastikas to show their contempt for fascism. The same symbol can mean different things to different people. Obviously, then, the symbol is not the thing symbolized.

Always be aware that, as semanticist S.I. Hayakawa says, "The symbolic process permeates human life at the most primitive and the most civilized levels alike." Be concious of symbols, and don't be mis-led by them. What people wear often symbolize their occupation or affiliation. But because a woman on a college campus wears Greek letters on the seat of her pants does not necessarily mean that she is going to college or that she is a member of that sorority. Symbols, like everything else, mean different things at different times. Beards and long hair no longer symbolize protest. Wealthy people used to avoid the sun to show that they were members of the leisure class. Now they get suntans to look like the leisure class.

Obviously, we often need and use symbols to tell us how to react to various situations and circumstances. Road signs warn us about a curve or an intersection. Road maps tell us how to get some place. But even the best maps have shortcomings, sometimes even mistakes. A map is not the territory. Certainly, a map is not the whole territory. A map does not contain everything that is in the territory. What is more, we can have maps of maps.

You may have heard a conversation like this:

"This can't be the road."
"Why not?"
"Because it's not on the map."

The person here identified the map with the territory. What the person may have had was an incomplete map. Your job as a writer is to draw accurate maps, maps that are clear and easy to follow, maps that measure reality with precision and care.

Look at this example of how a writer draws a map that describes how laser fusion creates energy:

The main laser bay is in a giant clean room two stories high and nearly the size of a football field. To take the analogy a step further, a single low-power laser beam begins at one end zone, is amplified, and is divided by mirrors into six separate beams. Each beam is then amplified further and directed through one of six long tunnel-like chains of optical components. Just beyond the 50-yard line, each beam is divided again, this time into four beams, and all 24 are directed toward a four-foot stainless steel sphere right about where the opposite goal line would be.

Inside the hollow sphere, all the beams converge on that single thermonuclear fuel pellet barely visible to the naked eye, and . . . pow! In that small fraction of a second, the hydrogen isotopes within the fuel pellet are fused together by an almost incredible amount of instantaneous energy—6.6 trillion watts to be exact.

It is an accurate and effective map. By using the analogy to football, the writer draws an accurate picture of the laser beam's path. To use Korzybski's metaphor, the author's verbal world stands in relation to the real world as a good map does to the territory it is supposed to represent.

But even so, the map is not the territory, and the word is not the thing. General semantics teaches us not to identify words with the things they signify. That sounds so simple, but this identification is a difficult habit to break. Not breaking it will hurt you as an observer because you will not think to ask more questions. It will hurt you as a writer because you will not be specific enough in your description and word choice.

The habit of identifying words with what they represent began way back when we began to speak. If you pointed to Bessie with a "What is that?" look, your mother told you Bessie was a cow. If there were other cows around, you may have learned immediately an important semantic principle: cow1 is not cow2 is not cow3. Cows are not all alike. As a matter of fact, one cow is vastly different from any other cow. Not only does it have a different psychological framework and disposition (some cows are better-natured than others), but every part of the cow is a different size and a different shape. If you were to take pictures of cows' stomachs, for example, you would find no two of them exactly alike.

Obviously, to get along at all in this world, we need to be able to identify a cow when we see one. We need, therefore, to generalize and to categorize. But it is equally important to realize that things are not what we say they are, and that one thing is not the same as another, even though we give both of them the same name.

For example, in all of this discussion about cows, if you are like most people, you probably had a picture in your head of a milk cow or a dairy cow. Actually, any animal of which the male is called a bull has a female that is called a cow. We could have been talking about a cow moose, or a cow seal or a cow alligator. If someone told you she saw a cow walking down Main Street, would you think to ask what kind of cow? And when you wrote your story, would you bother to indicate what kind of cow it was?

Much, of course, would depend on the context. In some stories or in some circumstances it may not be necessary to describe what kind of cow it was. The fact is, words have meanings only in context. You as the writer must always supply that context. Remember, words have no meanings; people bring meanings to words. To state it in another way, what we know is a joint product of the observer and of the observed. What we see is not what we look at; what we know is not what we know about. When we observe things and give them a name, we take them out of their context. We separate them from their environment. When we observe, we abstract; that is, we leave things out.

Usually people leave out the things they do not want to see. Sometimes they even put in things they want to see. Be aware of this in your own perception of things and in the way your readers perceive what you write. Just as you see things only in the context of your own experience, so will your readers. Provide that context, and that means that you must try to know who your readers are. Too many writers pay no attention to their audience.

Notice how writer Jim Scott relates a scene to what is familiar to his audience:

> Suddenly, the geese rise simultaneously from the field, like a congregation at the motion of a minister's hand. They tilt their gray wings at the same angle and, sounding like a thousand schoolchildren at recess, cross the pale, blue sky.

The geese didn't rise "all at once." They didn't rise "together." They rose "like a congregation at the motion of a minister's hand." No one has trouble imagining either that or the happy, spontaneous racket of schoolchildren at recess. By comparing the sound of the geese to what we all know, Scott helps us all hear what he enjoyed hearing.

Too many writers do not include color and context. Too many writers are content to be vague and abstract. Use examples, specifics, cases, data, descriptions, anecdotes, similes, metaphors. Always be conscious of your level of abstraction.

☐ THE ABSTRACTION LADDER

One of the prime purposes of general semantics is to make people conscious of their acts of abstracting. Every word leaves something out, even a concrete word like Bessie. But Bessie is more specific than cow, and cow is more specific than animal, and animal is more specific than organism. Semanticists say that when we get more abstract, we are climbing the abstraction ladder.

When you use words carefully, you are aware of their level of abstraction. The further down the abstraction ladder you go, the more concrete you become, and the more easily you are understood.

Notice the difference between these two statements:

I spend a fortune each year on the food I buy for my pet.

I spend 75 cents a day on catfood.

The second sentence has six fewer words and much more information.

Note the specifics Jim Scott uses when he takes us on a fox hunt:

It is dusk in early autumn. Junior Garrett and Jim Sparks are driving along a narrow stretch of winding road between Englewood and Boydsville, pulling a trailer full of foxhounds behind a '69 Ford pickup. The narrow dirt and gravel road is rutted, and the leaves of the hickory and sycamore trees that border it are powdered by the dust raised by tractors and pickup trucks. Beyond the trees are undulating fields of soybeans and milo, stitched into squares by barbed wire fences.

The road is narrow and winding. Scott could have told us how many foxhounds were in the trailer, but he chose a different picture with a little alliteration: "a trailer full of foxhounds." He tells us "a '69 Ford pickup" was pulling the trailer, not a truck. He names the trees that are powdered by dust and how they got that way. Then he paints an exquisite picture of a quilt of moving milo. Scott is specific, concrete; he shows us rather than tells us.

Look at this dormitory scene at Ft. Leonard Wood, Mo., painted by Paula Shepard:

Overhead lights glare off the polished, dustless barracks floors. Beds have been tucked and folded, neat as the seal of an envelope, tight as a clenched fist.

Specific, precise, graphic.

But that's not enough. Try to do more than just pile up specifics. Tell us what they mean. In other words, you need at times to generalize and to categorize. It is not wrong to become more abstract. On the contrary, it is necessary. Hayakawa says: "The interesting writer, the informative speaker, the accurate thinker and the sane individual operate on all levels of the abstraction ladder, moving quickly and gracefully and in orderly fashion from higher to lower, from lower to higher, with minds as lithe and deft and beautiful as monkeys in a tree."

To move gracefully and in orderly fashion up and down the abstraction ladder, the writer must first of all be aware of the process. Professor Kenneth Johnson speaks of the roller-coaster technique for writing and speaking. It involves a more-or-less systematic variation in the level of abstraction. He says if you give readers only specific information, they may ask, "So what? What does it all add up to?" They are asking for an interpretation, a generalization. If you give only generalizations, they want to know how you arrived at the generalizations. They want some specifics, some evidence.

In Paula Shepard's story on today's Army, for example, she moves from specifics about the living conditions in the barracks to a generalization about boot camp life.

> Today's recruits still live in open bays, but only eight, nine or 10 sleep in each. Platoon leaders and their assistants share the privilege of a smaller, separate room. Barracks are all brick now, steamheated in winter and air-conditioned in summer. And soldiers spend their dozing hours on wide, thick beds that Katt says are far more comfortable than the thinly padded folding metal cots he remembers.
>
> Boot camp was more rigorous all around three decades ago, he says.

The point is made. Now on to some more specifics. The insightful writer does more than look for facts and details. Look for the inference, the judgment that gives meaning to those specifics.

☐ REPORTS, INFERENCES, JUDGMENTS

Usually, you are reporting information that can be verified. The language of reports is the language of science. Even though words mean different things to different people, we must and we do agree upon the names of certain things: inches, yards, meters, pounds. What we need is a reasonably accurate map of the territory.

Dictionaries, then, are useful maps, even though most of the time, context determines the meaning. Using a word in its most commonly accepted meaning is simply a common-sense thing to do, especially when we are writing.

For example, when Harper's Magazine called Clare Boothe Luce a "courtesan" in an article title, columnist William Safire and others took editor Michael Kingsley to task. The article was an excerpt from a book by Wilfred Sheed that contained this passage: "As a bridge-figure between the courtesan and the career girl, Clare has sometimes seemed a funny kind of feminist, and the women's movement finds her a difficult patron saint."

The most common meaning of courtesan is prostitute, a particular kind of prostitute who sells sex to the high and mighty. Kingsley told Safire that he thought a courtesan was a member of a court whose role was to serve a great rich man. "The sexual connotation is only one part of it," Kingsley said.

Safire then makes this important point about English usage: "Words not only mean what you want them to mean; words mean what they mean to most people who understand them."

He adds: "That was Lewis Carroll's satiric point, as Humpty Dumpty dismissed Alice's objection to stretching words until they lost their meaning and became sources of confusion."

The language of reports must be clear. The writer of reports, the reporter, must deal with observable data and describe them in agreed-upon terms.

An inference, on the other hand, is a statement about the unknown made on the basis of the known. We may infer that the person standing in front of a university class is a professor. We may infer that a person holding an open book knows how to read. We may infer that the dead man with the deep knife wound was murdered.

Making inferences is essential for survival. Intelligent people try to make intelligent inferences. What is more important, they know when they are making them. So do good writers. In addition, if they make an inference, they test its accuracy.

For example, if you were told that an employee did not receive notice that his employment had been terminated until late September, you would not write that he had been fired in late September. He did not say he was fired, and second, he did not say when he stopped working.

If you were told that it took two hours for employees of the Fire Department to put out the blaze, you would not write that firefighters put out the fire two hours after it started. You would be inferring that the employees of the Fire Department were firefighters (actually, they may have been secretaries; the firefighters may have been on strike), and second, you don't know when the fire started.

You need to make inferences; you need to have hunches. But like a good scientist, you check them out. Far too many times we make inferences without knowing we are making them.

Look at this story:

The musty smell of damp sawdust rises from the floor as one of 41 horses on Alice Thompson's farm stomps his feet in the chilly barn. Birds scatter from beneath the eaves when the metal doors bang open, letting in a rush of cold air.

It seems an idyllic setting, the classic country farm.

Yet here there is a sense of the supernatural.

Here have been recorded telekinetic and extrasensory experiences for over 20 years.

Telekinesis is the power of the mind to move objects. But it is a power many scientists doubt.

When the writer says "there is a sense of the supernatural," she has made an inference. The word itself is an inference, because no one could demonstrate scientifically that the supernatural exists.

Then the writer tells us what telekinesis is, and follows with a statement saying that many scientists doubt its existence. The writer confuses fact with inference.

> A report can be verified.
> An inference is based on a report.
> A judgment expresses approval or disapproval.

Another story begins:

Claude Christian is a skilled worker. He fixes cars, and he does it well. But Claude is unemployed.

If Claude Christian does indeed repair cars so that they run well, he could properly be called a skilled worker. But the writer is making inferences. She does not demonstrate that what she writes is true.

Now look at this carefully drawn inference in a story about the old buildings of a state mental institution:

Bars used to surround the 3-by-7-foot pens that, during the 19th century, housed three people. There was no heat. There was no light. No beds, no toilet facilities, no cafeterias, no exercise areas—no hope.

First the writer gives concrete specifics; she demonstrates the point she's leading up to. Then comes the poignant inference—"no hope."

The point is, of course, that non-fiction writers should not ask readers to *believe* anything. Effective writers neither make inferences unknowingly nor make them without demonstrating the facts from which they are drawn.

A judgment goes a step further than an inference. In the language of general semantics, a judgment shows approval or disapproval. A report cannot say, "It was a marvelous cruise." That is a judgment. A report would describe what the cruise cost and what specific benefits were offered.

People often make judgments when they think they are reporting facts. If you say, "Tom is a liar," you are making both an inference and a judgment. You infer that Tom often knows the truth but deliberately misrepresents it, and you make a disapproving judgment of Tom.

Many words contain or imply a judgment. They are direct expressions of approval or disapproval. For that reason these words are precarious, the most dangerous of all words. Hayakawa calls them snarl-words or purr-words. If someone says, "He always was a radical," that person is probably expressing disapproval. "She's a sweet person" expresses approval.

Look at the approval this reporter is showing in a front-page news story:

> Boone County Southern District Judge Kay Roberts claimed she was new at politics, but Friday night she put on a masterful show.

By calling it a masterful show, the writer also tells us he liked what he saw. Later in the story he writes:

> Yet it was Judge Roberts who stole the spotlight.

Again he shows approval. Had he written that Judge Roberts "dominated" the discussion he would have shown disapproval.

In some writing, authors are expected to make judgments. What is important is that writers recognize when they do. When you use words that imply a favorable or unfavorable judgment, your writing is said to be slanted—and "slanted" is rarely a purr-word.

Look at these example:

I am firm; you are obstinate; he is bullheaded.

We are careful with our money; they are stingy.

I am cautious; you are timid; they are scared.

I am slender; you are slightly thin; she is skinny.

Another word for this kind of language is that it is *affective*. It contains hidden emotional content. It is difficult to believe that "that mangy cur," "that lovable pup," "that silly pooch" and "that vicious animal" can all refer to the same dog, depending upon the emotional attitude of the person using the words.

Why is it that we often read that unions demand a pay increase, although industry requests or seeks to raise the price of its products? Here is a letter to a newspaper charging that the news media use slanted or affective language:

> In nearly every reference to the desperately needed budget cuts the president has proposed, the media use words such as "axe," "chop" and "slice." With Social Security and income tax hikes, the news media have never referred to these tax increases in a similar manner. I am sure that after every tax increase every average worker feels the pain of the federal government hacking away at his take-home pay.

The writer, of course, shows his own bias, but he is not pretending to be a reporter. Here are two sentences written by a reporter in an investigative piece for a city magazine about the pornography racket:

> · Transactions are almost always in cash. The clientele is mostly white and mostly weird-looking.

The statements are not precise. The writer does not bother to tell us what makes someone "weird-looking." If those same people had been gathered in an art gallery or in a classroom of adults, would have they seemed "weird-looking"? Who was it that said beauty is in the eye of the beholder? The writer was not, of course, telling us how the people in the pornography store looked. He was telling us that he disapproved of the way they looked. And probably, he disapproved of them period.

☐ DIRECTIVE LANGUAGE

Closely related to affective language is directive language. Directive language tries to make something happen. It tries to influence our conduct, to control future events. Sometimes directive language simply commands: "Come here!" Other times, it is more subtle: "Good athletes do not need steroids." "Responsible people don't drink and drive."

Directive language usually contains affective language, especially in advertising and in political propaganda. Sometimes it contains a good deal of wishful thinking. "Tired of paying taxes? Vote for Jeremy

Smith." The careful writer knows when to use and when to avoid directive language.

☐ ALLNESS OR EITHER-OR THINKING

Beware of what some semanticists call the "allness" syndrome. This common syndrome occurs when you unconsciously assume that you have written all there is to say on a subject. General semanticists urge the conscious use of "etc." to indicate that you are aware that you cannot know or write everything about a subject. Obviously, you should rarely write "etc." into your copy, but you would do well to keep it in mind.

Remembering "etc." will help prevent you from using such words as *always, never, every, all, completely, every time, constantly.* The careful writer includes details and exceptions. Like the scientist, look for differences, for inconsistencies. It is too easy to see similarities.

Also, be careful of either-or thinking. Our language is loaded with polar terms because so much of life seems to be either-or: Life or death, day or night, land or water, hot or cold. This also appears to be true at higher levels of abstraction: induction or deduction, realism or idealism, capitalism or communism, Democrat or Republican.

It is perhaps natural then to think of things erroneously as black or white, good or bad, normal or abnormal. If you are not for me you are against me. The list goes on and on. "Reality" is not that simple. There are many levels of values, many shades of colors. Few things are either this or that. The scientist asks to what extent, to what degree, how much? Train yourself to do the same. Hayakawa tells you why: "The essential feature of the multi-valued orientation is its inherent capacity to enable us to see more deeply into reality, or to appreciate its finer shadings and subtle nuances of possibilities." And if you perceive reality in this way, you can find the right words to convey it to your readers.

☐ THE NEED FOR INDEXING

One practice that may help you avoid either-or thinking and other problems of communication is what general semanticists call *indexing.* Again, this indexing will not actually appear in the writing, but it is a device to keep the writer conscious of necessary distinctions.

1. *The What Index.* No two things are the same. Remember cow1 is not cow2 is not cow3. Freedom of the press in Cuba is not freedom of the press in the United States is not freedom of the press in Korea. Palestinian1 is not Palestinian2 is not Palestinian3. Labor leader1 is not labor leader2 is not labor leader3.

You can never learn this lesson too well. Mental indexing will help you avoid stereotyping, which always involves a prejudging. Some prejudgment is necessary. But the writer should be a discoverer. What is a "typical" farmer, a "typical" midwesterner, a "typical" teen-ager? The writer, like any other artist, sees reality freshly, differently, always for the first time. No one is just another reader.

2. *The When Index.* Nor is that reader the same person day after day or even moment to moment. The only sure thing is change, and that is true of people as well as of things. Professor Max Otto wrote: "We dip an intellectual net into fluid experience and mistake a catch of abstractions for quivering life."

Not even Mt. Everest is the same as it was. The Ozarks were once higher than the Himalayas. Eldridge Cleaver1992 is not Eldridge Cleaver1972 is not Eldridge Cleaver1962. You must allow for the change in things; you must allow people to change. They do.

Reporters, who primarily are chronicling change, can never capture all the change around us. People generally want things to remain the same because that is what they are used to. But writers can help people adapt to the change around them by constantly finding it and pointing it out. After all most things change gradually, and the change is difficult to see. But all change is easier to digest when we see it happening gradually, rather than in the form of disaster, violence or revolution.

3. *The Where Index.* Geography, climate, location have an effect on things as well as on people. Persons and things change depending on where they are at the time. A blossom on a tree is different from a blossom in a vase, is different from the blossom in a vase with water. S.I. Hayakawa in California was different from Hayakawa in Washington, D.C. Former Secretary of State Alexander Haig in a staff meeting was different from Haig in the Pentagon, was different from Haig in a Senate hearing room, is different from Haig in private life.

The what, when and where indices remind us that words are static in a world of dynamic process. The things or the people about whom you are writing continue to change, even as you write about them.

4. *Other Indices.* As with the other indices, remember the following when gathering information and when writing. Most of the time you are better not to say them. But your words should indicate that you are aware of them.

a. As Far as I Know. We always need to be reminded that it is nearly impossible to be certain about anything in this changing, moving, shifting world. Look at these statements:

The man is not dangerous. (as far as I know)

The gun is not loaded. (as far as I know)

That cat does not scratch. (as far as I know)

Too many times reporters do not ask the next question or do not ask just one more person. Too many times we find the answer that we are looking for and record it as fact.

We must remember that when we describe something as "red," we do not actually know that it is red. Redness is in our heads, a joint product of our nervous system and of certain characteristics of the thing we have called red. Mostly, color is determined by the way light hits the object. Actually, the object is different colors at different times. The object would not be red under ultraviolet light, nor would a colorblind person call it red.

Remembering "as far as I know" will remind you to ask more questions and to record the answers more precisely.

b. To a Point. In the world outside our heads, things are true in varying degrees, at various levels, to a certain extent. This consciousness should help you be aware that you have not said the last word on anything—because, of course, you haven't. Note these statements:

Her clothes were out of style. (true to a point)

He didn't need the money. (true to a point)

She left school because she hated her math teacher. (true to a point)

A reporter wrote this sentence about the results of a new sewage disposal plant: "Neighborhoods with old facilities won't be bothered by those distinctive odors anymore." That may be true—to a point.

The truth is evasive, seldom simple, usually many-faceted. Demonstrate this in your writing.

c. For Me, In My Opinion. After all, everyone reacts to everything differently. And even that universal statement probably has some exception. The Latin expression is "De gustibus non est disputandum": Do not argue about taste. Remember, much of what people say is purely a matter of taste. Knowing this about others and about yourself will help you to be more precise in your reporting and writing. Read these statements:

This is a classic example. (to me)

The escargots had a touch too much of garlic. (for me)

That guy was really funny. (in my opinion)

Opinion, like the inference, is legitimate and useful. Do not be afraid of opinions; just recognize them for what they are.

These are some of the ways that general semantics can help you to write what you want to write in order to mean what you want to mean. To understand words and what they do to people, you must first understand what words do to you.

Etc.

☐ QUESTIONS AND EXERCISES

1. Discuss what it means to say that a writer should be a scientist and take a scientific approach to language.

2. Read the front page of a daily newspaper, and underline every inference that you find that is made by the writer.

3. Make a list of commonly used snarl-words.

4. What does it mean to take readers and listeners up and down the abstraction ladder? Why is it important?

5. Discuss the importance of indexing. Also, what are the possible pitfalls of indexing?

"A Case of Mommie Dearest," September 23, 1982. Copyright © 1982, Time Warner Inc. Reprinted by permission.

"The Despair and Triumph of Mike Criner," by Cal Fussman. Reprinted by permission of Cal Fussman.

Excerpt from golf tournament story, by Jim Litke. Reprinted by permission of The Associated Press (AP).

"Income Declines Precipitously with Age." Copyright © 1992, Wayne Vincent & Associates. Reprinted by permission.

Excerpt from the Philadelphia mass transit system story, by Ricky Tulsky. Reprinted by permission of the *Philadelphia Inquirer.*

Excerpt from "Thomas May Have the Last Laugh After All," by Barbara Reynolds, September 13, 1991. Copyright © 1991, *USA Today.* Reprinted by permission.

Taken from the A CONSERVATIVE VIEW column by James J. Kilpatrick. Copyright © & Dist. by UNIVERSAL PRESS SYNDICATE. Reprinted by permission. All rights reserved.

Taken from the ON THE RIGHT column by William F. Buckley, Jr. Copyright © & Dist. by UNIVERSAL PRESS SYNDICATE. Reprinted by permission. All rights reserved.

Excerpt from William Raspberry column on Urie Bronfenbrenner. Copyright © Washington Post Writers Group. Reprinted with permission.

Excerpt from "The Real Palm Beach Story," by Susan Estrich, April 18, 1991. Copyright © 1991 by The New York Times Company. Reprinted by permission.

Excerpts from Bernie Miklasz's article on the Chicago Cubs. Reprinted by permission of the *St. Louis Post-Dispatch.*

Excerpt from editorial. Reprinted by permission of the *Gainesville Sun.*

Excerpt from July 4 editorial. Reprinted by permission of the *St. Louis Post-Dispatch.*

Excerpt from editorial. Reprinted by permission of the *St. Louis Post-Dispatch.*

Excerpt from the Philadelphia Museum of Art parking lot story, by Dick Pothier. Reprinted by permission of the *Philadelphia Inquirer.*

Excerpts from article by Dave Barry. Reprinted by permission of *The Miami Herald.*

"Punctuation Rules." Reprinted by permission of Iowa State University Press.

Index